FIFTY SIX
THINGS
THE LEFT
WILL
TAKE AWAY
FROM YOU

STARTING WITH THE LETTERS T AND X
(THEY'RE CHRISTIAN SYMBOLS)

A CATALOG OF COMING CONFISCATIONS

WYNN WILLARD

Fifty-Six Things The Left Will Take Away From You: A Catalog of Coming Confiscations
Published by Pheromone Industries, LLC.
Florida, USA

ISBN: 978-1-7351580-0-6

POLITICAL SCIENCE / Political Ideologies / Conservatism & Liberalism

PHEROMONE
INDUSTRIES

Every effort has been made to accurately cite and
quote sources. If you believe there is an omission
or error please contact the author.

For Sam: friend, father, builder, dreamer and doer

CONTENTS

CONTROL YOUR BELIEFS

REDEFINE "FAIRNESS"

ATTACK YOUR FOUNDATION

TAKE WHAT YOU HAVE

CONTROL THE FUTURE BEFORE IT ARRIVES

FOREWORD

PSST ... WANNA BUY A BRIDGE? STEP OVER HERE, TO THE LEFT.
I can solve the perennial affordable housing problem in
the US while freezing the carbon footprint of all housing for
at least forty years. Sound good? *We take all private homes in
the US and put them under government control so that each can
be divided to house between two and eight times more people.* In
essence, each home turns into multiple public housing apartments. Of course, *to be fair* to those with property interests,
there will be a vote before proceeding, where it is expected
that the tyranny of the majority—the many gaining housing—will overwhelmingly elect to receive subsidized or free
housing. To review, this policy will greatly expand housing, reduce the effects of income inequality, and help control
climate change. ELECT ME!

But you won't elect *me*, because while I am being sarcastic, others are truly out there working this perverted agenda. Overcoming inequality and attempting to control climate change while promoting political correctness and government solutions have quickly become hallmarks of the Left. What they never plainly say is that overcoming inequality means taking from the rich(er) to give free stuff to the poor(er); that attempting to control climate change means reducing carbon emissions by restricting personal freedom to drive/fly, spend/consume, and own/control; and that political correctness and government solutions mean that traditional self-reliance, family, and church must be discarded.

Medicare for all! Health care paid for by others is a human right! Let government take it over! Forgive student debt! Taxpayers and bank shareholders should pay those debts! Fight climate change! Eliminate fossil fuels! Shut down the greedy gas and oil companies! Don't use plastic bags! Don't fly! Use mass transit! Don't eat meat!

The Left's radical, destructive agenda is facilitated by promising free stuff and airy slogans that appeal to the masses that believe they deserve more. From whom, they don't care, and if one political party or the government will offer it, that's who they will take it from. Then financial and psychological dependence kick in, and the trap is sprung. African Americans are the archetypal example, and the Left and the Democrat party would like nothing better than to pull every identity group into the fold, gaining more and more power as they go.

God help us if their success continues.

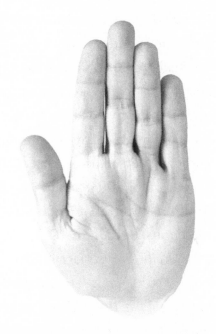

FORBIDDEN
FRUIT

DO PEOPLE ON THE LEFT WAKE EVERY DAY overtly plotting to take away the comforts, fundamental truths, freedoms, and human rights you treasure? No, probably not, at least for most. But they start with different values, and whatever those may be, they are overwhelmed by the pursuit and exercise of power. Even if they start out expecting to exercise power for good reason, power corrupts swiftly and surely. Corrupt use of power can be as simple as denying an opponent a voice. Understand that decisions to confiscate what you have don't have to come from a complete 100-0 bias. All it takes is a slight but persistent stacking of the deck; 51-49 will do, and it even sounds more defensible. *It was a close call, but our decision came out against you, sorry. You'll need to comply, starting right now.* The 5-4 decisions of the US Supreme Court hold the same effect as the 9-0 ones.

It is also not necessary for every person on the Left—including maybe your mother, your spouse, or your closest friend— to actively campaign. Not everyone needs to be a fighter on the front line. No, all it takes is a *vote*, and that doesn't even require being informed. Millions of votes get cast on the basis of misinformation, deceptions, half-truths, and bald-faced lies.

That misdirection is what this book recounts in example after example.

The Left has a relatively short list of categories of things to deny you, but when the list includes things like your thoughts, your property, and your individuality, it looms very large. A good argument can be made for about a dozen broad subjects or themes, and even with that some are subsets of others. Here is that list, with explanation following:

THEMES OF THINGS THE LEFT WANTS TO TAKE AWAY FROM YOU

✔ Achievement/Individualism/Self-Reliance
✔ Animal Use
✔ Carbon Emissions
✔ Family Sanctity
✔ Gender Differentiation
✔ Guns
✔ Inequality
✔ Nationalism/Patriotism
✔ Politically Incorrect Thought
✔ Private Enterprise/Capitalism/Private Ownership
✔ Religion
✔ Wealth

Of course, **POLITICALLY INCORRECT THOUGHT** is the ~~granddaddy~~ … uh, ~~grandmother~~ … uh, better said, *non-binary* most awe inspiring and all-encompassing of all subjects to be eradicated. Any of the other subjects—family sanctity, guns, religion, and so on—may be dismissed as mere fallacious manifestations of politically incorrect thoughts. So "politically incorrect" serves as the joker in the game playing by the Left.

The nature of political correctness is that it eliminates options and answers by declaring them unacceptable in advance of any further consideration. The result is that there is only **one** proclaimed correct path. If you are a politically correct Democrat you know there can only be one answer to the issues of abortion, the women's "pay gap," "gun violence," free health care for undocumented aliens, legalization of marijuana, border walls, climate change, and on and on.

Where there is no politically correct answer and one is needed, one will be *created*. Take the example of "hate speech." Hate speech appears nowhere in the criminal code because **it is not a crime**. But according to the Left, it should be! Hate speech doesn't even get a legal, official government definition.[1] To the contrary, the First Amendment of the US Constitution protects speech regardless of how offensive or hateful some may find it. To the Left's abject disappointment, hate itself is not a crime either. Per the FBI, a "hate crime" only exists if it is *first* a crime, like assault or murder, and then *also* shown to be motivated by the offender's bias. What is the offense of "hate speech"? Short of any call to imminent violence, it is only in the perception of the offended. But the Left will not be stymied, so they now try to conflate speech with behavior. Actions appear *so much more real* than words and unspoken thoughts. Get it? Offensive *speech* will be termed hateful *behavior*! That is good enough for colleges nationwide, who patrol the "behavior" with speech codes threatening shaming and expulsion for "offenders."[2]

If government won't strip people of their God-given rights, then private organizations on the Left will try. The National Hispanic Media Coalition holds that hatred may be *inferred* from distorted facts and bad arguments. Divisive language, as defined by them, is hate speech.[3] The Southern Poverty Law Center declares pro-family groups against same-sex marriage as "hate groups."[4] The American College of Pediatricians earns their same designation. A whole slew of media organizations and commentators have deemed Trump "Make America Great Again" hats as hateful expressions of racism and white supremacy. And social media giants such as Facebook and Twitter regularly deem conservative viewpoints offensive and in violation of their "standards." In one example, when a Fox News co-host and combat veteran dared tweet the Islamist manifesto of a suspected terrorist *murderer* at Navy Station Pensacola, it was the *conservative* that was banned for exposing the killer's hateful own words.[5]

ACHIEVEMENT/INDIVIDUALISM/SELF-RELIANCE is anathema to the Left. Achievement weighs heavily on non-achievers, who respond, "do you think you are better than me because you've *achieved* things?" Individualism does much the same: it uncomfortably reinforces that while we are all created equal, what happens next is a product of initiative, effort, and persistence. Naturally, the Left finds that last statement incredibly politically incorrect ... and offensive, and hateful. The Left says what happens next is a product of your skin color, gender, and ethnic background—and that the white supremacist patriarchal ruling class still stacks the deck in society to hold everyone else back. Achievement is therefore unattainable, and individualism may only be a benefit if you enjoy white privilege and were born with a penis. If a great résumé is an asset and you don't have one, this is the Left's reaction: "F*ck résumés!" With the Left, achievements are not to be noted or honored, because everyone does not have them, and that's *unfair*! It's *discrimination*! In truth, it's a race to the bottom as societal standards are cast to the wind.

Another strategy is to change the rules, as the College Board attempted for the often-pivotal SAT college admissions test. Rather than scoring only test achievement, they were poised to report the student's "adversity score," which was to be used to discriminate *against* those with high achievement scores, but lacking the adversity (*cue "Nobody Knows The Trouble I've Seen" music*) sometimes associated with minority candidates.[6] "Minority," *with the exception of Asians*, of course. Criticism from those still valuing achievement ensued, and the College Board went through the motions to listen. But the Left is not taking anywhere near a loss: the adversity score won't be reported to students and parents, but the school and neighborhood environment ratings composing that adversity score will *still* go to the colleges to let them to do the dirty work on their own.

Self-reliance sounds closely related to individualism, but it provokes an entirely different set of objections from the Left.

The Left works hard to gain and cement power by manning and expanding government, so anyone opting out through self-reliance is not only **not** beholden to them, but they are hard to predict and control. Though it is tough for the Left to admit, there have been wildly divergent economic success results among immigrant groups to the US. Even if we give a blanket pass to all blacks as immigrating here as slaves and being held down by The Man to this day, and we limit our comparison to Hispanics versus Asians, we find Asians much more successful.[7] Yet the Left clearly favors Hispanic immigration—even if *illegal*—more than Asian immigration. The Left has even been credibly accused of suppressing college admissions of Asians to throttle them back.[8] *Hmm.* Which group is more reliant on their big government programs? Which group is easier to control? *Is there really any argument?* Do you think this is a mere coincidence?

The goal of the Left and the Democrat Party is to increase reliance on government. What's in it for them? They **dominate** government. It's their tool. They get to exercise their "leadership," which translates to they get to exercise their *control*—and they get to build their **power**. They profit by being those who hold the purse strings of a massive government budget, with the power to reward those who are loyal to them. And, as seen over and over, somehow politicians and their families get rich far in excess of the government paychecks. Check out the fortune of the Biden family for a lesson in creative monetization.[9] [10]

Every instance of self-reliance takes away an opportunity

for the Left to build and wield its power. Self-reliance, family, religion and the influence they hold are all the enemies of the Left. It is the same for private enterprise, and by extension, wealth. All are sources of power competing with government, which is the one the Left has come to control.

GUNS is actually a subset of **Self-Reliance**. Americans with guns have less need for police—*government employees with badges and guns*—to protect them. Americans with guns are potentially dangerous to corrupt politicians who do not abide by the Constitution and its protections of individual rights. That was the purpose of the Second Amendment: to enable an armed populace to resist government tyranny, which was fresh in the minds of the Founding Fathers. Has that concern become obsolete? Hardly. In the last completed century, more people were killed by their own governments than by foreign armies—and that was a century with two world wars.[11] *But wasn't that in other countries, not the US?* Yes, but the threat of political correctness here, today, in the US is the *real* threat of totalitarianism.

What is totalitarianism? Merriam-Webster defines it as "centralized control by an autocratic authority" and "the political concept that the citizen should be totally subject to an absolute state authority." Have you heard Senator Bernie Sanders talk about his Medicare for All plan, where 150 million Americans would be **forced** to give up their health care plans from their employers to be put into a government system, prone to all the deficiencies of that other great government health care provider, the Veterans Administration? Bernie is an admitted socialist, but he has yet to cop to being the true totalitarian that he is.

The Left doesn't like guns. But *not* because of compassion for victims killed by guns—if so, they would publicize and mourn and fight every gang murder in Chicago, *but they don't.*

The Left doesn't like guns. But *not* because of the physical tool guns represent—if so, they would have to concede the same type tool is carried by our military to protect our sovereign freedom, and by everyday citizens to defend themselves and avoid violence hundreds of thousands of times every year, *but they don't.*

The Left doesn't like guns. Because they *diminish their control.* The first rule for totalitarian leaders is to confiscate the guns and eliminate the dissidents.

FAMILY SANCTITY gets in the way of the Left's power trip. The family is the strongest bond ever to unite humans. Its power transcends governments and laws—across continents, and across generations. No one can deny a mother's love, even when the son or daughter is judged harshly by others, including the courts. It's not US Senators or state judges or city mayors that people carry pictures of in their wallets or hang on their walls. It's family. Family comes first.

Can there be exceptions? Yes, the state takes charge over orphans, where no parents are present. The state also takes charge if the parents are present but unfit at any point, or for always. But without taking physical charge of children, the state increasingly limits the role of parents. Want to homeschool your children? *Eleven states say no* if the parent doesn't have a high school diploma or equivalent.[12] One goes on to require either college credits or completion of a course in home-based study. Want to opt your grade-school children out of gender fluidity lessons? *California says no.*[13] Want to teach your children that the Bible says homosexuality is wrong without being contradicted by their schoolteachers? *Good luck with that* in all fifty states.

Want to keep your children under your roof and avoid child protective services carting them off? *Be careful.* There are nearly **eight million** children referred each year, and the largest portion comes from those same schoolteachers— *government workers with chalk*—who are sure they know how to raise children better than the parents.[14] Want your children to respect America and its institutions? *Grade-schoolers by the millions are taught that America is a white supremacist, racist society!*[15] If children haven't been fully brainwashed with Leftist hogwash before they get their diplomas, America's higher education system then gets its chance. There, Democrat professors outnumber Republicans by a factor of *ten.*[16]

The Left is behind all of this. Of course, they have more than one anti-family strategy. For the black community, Democrat and Left programs have reduced the formation of families drastically. Today, just 31% of black children are born to two parents, and in 1965, about 76% were.[17] [18] For many black children, the government is a much bigger factor in their lives than their biological fathers are. That is the plan. And lower family formation is not limited to blacks. The Obama years saw middle class wealth decline and student debt soar.[19] [20] [21] Not surprisingly, family formation was pushed off to attempt to first establish financial health.[22] Cynically, leading Democrats call for "free" stuff to ease the pain, and even if that helps family formation, those beholden for accepting the goodies will end up under the Democrat's spell either way.

RELIGION has been a threat to totalitarians from the start. What good does it do to set the laws and the punishments for your own purposes if people can claim a superior law set by God? Even people *willing to be* **killed** for adherence to a higher law are a problem because dead martyrs energize causes and attract followings. One of the Left's most active endeavors is to beat down the influence of religion. The politically correct Left allows only *one* correct viewpoint—a core tenet of totalitarianism—and it does not include religiousness.

China, the world's most populous country, is officially atheistic, even nearly a half-century after the death of old-school Mao, who first established state atheism in 1949 and eventually banned religion outright in 1966. Those too objectionable in their beliefs, such as many Uighurs, still today get thrown in "reeducation" camps by the millions.[23] Stalin led multiple campaigns to eliminate religion in the Soviet Union.[24] Occasionally Hitler is mistaken to be only against the Jewish religion, but he despised Jews as an inferior *race*, while dismissing Christianity itself as mere superstition destined to be overtaken by science.[25] [26] The time was simply not right for him to persecute Christians, as they were the vast majority of those he needed to wage his war for him.

The Left in the US is in much the same position as Hitler vis-à-vis battling the majority's religion. This country was overtly founded on Judeo-Christian principles. How to overcome it? For many, many decades, the Left has used the courts, which tend to be more liberal than the legislative and executive branches. The Supreme Court itself tipped the balance in 1947 when it greatly expanded the separation of church and state concept by extending it to the states for the first time.[27] Dozens of Supreme Court cases followed, with extensive changes and liability created for government entities like schools, town councils, and even entire states, all trying to avoid the next liberal protest or lawsuit.

The current favorite weapon to sublimate the power of religion to the power of government is to rebrand religion as *discrimination*. No opportunity is missed. The Left has sued over messages on *cakes*. Religious prohibitions against homosexuality are decried, sensationalized, boycotted, then litigated. Christian business owners are directed, against their beliefs, to offer morning-after chemical abortion drugs to employees as "health care." The US Government itself threatened Catholic nuns with tens of millions of dollars in fines for the same after granting exemptions to thousands of other organizations.[28] Support for abortion is equated with enlightenment.

Who's next? Lately, it's the Salvation Army, one of the largest providers of homeless shelters, food banks, and broad social services. But they are an evangelical Christian organization at odds with the Left over sexual politics. *So no more holiday bell ringers outside of Nordstrom's. Oh, and let's make sure government investigates the Salvation Army—for discrimination![29]*

PRIVATE ENTERPRISE falls in the same camp as **Self-Reliance**, **Family Sanctity**, and **Religion**. Each is a source of power able to oppose government. In the view of the Left, all four must be choked out to allow government to dominate and expand. **CAPITALISM** is the economic organizing system that allows private enterprise to flourish—put your individual capital at risk, and either lose it or see it succeed and collect the rewards for your own. **PRIVATE OWNERSHIP** is the concept that goods—cash, land, cars, phones, and even ideas—may be possessed by the individual and not be subject either to uncompensated public use or government confiscation. In summary, capitalism permits private enterprise—which may be corporate entities, or partnerships, or individuals—to put an investment at risk and keep the proceeds in respect of the concept of private ownership.

Private enterprise is particularly hated by the Left because, unlike government, it can actually **create** value. A prime example is Apple. When its stock went public in 1980, a share was valued at $22. With stock splits, that initial share would on January 1, 2020, be fifty-six shares, with the value of that single original share growing to over $16,000.[30] In contrast, the money the government spends represents a *destruction* of value. Spending money does not create value, it's saving and investing that does. Worse, government taxes and fees destroy value for those who could otherwise save or invest that same money. Every dollar to government reduces the capacity for capitalism to operate and private enterprise to create value.

If you played the board game of *Big Government!* to beat your opponents to death, you would win by closing down the ability of private enterprise to even participate in the economy.

Wow, that sounds harsh, like the Soviet Union, or North Korea. Better put some lipstick on that pig! *Don't call it a shutdown of industry and private enterprise, call it something like "Medicare for All" and appeal to the have-nots to get their "fair share."* The Medicare for All plans espoused by leading Democrats don't allow private industry to compete with government in providing health care; they require even those people with company (private enterprise!) provided health care to give it up. That denies private industry the chance to create value for their investors, and it makes them smaller so that they wield less power vis-à-vis government. As a result, that company is less influential and its investors are *less wealthy* and *more dependent* upon the government. *Brilliant!* Keep in mind that the Left wants to eliminate the health insurance, pharmaceutical, and hospital private enterprise industries in favor of government providers, as well as the coal, gas, oil, and plastics industries.

And isn't private ownership itself a bit old fashioned? Isn't public mass transit morally superior to private automobiles? Don't single-family homes have a massive carbon footprint compared to apartments housing the same number of people? Does anyone really need a second or vacation home? Is it really possible to "own" land if it will survive you and continue on without you? Can't we dispense with income inequality and just give everyone the same? The Left is already working to ensure that private ownership is reduced and limited to make government—*the government they control*—more powerful.

WEALTH is a subset of **Private Enterprise/Capitalism/Private Ownership**, and of **Inequality**. Like **Guns**, it is such a lightning rod that it merits its own classification. Taking punishment as an element of two of the Left's favorite whipping ~~boys~~ persons, wealth is increasingly vilified at every opportunity. No matter that the collective wealth of Americans is the wealth of America itself and that it creates the essential economic foundation of America's freedoms and greatness.

Leading Democrats, courting any number of have-not identity groups—blacks, young women, millennials, debt-laden college graduates, et al.—divide America by preaching income inequality as the blameworthy source of their lot in life. A Bernie Sanders' speech is a nonstop rant on the topic. "The top one-tenth of 1 percent now owns almost as much wealth as the bottom 90 percent," he rails. Except the study he paraphrases does not include the vast Social Security payments to many of the 90%, so his assertion is a lie.[31] Bernie also would have his acolytes believe the even bigger lie that Bill Gates and Steve Jobs and Jeff Bezos all assembled their wealth at American's expense, rather than to America's benefit. Who of the bottom 90% have not benefitted from personal computers, smartphones, and Amazon? And how is it that those three people have somehow taken wealth from the bottom 90%? They succeeded by growing the pie, not by taking a bigger slice for themselves.

The solution for this is to allow **more** people to create wealth for themselves and society. That comes through improved education, lower taxes, deregulation, and assurances of personal freedom without government interference. The Left is against all of that. Their solution is for government to *take more*—and not just from "the top one-tenth of 1 percent"—so that they may dole it out to those they deem most worthy, *or most likely to vote for their destructive policies.*

INEQUALITY spans everything from inequality between the rich and the poor, between the sexes, among national and ethnic origins, and of course, between the races. No matter the occasion or the achievement, the Left claims inequality is ubiquitous and insidious. "Racism" is such an in vogue shorthand for inequality that it has been co-opted to describe not only inequalities between races, but as a sort of tainted topping that poisons any main ingredient: Democrat Senator Elizabeth Warren charged President Trump with advancing "environmental racism, economic racism, criminal justice racism, health care racism."[32] With his "environmental racism" does Donald Trump actually have the power to make it rain only upon black people? If "economic racism" includes black median household income at all-time highs and black unemployment at all-time lows under President Trump, just what is economic racism, other than another Left-wing false talking point with a false label as well?[33]

Inequality is the Left's great divider, used to prey upon human nature suspicions that somehow, somewhere, someone else is getting a better deal, or even just the same, but not deserving it. Democrats' embrace of identity politics shamelessly promotes inequality across the board as just heard in Senator Warren's baseless aspersions. The so-called women's pay gap is easily debunked when the comparisons are actually of equal jobs and equal tenure, but it is trumpeted nevertheless.[34] The so-called racial injustice of the criminal justice system melts away when the higher incarceration of minorities is matched with the higher commission of crimes by minorities—and when the system is acknowledged as broken and corrupt to varying degrees for *all* caught in its web, regardless of race.[35] [36] The Left wrings their hands over potential hate crimes against Muslims when the majority of real hate crimes are against Jews and four times that of against Muslims.[37]

The Left's dirty secret of inequality is that in contrast to America's long-held value of providing **equality of opportunity**, the Left insists upon **equality of outcomes**. To them, equality of opportunity is de facto *inequality*, because we all know *America is a racist, xenophobic, misogynist society where privileged white European men stack the deck against everyone else*. The Left demands equality of outcomes regardless of equality of inputs. Did you sacrifice and pick a less expensive public college and work part-time to minimize your college expenses? *It doesn't matter—you should pay to take on the massive debt run up by your less responsible peers who made neither concession.* Have you avoided smoking and drinking and watched your weight to preserve your health and minimize your health care expenses? *It doesn't matter—you should pay for the health care of all the wheezing Walmart shoppers filling their carts with cigarettes, beer, sugared sodas, and fatty foods.* Are you an Asian student with a flawless transcript who missed getting into an Ivy League school because too many Asians outperform their black and brown competitors? *It doesn't matter—you should understand that the bar should be higher for* *you and lower for them, regardless of how hard they worked—or didn't. Anything less would be **racism**!*

NATIONALISM/PATRIOTISM, like **Wealth**, is a subset of **Inequality**. The Left doesn't like either because it doesn't like America. The Left doesn't like America because they say it is hopelessly racist, xenophobic, and misogynist. They believe America has *zero* moral authority. President Obama was celebrated for bowing to foreign kings and determining that America should be diminished by his many ways so that other countries could work to catch up. He advocated competing less and acquiescing more. President Trump is reviled for putting an "unworthy" America first. His brand of nationalism is frequently compared to Hitler's, with no acknowledgment of the contrast in underlying values. He is competitive at every turn, and under his leadership, America's economic performance greatly outdistances the world's. This upsets Lefties, liberals, and Democrats who want Americans to be poorer and more dependent upon government.

While patriotism doesn't have the same degree of outwardly focused competitive energy as nationalism, even celebrating America at no other country's expense is unacceptable to the Left. Many opposing voices were surprised to hear that the original thirteen star "Betsy Ross" flag was reprehensible because it was created during a period of slavery—the apotheosis of inequality.[38] They were then further schooled that the *current* flag is also offensive because America retains the stain of slavery even after nearly 400,000 Americans—including one US President—gave their lives to end it over 150 years ago.[39] Some of the most visible of this criticism came from National Football League players who seemed ironically oblivious to protesting a nation that has enabled them to become multimillionaires on a skill set that encompasses little more than pushing, running, chasing, and, *occasionally*, throwing, jumping and catching.

Overcoming **GENDER DIFFERENTIATION** would appear to be a cause with narrow support, yet it seems a badge of honor with the Left, almost as if the more obscure the cause, the greater the honor in suffering for it. Democrats court the LGBTQ population, as detailed plainly in their official political platform. But it is not the chief LGBTQ constituencies that have led the fight against gender differentiation. Is there a vocal Lesbians or Gays or Bisexuals Against Gender Typing that we are unaware of? Leading it is the transgender population, which is a distinct minority of the LGBTQ population and just a *sliver* of the general population—so what gives?

This issue is a great example of willfully walking the plank and drowning to demonstrate support for ever more extreme demands of the LGBTQ crowd. *How did we survive so long without announcing our preferred pronouns?* Were we gravely offending countless others year after year for callously not asking whether they wanted to be referred to as "ze" or "they"? Think of how much the stress levels for the gender dysphoric have dropped now that they may use the same old bathroom at Starbucks, but there is no longer the abject humiliation of the former sign "Men" that used to hang on the door![40] Just think how much the psyche of women will be lifted by competing in sports against people with male DNA—now they are *truly* being treated equally![41] *Hopefully, women's sports can soon be abolished to cement the gains of women and trans people!*

What red-blooded American male high schooler will miss the chance to identify as a woman on the days of gym class to get access to the girl's locker room and showers? One day, in a better world to come, there will be only one locker room, and he/she/ze will no longer have to keep up the charade to reap the same benefit.

ANIMAL USE is another cause with a badge of honor for the Left. Who cannot be moved by those doleful animal commercials—the ones that film animals freezing, starving, and suffering abuse *for just a few hours or days longer* to dramatize the appeal for your money rather than rescuing them at once? Animals have been used by humans for time immemorial. Was that wrong? The Left says yes! Fur protests have gone on for decades. The defense there was that the animals were used for a nonessential purpose, so throwing paint on the wearers was justified. But is using a steer for a beef patty an *essential* use? *Eat a plant!* Who decides?

Just as the Left says America has no moral authority over other nations, the animal rights extremists of the Left say humans have no moral authority over other species. It's unclear whether they applaud at *Planet of the Apes* movies, or feel a little betrayed for witnessing one master replacing the other. Activists have recently succeeded in stopping greyhound racing in one state. The broad language in that legislation leaves it an open issue whether hunting, keeping livestock, or even having pets represents the same transgression against "the humane treatment of animals."[42] *Love little Mittens and not-so-little Fido while you can, because the Left says you are not worthy!*

CARBON EMISSIONS is the true bookend to **Politically Incorrect Thought**. Both are overarching and all-encompassing. There is not much you can buy or do in today's world without leaving a carbon footprint. If carbon footprints can be made bad, then they are something to be regulated, and may be subject to political influence and control. That is where the Left is taking it.

If you are looking to build government power and put your own people in place to be the ones controlling that government power, carbon emissions is a genius move for multiple reasons. First, it plays on the ignorance and gullibility of the masses. The public can't measure global temperatures or determine the reliability of those current and historical measurements. They can't easily determine whether man versus nature is causing climate change, or judge whether man has any chance of changing any trends. They can't assess whether one nation may be more responsible and more liable to fund any possible solutions. So *"experts"* will feed them all they need to know. Second, it plays on the inherent goodness of people. *I can make a difference? How?* Third, it is so pervasive that it permits all-encompassing scope and use of power to be exercised. There is almost nothing immune to regulation with carbon emission "corrections." Fourth, it is, therefore, an unprecedented opportunity to vastly grow government. Win-*win*-**win**-**WIN**!

Fighting carbon emissions allows the Left to exercise

imagination in the most creative ways. What if they decide that it's okay to create a carbon footprint so long as you compensate for it somehow? Take a flight to Houston and pay a new "carbon offset" for the privilege. Pay whom? *The government!* The Obama administration supported something called cap and trade, which would have dramatically increased residential home heating bills out of the blue. A less imaginative solution is a plain old tax on carbon. The Democrat Party platform in 2016 referred to all this as pricing carbon to reflect its "negative externalities."[43] You can easily guess who will define and price out the "negative externalities."

When in power, it's also the Democrat party and their Leftist advisors, "experts," and extended family members who will seek to get government contracts created to reduce carbon footprints. This is a major part of the Green New Deal that the socialist members of the Democrat party are pushing on an unsuspecting public. Its price tag is staggering—in the tens of *trillions.*

Having read this **FORBIDDEN FRUIT** *introduction, you now know the range of the motivations of the Left to take many, many things away from you. With that, the rest of the book details, one after the other, fifty things you take for granted that will soon be gone unless you push back and make your voice heard.*

However, launching straight into the many things the Left will take away from you risks accelerating your awareness at too many multiples of the force of gravity for your own good. Instead, to just start things moving and catch up those who may not have had their feelers out, here first is a sampling of some six significant things going, going fast, or **already gone.**

ALREADY
GONE

NO PLASTIC BAGS

VIOLATION:
Carbon Emissions

THIS CONFISCATION FROM THE LEFT is well underway. Thirty years ago, a trend took hold in the food and beverage industry: plastic containers replaced glass, greatly reducing weight for both consumer convenience and lowered shipping costs. Of course, there was an outcry from environmentalists on the Left that plastic was bad for the environment, but it was overcome when the facts were permitted to speak for themselves: glass consumed more resource (it had to be thicker to prevent breakage), took up more room in landfills, and filled trucks faster so that more trucks had to be used to ship, thus taking more fuel for transportation. Plus, consumers preferred plastic. There was really no argument *against* plastic, other than an uninformed emotional one that plastic was somehow inherently bad or was using "evil" oil to be manufactured.

Thus defeated, for nearly as long, the Left has been instead on a crusade against plastic shopping bags, which are most used for groceries. Europeans, who the Left hold up to be smarter than Americans, were already using reusable cloth bags to avoid using any disposable bag, whether paper or plastic. How could America go *backward*, shifting from paper bags to *plastic*?

As with the food and beverage containers, the facts and simple math win the day: plastic bags weigh as little as one-seventh to one-fifth as much as paper bags.[44] Again, that drives down transportation costs and many multiples of carbon emissions. Manufacture of paper bags is actually much more resource-intensive than that of plastic bags. In fact, plastic bags can be manufactured from a by-product of natural gas production, turning the by-product from waste to precious material. Plastic bags are better for the consumer waste stream because they have much less bulk than paper bags. Landfill technology ensures that waste is truly entombed — *nothing degrades* — so paper degradability is not an advantage. In addition, plastic bags are repurposed in most homes to contain pet droppings and to line wastebaskets.[45] Data available from Canada says they aren't a significant factor in litter, either. Paper bags are typically useless as soon as they may get wet. Moreover, paper bags require land to be cleared and trees to be cut. That doesn't sound very green.

So why haven't plastic bags won versus paper as plastic containers did over glass? It's tough to say for sure. Perhaps it makes it easier to deceive the public with substituting something seemingly "natural" (paper) for something "unnatural" (plastic). Glass didn't have that "natural" advantage. In the end, legislators are people and just as ignorant as the general public in matters of science and economics. Worse, they are subject to a biased Leftist environmental lobby—a lobby that is intrinsically against anything associated with the gas and oil industry—that tells them that paper bags are superior. Of course, they would love for Americans to discard *both* types of bags in favor of the European model with reusable bags that must be carried back and forth for every shopping trip. But it is seldom clear that most reusable bags are any greener than the paper or plastic bags they replace. Cloth must be manufactured, and to aid in water resistance and strength those bags used for groceries are often made of environmentally unfriendly multilayer construction containing ... *wait for it* ... **plastic**. They are also much heavier to last longer. Ironically, the only truly green reusable bag may be one made of a single type of *plastic* (like polyester) that gets used *hundreds* of times.

So what has happened with our great and wise legislators? Against all the facts pointing the opposite direction, eight states have banned single-use plastic bags. With Hawaii and California leading the way, six more states—Connecticut, Delaware, Maine, New York, Oregon, and Vermont—voted for bans in 2019 alone.[46] Contact your legislators and ask them how many trucks it takes to transport two million plastic bags versus two million paper bags. They won't know, because they would not cast their vote based on relevant facts. The answer is that it takes *seven* trucks to transport the paper bags and only *one* to transport the plastic ones. That mass and volume differential makes any case against plastic almost impossible. Keep in mind that extra mass must be transported and consumes energy at least three separate times—to the store, from the store, and to the landfill—before also filling up the landfill faster.

If plastic can be so easily outlawed for bags, why should the case not also apply to plastic used in other consumer goods? Let's start with your *clothing*. Why not a ban on plastics like polyester and acrylic and nylon in favor of cotton and wool and burlap? Perhaps there can be a government "buyback" program where you will turn in your irresponsible, dangerous-to-the-environment and threat-to-mankind shirts and slacks. *But wait, we are getting ahead of ourselves ...*

NO VALEDICTORIANS

VIOLATION:
Achievement/Individualism/Self-Reliance, Inequality

TALK ABOUT NO-BRAINERS! The big picture is the Left doesn't want to reward academic achievement because educated and accomplished people are more self-reliant and less dependent upon government. However, the more acceptable thing for them to say is that not all have the privilege and background to be able to achieve, and though the Left can't fully prevent achievers from achieving, they can work to devalue achievement as a currency.[47] [48] [49] [50] This is all about a dumbing down of society—a stoop down to the lowest common denominator.

High schools have been declining to name valedictorians and salutatorians for the last twenty years, and it seems to be gaining steam. But the old practice dates to the Revolutionary War era in the US. One graduating student was honored to be selected to provide a last valedictory address—literally, a goodbye—at commencement. Through the years, the way virtually every school in America selected their valedictorian was to name the student with the highest grade point average. Number two was the salutatorian.

Lately, schools have not only stopped naming valedictorians, but about half have stopped even doing class rankings based upon student grade point averages.[51] The authority on college admissions, the College Board, provides this absolutely nonsensical explanation: "Most small private and competitive high schools have done away with it because they feel it penalizes many excellent students who are squeezed out of the top 10 percent of the class and then overlooked by elite colleges."[52] Did you get that? *Measuring class rank results in 90% of the class* *not being in the top 10%.* And perhaps it is most unjust for the students in the *second* 10%—those ranked 10.1-20.0%—*who by definition cannot be in the first 10%.* Maybe the 30%-ers are also upset they are *not* the 20%-ers. *When will it ever end!*

Most certainly, it is not the act of class ranking that squeezes students out of the top 10%, but their lower measurement of achievement versus those in the top 10%. The students perform—*or not*—and the ordering of their results allows only one to be first, and only 10% to be in the top 10%. The Left hisses: that's **inequality**!

So let the excuses begin! What are the various and sundry ways that students—nay, even *society*—may be damaged by rankings and valedictorians? The College Board has already advanced that "excellent" students may be "overlooked." Other experts say it can contribute to heightened anxiety for students. It also permits "hyper-competition," where to gain a bit of grade point average, students are *forced* against their own wills to give up *non-academic* activities. More students may also be *forced* to take harder honors courses that may count more heavily. School officials at an Ohio school announcing the elimination of valedictorian for 2020 said it was done to reduce the "competitive culture" and to discourage "a disturbingly large number of students" from taking honors and summer courses. They added, it's about "mental well-being," "what it means to be happy," and naturally, "the whole child."[53][54]

Of course, it takes somebody wiser and more enlightened than secondary school personnel to pronounce what is really driving the change. A University of Chicago professor reveals that class rank is to be put aside for new factors to describe students, like whether they "speak English as a second language or come from challenging homes."[55] Another from the University of Kentucky reports that academic achievements may spring from "opportunities and privileges," so talent can only be credited so much before "non-merit factors of race, gender, income, connections, and luck" must be considered.[56] And there we have it: *achievement must be discounted because it is a result of white privilege and discrimination.* Note that this is in alignment with the College Board's practice to provide the components of an "adversity score" along with every graded student SAT score to allow colleges to consider the very factors the professors recount. Achievement, *hell.*

Isn't it interesting that the arguments about measuring excellence in secondary school *academic* achievement seem not to apply to secondary school *athletic* achievement?[57] Don't schools celebrate their success in sports and the individual athletes with the highest achievements? Aren't there awards dinners? Isn't that disregarding the "mental well-being" of the athletes? Don't schools tally statistics and create *rankings*? Doesn't that create a "competitive culture" and fuel "heightened anxiety"? Don't schools promote these athletic achievements to prospective colleges for the students?

Instead, can't they provide an "adversity score" for the *short* students who couldn't make the basketball starting team? Shouldn't there be *sports* scholarships available to students who have demonstrated *no sports talent*, but with *other factors* credited instead—like a nice personality or a pleasing smile or a home *without* a basketball hoop?

Academic achievement is to be despised, says the Left. In the words of Barack Obama, it's another case of "you didn't build that." Academic achievement is more prevalent with white people, *obviously* owing to white privilege and a systemically racist American society; and with Asian people, *obviously* owing to them valuing education *too highly* and just working *too hard*. Blacks and Hispanics tend to score lower on the SAT and other measures of academic achievement, *obviously* owing to nothing in their control. That means to use and value measures of academic achievement is to be *racist*. And that is why there can be no valedictorians, no class rank, and no talk of individual responsibility and achievement.

Racist, STOP!

NO GUNS ON MILITARY BASES

VIOLATION:
Guns, Achievement/Individualism/Self-Reliance

IT IS IMPOSSIBLE TO SEPARATE the image and definition of "soldier" from guns—except on American military bases, where soldiers are *banned* from having guns. Yes, *soldiers need safe spaces too*, the Left tells us. Well, it's not actually safe space for the *soldiers*, but for the *commanders* looking to limit liability for themselves and to avoid criticism from the Left for violating their feelings about "gun violence."[58]

Bank tellers used to bear a combination of nervous titters and real worries for the danger of their jobs—until it was revealed that it was *much more* dangerous to work as a clerk in a convenience store. Imagine going to work for a large, multinational organization with this record of fatal incidents at its facilities:

- ✔ 2009 - Fort Hood (13 dead)
- ✔ 2011 - Fort Hood (planned bombing thwarted)
- ✔ 2013 - Quantico (2 dead)
- ✔ 2013 - Washington Navy Yard (12 dead)
- ✔ 2014 - Fort Hood (3 dead)
- ✔ 2015 - Chattanooga (5 dead)
- ✔ 2016 - Lackland AFB (2 dead)
- ✔ 2019 - NAS Oceana (1 dead)
- ✔ 2019 - Pearl Harbor (2 dead)
- ✔ 2019 - NAS Pensacola (3 dead)[59]

Is it the 7-Eleven convenience store chain? A bomb-defusing company? *No, it's the US military!* Bank tellers, convenience store clerks, and bomb squad technicians can all rest easy.

Somehow, American military facilities, ranging from bases to supply depots to recruiting offices in strip malls, have been made "gun-free zones," aka *kill zones*, with the acceptance of the military's own top brass. After the Chattanooga killings at both a recruiting station and a naval reserve support center, the Left offered a rare, accurate assessment of why the military accepts the carnage. The policy is in place, said the executive director of the Coalition to Stop Gun Violence, "because the commanders want it." He added, "they want to be able to regulate who has guns," and he went on to cite discipline, mental health, and substance abuse concerns. "There's clearly a risk-benefit approach that the commanders are applying," he posited.

Is he on target? Then US Army Chief of Staff General Ray Odierno himself considered that arming troops could "cause more problems than it solves," saying "we have to be careful about over-arming ourselves" and expressed his concerns about "accidental discharges and everything else" that goes along with his own soldiers being armed.[60] Army General Mark Milley rose to be Chairman of the Joint Chiefs of Staff after he professed much the same: "Arming our people on our military bases and allowing them to carry concealed privately owned weapons—I do not recommend that as a course of action." To be clear, he doesn't support them carrying *government-issued* weapons, either. Pressed on how he was protecting his own people after a second tragedy at Fort Hood and then two at Chattanooga, he used the first mass shooting at Fort Hood where thirteen died and forty-two were wounded to make his point: "Those [*civilian*, not military!] police responded in eight minutes .... I am not convinced from what I know that carrying privately owned weapons would have stopped that individual."[61] Not *convinced*? Not *sure*? Need some more facts or some more time? *May the fifty-five shot down offer an opinion?*

Let's back up for a moment. American soldiers are trained in gun safety, as well as in combat use of firearms—trained by likely the best trainers in the world. And the alternative to the status quo of only a relatively few military (or civilian) police at major installations and no one at small recruiting offices being armed is not just concealed carry of personal weapons by the rank and file, but open carry of a sidearm, just like the police. Yet time and again, *our own soldiers are unarmed and shot down like dogs on their own home turf?*

Some jawboners like to blame President Clinton for the early 1990s regulations specifying that no military personnel other than military law enforcement shall be armed if not in the theater of war or in response to imminent danger.[62] That is false, and it appears that there has been no time post-Vietnam, and perhaps before, that has seen soldiers walking around installations armed. The generals themselves *do* want it. After the 2013 Navy Yard massacre, the Department of Defense issued a report with fourteen recommendations. None included arming soldiers, though one notably did suggest signage be "posted conspicuously" as reminders of the prohibition against carrying firearms illegally.[63] Following the 2015 Chattanooga murders, President Obama's Secretary of Defense approved the Marines' recommendation that recruiters no longer wear their uniforms, whether to present a less colorful target, or to avoid pushing crazies over the edge.[64]

Congress had no taste to change it, even with Republicans controlling both houses of Congress.[65] In 2016, a new Obama Department of Defense directive did come down that opened to base commanders the decision to arm additional personnel. But the directive made it clear that was by no means mandatory: "*if* the commander determines that carrying such a firearm is *necessary* as a personal or force-protection measure" (emphasis added).[66] [67] It was simply window dressing that was also not to be so effective as to raise the ire of the Left.[68] After the second Fort Hood tragedy in 2014, Democrat Senator Murphy of Connecticut had already said, "I doubt there's going to be much support in Congress to allow military personnel to carry weapons on base," and for once, he was speaking for both sides. Even Trump, who campaigned on eliminating these gun-free zones for the military, has gone silent.[69]

No guns on military bases is a perfect example of Big Government limiting the power of the individual. It is safer, and more predictable. Keep people controlled, and require them to depend on government, rather than on themselves. Eight minutes for a response, and thirteen dead and forty-two wounded is just an *expected* collateral damage for that *comfort* required by those at the top of government. Think of it this way: soldiers with guns win the risk-benefit analysis when they are between the generals and an opposing wartime force, but badly lose when they are between the generals and a drive to the officers' dining room in a liability-laden and politically charged "peaceful" homeland.

The whole mess is a microcosm of the same gun control issue for the general population. The Left insists that guns are only suitable for law enforcement and that individuals should place their trust in government to protect them. Look to the list of casualties right here, or check in with some Native Americans to judge how that works out for the "protected."

NO MEN'S ROOM-OR WOMEN'S ROOM

VIOLATION:
Gender Differentiation, Inequality

IN A DEMOCRACY, PEOPLE ARE GRANTED A VOICE in the matters that affect them. While there is a concern for the "tyranny of the majority"—that perhaps 49% of the population could be held hostage to the wishes of the majority 51%—there are also protections for that, such as initiatives requiring 60%, or even a supermajority of 67%, to be evidenced for passage. Surely, no one would *reverse* the majority rules concept for the 49% instead to prevail—and it would be utter lunacy and anarchy for just **4.9%** to hold the power. Certainly, it is to be understood if we reject that.

So what about an instance where just **0.6%** win the day over the other 99.4%? That is the situation already set in motion with the move to "gender-neutral" bathrooms based upon the feelings and fears of transgender people, who total just 0.6% of the population.[70] [71] [72] Could the transgender population be perhaps twice that, at 1.2%, doubling their "vote"? *Maybe*, but even a Harris poll commissioned by GLAAD, an LGBTQ advocacy group, puts it at no higher than 2% in the highest occurring age group, and at 1% or less in two others.[73] Plus, nowhere near all of the trans people have complained of problems with mainstream "gendered" bathrooms. The U.S. Transgender Survey in 2016 talked to over 25,000 and seemed to accelerate things when it reported about 10% said they had been denied access to a restroom, and 12% self-reported they had been verbally harassed in the restroom. Less than half (48%) said they sometimes feared and avoided public restrooms, while 11% said they always did.[74] Those 10, 11, or 12% represent about 0.07%—just seven out of 10,000—and even the 48% represent just thirty out of 10,000 of the US population.

That's not to say even the seven are not important, just that any solution might be well served to be proportional to the problem. Men "of height" in the US 6'6" and over are about as tall as the standard opening for most all residential doors, constantly risking head injury, or just humiliation for not fitting in. They compose about the same 0.07% of the population as the transgender people "denied," or "verbally harassed," or "always avoiding."[75] Shall all homes and apartments be required to be retrofitted immediately to facilitate accommodation of any future 6'6"-ers or larger? *Maybe they need their own survey of problems and fears!* Has anyone made a documentary film about their burden? *Why won't Congress act?*

Keep in mind many, many facilities *already* have gender-neutral, or unisex, bathrooms with privacy: they are labeled "family" bathrooms. If "family" is uncomfortable or somehow offensive, just a twenty dollar sign change could fix it. *Voila!* Done.

No, instead, the Left insists that this wrong must be righted, and no expense or former convenience may be spared. For this, a trip to Portland, Oregon, is instructive. Portland Community College's Queer Resource Center covers the topic exhaustively in documenting their victorious quest for "multi-stall all-user restrooms." "Transgender and gender-diverse people experience harassment, humiliation, denial of access and physical violence in public restrooms," they say, but apparently in these multi-stall all-user restrooms that force all genders into a small, confined space, those problems are magically vanquished forever.[76] It's *fabulous!* They also assure that Portland State University, University of Oregon, and Western Oregon University have the same magical no-conflict restrooms.

Across town, at the Portland Building that houses the offices of the City of Portland, it was announced that the $195 million renovation had done away with men's urinals as an artifact of a less-woke era. This building would also prominently feature multi-stall all-user restrooms, but some floors would retain separate men's and women's rooms. However, to permit "flexibility we need for any future changes in signage," the City Chief Administrative Officer noted *none* would include any urinals.[77] This gets to the next unforeseen consequence of gender-neutral bathrooms—there is yet no consensus on what is the ideal design, whether from a queueing, sexual politic, cultural, or aesthetic (*think shart in the stall, not art on the wall*) standpoint.

Those 0.6% of transgender beings have touched off a war between the *two* genders that we are not even to acknowledge: *men and women.* In 2017, two queueing theorists at Ghent University in Belgium announced that unisex bathrooms would result in shorter waits for women.[78] The *New York Post* led their story with "Ladies, the wait could be over. Unisex bathrooms reduce waiting time by 63% overall."[79] Yes, but that neglects that in the same scenario, the time waiting for *men* went up over 400%! In fact, there was no unisex scenario that benefitted men, with the Portland Building approach eliminating all urinals coming out the worst. Even taking two existing men's and women's rooms and knocking out the wall between to open it to both sexes resulted in more waiting time for men, because the women otherwise waiting for a toilet in the women's room now snagged the men's toilets that either were used for those men with a need to sit down, or as "overflow" for occupied urinals.

Of course, those speaking for our transgender friends just brush off that dust-up. Again, from the Queer Resource Center: *"Is this sexist because women are losing access to a restroom?* No, creating an all-user restroom actually addresses the power dynamic of cissexism, which privileges cisgender people over transgender people." In other words, "you were stepping on our toes all along, so don't even talk to us about *sexism.*"

Those deciding gender-neutral restroom design are still toying with eliminating urinals based on feminist views that women should be equal at any cost.[80] This is not limited to architects and civil planners. A California high school vice principal related the administration "didn't want urinals in the gender-neutral bathrooms because both female and male students can use a regular toilet," so they put a sheet of plywood across the urinals to block access. The result? The frustrated boys just constantly peed on the wood.[81]

The physiological and cultural reality is that men use the

bathroom faster, on average, by a factor of two or three times. They most often walk to a urinal, unzip, point, urinate, shake, zip, and go. Women must open a door, step in, close a door, perhaps clean or line a seat, take off clothing, sit, urinate, wipe, flush, stand, dress, open a door, and wash hands or go. That doesn't include tending to menstruation needs. Eliminating urinals or downsizing men's rooms to "equalize" the bathroom time is a superb example of bringing one down to raise another up, as if men should be penalized for their physiology.[82]

If you don't believe politics is embedded in the issue, understand that the Left now also attributes America's restroom history to *racism*: our restrooms are separate as a residual of keeping black men from white women. A feminist professor at the University of Chicago Law School goes further to say the sexes can never be equal so long as separate restrooms exist because men do so much networking there.[83] *CAUTION: men, no matter what the professor says, DO NOT invite female colleagues into the restroom to "network"!*

Two more professors (London School of Economics and Political Science, and University of North Carolina, Chapel Hill) whiff on the whole waiting time of gender-neutral restrooms before they note some still lingering problems and air their own recommendations of "design, nudging, and dialogue." They like full-length stall doors. They debate urinals, noting that since they just *offend* some *women*, they may have to go. Oh, and *did you know? Men are filthy.* They need to be encouraged to *aim.* Better, they should be trained to **sit** to urinate, extending the same consideration Japanese wives have received from their husbands—another great example of bringing one down ....[84]

To all this, the Left may thank one of their own for one possible men's strategy to effectively deal with these "helpful" sexist suggestions. The great activist, professional agitator, and Hillary Clinton mentor, Saul Alinsky, had a novel recommendation to organize Rochester's black community against the establishment. He urged them to picnic solely on baked beans and then raise a stink by going to the white man's symphony orchestra to pass gas. *It's not illegal! It will make an unforgettable impression!*[85] While they were too proud to do it, he was not too proud to recount his story multiple times. *Men will win the war against the elimination of urinals when they inflict their "filthiness" on all who would seek a clean, **dry** seat.*

NO RELIGIOUS REFUSALS

VIOLATION:
Religion

RELIGION IS TROUBLESOME. The Founding Fathers drew upon Judeo-Christian principles to draft the Constitution, and the Left preaches that the Founding Fathers and their work are systemically racist (some of them had *slaves!*) and meant to keep any but God-fearing, property-owning, white males down. *Even though they were monsters, didn't those Founding Fathers at least say church and state must always be kept separate?*

Let's at least enforce that! Also, religion may be a source of power that the government and its Lefty Deep State administrators do not control. Allowing another source of power to flourish unimpeded is a big problem, and a needless giveaway. Further, religious people are shamelessly comfortable not believing in *science*—like to them the "science" of genetically predetermined homosexuality, or the "science" of unlimited and shifting genders.[86] Finally, religious doctrine may be *selective* in its beliefs—some things may be believed and accepted, while others may be disregarded and rejected. *Wait, doesn't that make religion **not inclusive**? And doesn't not inclusive mean **inequality**, and inequality mean **discrimination**?*

So religion is discrimination!

Yes, religion is bad, no matter how the Left looks at it. Religion should be governed by the state they say and, increasingly, *it is*. Take marriage. While marriage has not been exclusively religious- versus civil-based across history and cultures, it is religious-based for scores of millions of Americans who have married in America's predominant Christian tradition. No one in government has yet said that religious marriages must be discarded for only ones sanctioned by the government, though in typical government fashion, it collects a fee for a "license" even for religious marriages. And even when *citizens* and *legislators* agree that marriage may be defined just as religious doctrine has determined, the Left turns to a sympathetic *executive branch* or to *the courts* to overturn the will of the people and their religion.

In 1996, the Defense of Marriage Act passed both houses

of Congress by over 80% majorities and was signed into law by Democrat Bill Clinton. It defined marriage as only between "one man and one woman as husband and wife." Fewer than fifteen years later, in 2011, one person decided that should no longer be the law for the nation, and that person, President Obama, instructed his Attorney General not to defend it. In 2015, the US Supreme Court, with Obama's two liberal appointees, decided 5-4 that the people's wishes now amounted to discrimination.[87][88]

Wikipedia poppycock says that at the time of the Supreme Court decision, only fourteen states had not already legalized same-sex marriage on their own "by law, court ruling, or voter initiative," permitting a false impression that the majority of Americans, state by state, had chosen same-sex marriage. Nothing could be farther from the truth. At the time Obama made his pronouncement, thus emboldening liberal judges across America, only two states, Vermont and New Hampshire, had legislation signed legalizing same-sex marriage. Only nine other states produced legislation or voter initiatives to do the same even *after* Obama's dictate. All of the other states got there propelled by federal and state court decisions—**not** by voters or their elected representatives. Liberal California first allowed same-sex marriage by a state court decision in 2008. Voters quickly reversed it by *constitutional amendment* in November that year, with Proposition 8. The Left dug in, and in 2010 found a federal judge to declare the people's wishes *unconstitutional*. That was stayed on appeal until 2013, when the US Supreme Court let the judge's 2010 ruling stand, and gay marriages resumed. What was left for the *people's* legislature? To perfunctorily remove the terms "husband" and "wife" from marriage statutes.[89]

The point is, the Left will turn to the courts to do what the American people *choose not to*.[90] Religion is to be defeated by the soldiers of the judiciary. The US Supreme Court, on average, decides one religion case a year—dozens over the past half-century.[91] [92] Countless more are heard at state and lower federal levels. Perhaps the only restraint on the judiciary is the appointment of conservative, originalist judges by Donald Trump. In 2016, with a Supreme Court of only three conservative members owing to the death of Justice Scalia, the court refused to hear a case of Washington state law making it illegal for pharmacists to refuse to stock a drug—a spontaneous abortion pill—in violation of their own religious beliefs. The dissenting conservative justices labeled that of "great concern" for religious liberty.[93] In 2018, in a turnaround with two of Trump's justices on the bench, the court refused to hear another case—one *challenging* Mississippi's religious liberty law that shields citizens, government officials, businesses, and religious institutions from being penalized for acting on their beliefs in traditional marriage.[94] The law stands.

The Left was shocked. Since the court had redefined marriage as for any two of the human species in 2015, the Left had been on a modern version of Sherman's March to the Sea, laying waste to anyone and anything in their way. Obama's Solicitor General kicked that off with his assertion before the court that religious institutions could lose their tax-exempt status if they clung to their "discriminatory" views of marriage.[95] Governments halted contracting with faith-based adoption agencies because of their policies to place children only in traditional families with one parent of each sex.[96] *Comply, or stop "helping" children!* In Illinois, caseworkers were required, prior to placement, to determine that caregivers—even relatives—be unquestioningly LGBTQ-"affirming." *Transgenderism is not to be discouraged!* Minnesota and Arizona created *criminal penalties* for businesses that would not bow to the states' enlightened dictates on marriage. In Michigan, a farmer was kicked out of the town farmer's market because he wouldn't also host same-sex weddings.[97] Picking up where government left off, a prominent gay mega-donor to the LGBTQ cause said he would target conservative states with his wealth and influence to "punish the wicked" for their views on religion regarding sexual morality.[98] Now, the Left declared, this latest Supreme Court action again authorized *discrimination!*

The Left did not know then that they would go apoplectic just a few months later in 2018, when the court decided a Colorado cake decoration case in favor of the beleaguered baker, who refused a gay couple's business. While the court declined to set a binding precedent for other cases, a 7-2 decision found the state's Civil Rights Commission exhibited hostility to religion. That came on evidence a commissioner stated the baker could **not** act on his religious beliefs if he wanted to do business in the state. Sealing the decision was another commissioner's statement that "we can list hundreds of situations where freedom of religion has been used to justify discrimination. And to me, it is one of the most despicable pieces of rhetoric that people can use to—to use their religion to hurt others."[99]

According to the Left, religion is despicable, and it amounts to nothing more than rhetoric. Leave it to the dean of a prominent liberal law school to pronounce himself smarter than the Supreme Court in second-guessing their decision, including, as a Jew, defending a commissioner for saying religion was used to justify the Holocaust.[100] Perhaps he is more qualified in law than in history: Hitler did not object to Jews for the teachings of the Torah and the Jewish *religion* per se; he viewed them as an inferior *race* and insufficiently patriotic—along with Communists and Social Democrats—during World War I.[101][102]

The Left is by no means down and out. They still have plenty of acolytes on the lower courts, as seen with the countless injunctions where a single federal District Court judge may halt a Trump executive order nationwide. The Office for Civil Rights in the executive branch is best known for responding to charges of discrimination on the bases of race, sex, national origin, disability, and age, but it is also charged with protecting "conscience rights." These guard health care workers from being forced to do things against their morals or religion—like nurses forced to assist with abortions, or with "gender transitioning." While announcing it would be more open to these cases to defend religious freedom, the Trump administration also determined to expand the protection to more workers, such as medical schedulers.[103] A single District Court Obama appointee stopped that two weeks before it was to take effect.[104]

Consider one last story in assessing the Left's willingness to paint normal religious conduct as vile discrimination by all means at hand: religious liberty was not such a polarizing or partisan cause prior to the Left pivotally embracing same-sex marriage as another puzzle piece of their identity politics recruitment strategy. Perhaps in 2014, the president of Gordon College felt those times were not too far removed to hope to turn back to recapture some rationality and compassion. With just a few weeks until the effective date of Obama's executive order adding sexual orientation as a new form of discrimination, he joined notable Christian leaders in a polite letter to the president inquiring whether a "religious exemption" might be granted. He did not receive that exemption.

Instead, with the letter public, activists protested the thoroughly Christian college's policies prohibiting "sexual relations outside marriage" and sexual intercourse between homosexuals to proclaim Gordon's bigotry and discrimination. Next, the nearby city of Salem reneged on a contract allowing the use of one of their buildings. In the following month, a nearby school district banned student-teaching by Gordon students there in an ironic violation of the civil rights of those who themselves could be accused of nothing discriminatory. Altogether, annoying and unfair, but not catastrophic. But the next blow did spell potential catastrophe: while plainly outside its purview, Gordon's accreditation agency threatened to revoke accreditation unless Gordon changed its "discriminatory" sexual conduct policies.[105] Gordon held fast, and ultimately it was the agency that blinked when it was accused of discriminatory conduct to punish Christianity and violate federal law.[106]

Many on the Left do not understand how their wished-for discrimination laws to hold in check any of their scorned religious freedoms *du jour* can be turned around. About half the states bar sexual orientation discrimination by businesses. A Minnesota couple declining to make same-sex wedding videos first had their claims of that state's anti-bias laws violating their rights of free exercise of religion and free speech thrown out. The Appeals Court judge who reversed that, a Trump appointee, reasoned that the state's law could "require a Muslim tattoo artist to inscribe 'My religion is the only true religion' on the body of a Christian if he or she would do the same for a fellow Muslim, or it could demand that an atheist musician perform at an evangelical church service."[107]

Perhaps most scary—and convincing—to the Left would be using their anti-bias laws to force them to provide the same services they provide to Democrats to Republicans. *Couldn't Barbra Streisand be forced to perform at Trump's next inauguration?*

NO BAD WORDS

VIOLATION:
Politically Incorrect Thought

ISN'T POLITICALLY CORRECT INSTRUCTION *just an extension of being polite and respectful to others?* No, there is a difference. When your mother told you to pretend to not notice the babysitter's harelip, she was trying her best to teach you to be sensitive to maintain social decorum for all involved. Now, the politically correct Left would tell you that just thinking "harelip" is offensive—it's "cleft lip," *not something assigning an animal trait to a human being*—and reinforce their superiority in demonstrating your *ignorance,* themselves violating social decorum by spotlighting your indiscreet flaw. And then there's the whole other level of political correctness that assumes your *bad intent,* like where others on the Left may insist "harelip" is a deliberate *misappropriation of the noble Lepus genus, much more worthy than human beings.* Bad intent and/or ignorance are what political correctness is out to rid the world of, starting with *you,* if necessary. Also, mom started from the *widely held rules* she learned, while the Left starts from the *narrow exception* that may be declared by just one (*very offended*) individual.

This is not new; lists of politically incorrect words have been published for the last two decades, though just when you thought the last list had reached the pinnacle of the bewildered Theatre of the Absurd, there is a new one to top it.

But why does political correctness exist? What purpose does it serve? As related in **FORBIDDEN FRUIT**, the nature of political correctness is that it *eliminates options and answers by declaring them unacceptable in advance of any further consideration.* The result is that there is only **one** proclaimed correct path. It functions as an essential tool of totalitarianism, which is the rigid control demanded by an autocratic authority—the Left: your government, your academic institutions, your biased, progressive media, and the crazy proselytes they seek to create. *Control the speech, control the mind.*[108]

The most aware of you may have already noticed politically incorrect words in this discussion of politically incorrect words, and we've barely gotten started. "Mother" is a gender-biased term to be replaced with "parent one," or just "parent" in a pinch. "Crazy" is demeaning to the mentally ill, or is it the *mentally differently-abled*? If you spotted these and knew the reasons, congratulations, you are *woke!* "Or" is also politically incorrect, because it connotes *exclusion.* "Or" should not be used, ~~or~~ and it should be replaced with "and," which celebrates *inclusion. Did I make that up? It doesn't matter, for it is my feeling, and per the Left all my feelings must be validated and respected, because they are my feelings.* Finally, "politically incorrect" is itself politically incorrect because the addition of the word "politically" suggests it is only incorrect *in a political context.* In reality, anything politically incorrect *is* incorrect, apart from any connection to "politically."[109] And thus, we devolve, down, down.

Certainly, it is no new news that the Left finds many

words distasteful, disgusting, and even injurious. What follows is a sampling of words, expressions, and situations declared politically incorrect by *someone*. Forming the syllables and making the sounds you were taught as a young child is not okay if it comes out sounding like these bad words. Many are overwrought and ridiculous, though a few must be held up for their creativity and sheer audacity. All serve to foretell what the next wave will bring. Feminists and prescriptive mannerists were the first to make an impact, and ableists, atheists, and race-baiters quickly filled in behind. *Excess rules.*

Feminists would have no words containing "man" or "men" in them.[110] *What's wrong with those womyn?* Say goodbye to "mankind," "manpower," "man-made," "workmanlike," and surely, "chairman." Don't even try "man in the street," "right-hand man," or "best man for the job." *"Man*ufacturing"? *Excuse me, say "producing."* There can be no "sportsmanship," or even "fellowship." "Forefathers"? *Ha! Men*struation? *Who named that? Sisters, can't we all make free-bleeding work?*

Prescriptive mannerists run the lot from telling us "garbagemen" are instead "sanitation engineers" to saying "homosexual" is better said as "same-sex." There are only "Asians" where "Orientals" used to come from.[111] Even a major portion of Native Americans refers to themselves as American "Indians" — but apparently, they have not read the politically correct press that insists on "indigenous people," because saying *"Indian"* is *bad*. "Savage" is demeaning, because it is. There was never any "ghetto" anywhere, just an "economically challenged neighborhood." And those unfortunate plots of land formerly called "jungles" are now "rainforests," where the bemoaned destruction surpasses the mere linguistic.

Ableists pronounce that it is the person that is primary, not the characteristic or (*shudder!*) the disease. Here is the formula to avoid all embarrassment: take any description like "blond guy" or "poor people" or "disabled person" or "fat lady," and turn it around. *Start with "person" and then add the description,* but be sensitive to try to *turn any negative into a positive!*[112] Thus, "person *of* blond," "people *experiencing poverty,*" "person *of different* ability," and *"assigned female of generous proportion." See, you can do it!* "Colored person?" *Try again, it's "person of color."* Stick with it, and soon it will come *naturally.* A real talent may be demonstrated where the convention is turned upside down, such as rejiggering the proudly "healthy" to be the "non-disabled." *Touché!* There can be no such things as "victims," like "polio *victims*" — only "polio *survivors*" — unless, of course, someone is subjected to "gun violence," and then they are most definitely *victims.* Down syndrome "sufferers" are not sufferers at all, because that might imply there is *some* disadvantage that holds all the many positives in check.

Atheists, who yell "black" wherever the faithful see "white," are just too predictably tiresome to catalog here. Suffice to say, if your parents gifted you with a "Christian name," there are those who will insist it is instead only a "forename."

Race-baiters would be unhappy with atheists yelling "black." Despite a black sky naturally being ominous, or a black night filling some with fears (feelings that the Left tells us are not to be diminished), "black" as any descriptor that possibly conveys negativity is preordained racist.[113] NEVER say "blackball," "black-flag," "black hearted," "blacklist," "blackmail," "black-market," "black ops," "blackout," or "black sheep." (And just what conspiracy decided that *angel* food cake is *white* and *devil's* food cake is *dark*?)

At times the connection seems as far-fetched as someone with wavy hair taking offense with those who complain of seasickness. *"You talking to me?"* Blacks themselves use the N-word with each other, but disallow and disembowel any others for the same, in a sort of situational political correctness. Tales get spun to take *new* offense to *old* things: "call a spade a spade" entered English usage in 1542, but did not ever refer to blackness until a black Jamaican socialist author co-opted it in 1928. That doesn't stop it from being taught as a blindly racist insult.[114] Even worse is a kind of *sins of the fathers* association: the kids' counting chant of "eenie meenie miney mo" is also *verboten* for its generations-old former reference that shares the middle "ig" letters of its "tiger" replacement.[115] *No matter how many times Lady Macbeth laments "out, damned spot" the former stain can never be removed!* Of course, this is not all limited to black vs. white. "Indian-giver" is a *heap big* epithet that may no longer be spoken. Drunken leprechauns and "Irishman" apparently are still just fine, but please, no *no tickee no washee*, and no *"Chinaman."* And who can ever forgive

Ronald Reagan for disparaging Haitians and a whole culture by demonizing *"voodoo* economics?"

Tempted to yell "are you deaf?" to the parking lot attendant who promised not to park you in, or to emote "are you blind?" to the jerk who backed into you? Do you understand that there are *real* deaf and blind people—excuse me, *auditorily and visually challenged*—who are diminished by your thoughtless speech?[116] What are you, STUPID? *Wait, is that disrespectful to real stupid people—or the neuron-compromised?* For obvious reasons, please do not describe anything as "gay," "lame," or even "sick." It may cause *real* gay, lame, and sick people to go *psycho*! If you had a conscience, that would make you want to just curl up and *die*—and the real people who have done that are perhaps the only ones *not* to take offense.

Those serving something they called Jamaican Stew were told to send it back by students claiming to be Jamaican experts who determined the food was a micro-aggression (more to come . . .) because it did not meet their standard of authenticity.[117] Has anyone told the Irish to enforce their provenance over Irish Stew—or Irish Coffee—or risk losing their culture? Should Oscar Mayer wieners expect shaming from *real* sausage experts from Vienna? Is it possible to eat Crab Rangoon without being accused of appropriating the culture of Myanmar, or Burma, or India, or wherever Rangoon is right now? Is eating Danish *celebrating* white supremacy because it supports a country that is predominately white? Or is consuming it a way of *diminishing* the people of Denmark, *one bite at a time*? Dare we even speculate what eating Turkey means, with its 99% Muslim population? Moving from mere words to other forms of expression, consider *twerking*. Twerking—the suggestive dancing with squatting hip thrusting and buttocks shaking—is credited to the bounce music of New Orleans, but Miley Cyrus lit it on fire when she performed it on a music awards show in 2013. Just like Chuck Berry and Little Richard groused that Elvis stole their acts and was somehow unworthy, Miley was accused of culturally appropriating what was to be "owned" by black dancers.[118] So far, John Travolta and the estates of Fred Astaire and Gene Kelly have miraculously avoided being sued by The Hustle, The Waltz, and The Tango.

The Vagina Monologues is a play referred to as the "Holy Grail of Feminism." In a sign of the times, feminism lost out to transgenderism at ultra-liberal Mount Holyoke College. The student theater board found the play "inherently reductionist" and not inclusive of transgender students who may identify as women but don't have actual vaginas.[119] *Yikes!* After all, gender cannot be "reduced to biological and anatomical distinctions." GLAAD (once the Gay and Lesbian Alliance Against Defamation) now finds "biologically male" and "biologically female" oversimplify the infinitely complex topic of gender.[120] Say "designated," or "assigned" male or female, and back out of the room before another trap is revealed!

Words put in a larger context and used in specific situations may also be strictly unacceptable. *Pay attention!* Students at Harvard Law School are encouraged not to attend classes on rape law, lest they should have traumatic memories "triggered" or just find themselves upset in general. Even a lecture asking whether the facts constitute a *violation* of the law has generated the charge that the word "violation" is a forbidden trigger. Students may insist professors protect them from discomfort, and they get agreement because it would be considered negligent not to acknowledge their distress—potential or *real*. Rape law is avoided because the risk of injury from *discussion* is now considered virtually the same as the injury from the *act*.[121] Would you go to a doctor who opted out of classes to avoid distress from seeing blood?

There can be no better example of the totalitarian bent of the Left to enforce only one politically correct "right" answer than seen with the University of California (UC). Former Obama cabinet member Janet Napolitano, as president of UC, held seminars for deans and department heads to recognize and "interrupt" micro-aggressions.[122] For the PC-impaired, a micro-aggression is a "comment or action that subtly and often unconsciously or unintentionally expresses a prejudiced attitude toward a member of a marginalized group," according to Merriam-Webster. *You are so racist, you are* ~~blind~~ *visually challenged!* Their reeducation indoctrination highlighted the following as offensive:[123]

- "America is a land of opportunity." A form of coded racism that suggests people of color are lazy and need to work harder.
- "I believe the most qualified person should get the

job." Neglects the white privilege and advantages denied to others that hurt their achievement.

- "When I look at you, I don't see color." Devalues an individual's racial/ethnic experience and history.
- "There is only one race, the human race." Denies the significance of racial/cultural being, like saying "all lives matter."
- Asking "where are you from?" Communicates foreignness and not belonging.
- Asking "why are you so quiet?" A veiled order directing conformance to the dominant culture.

This is taught to the faculty to teach to the students. Not surprisingly, at one campus, UC-Davis, students were further indoctrinated. They were to affirm that the words "pimp," "bitch," and "slut," and the sayings "I'd hit that" and "I raped that exam" (?) were problematic. The clincher is that they were *required* to do that as a prerequisite to registering for their classes.[124] But hey, no thumbscrews or bamboo under the fingernails, *so not to worry*. Some might say Napolitano *had* to act. It seems one UCLA professor had gotten harsh criticism — and a *sit-in* — from a handful of students who reacted indignantly to being graded on their bad grammar. They charged that spelling and grammar corrections could only make for a "hostile campus climate" for students of color. Not only that, but the professor's corrections held no authority because they were only "perceived grammatical choices that in actuality reflect ideologies" — *his own*. One other professor did weigh in to defend, saying he did not consider correcting papers racist, but apparently Napolitano was not convinced — after all, one graduate student *cried*.[125] [126]

SAY GOODBYE

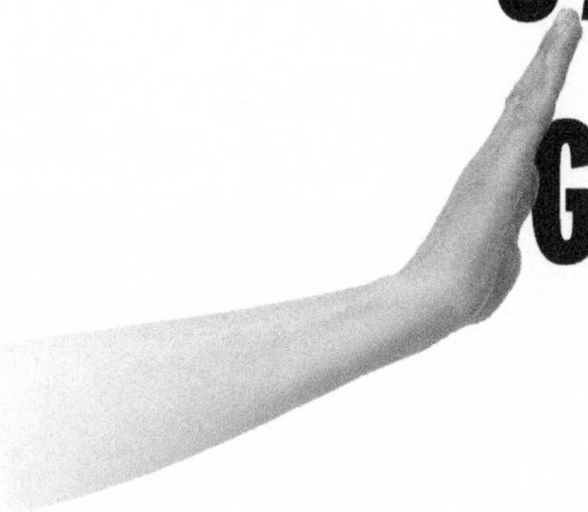

THE WORLD TURNED UPSIDE DOWN

NO LETTERS "T" OR "X" IN THE ALPHABET

VIOLATION:
Religion

AS MENTIONED IN FORBIDDEN FRUIT, the Left already bans statues, displays, names, and thoughts, so it can be no surprise that letters of the alphabet, if somehow deemed discriminatory or just generally offensive, could be banned as well. For starters, there are two letters connected to Christianity—and we know the Left wants to diminish religion broadly and Christianity specifically as a source of power in Americans' lives.

Christian principle is the foundation for much of the

Constitution and is the faith of almost all the Founding Fathers, who the Left view as racist, white supremacist, misogynistic, paternalistic, self-dealing, landed gentry setting down laws to preserve their places while diminishing all others'. That was *then*. What is *now* is the Left's determination to establish a secular society devoid of the "discriminatory" beliefs of organized religion and the power those beliefs may instill in the believers. Once, family and church provided the support for the poor and the sick. Today, government seeks to provide that safety net, and families and churches with "backward" or "unscientific" beliefs are chastised as unfit to serve in *all* ways if they fail to meet *any* of the Left's purity tests.

X is a known symbol for Christ.[127] It is the Greek symbol for letter *chi*, and is written as X. For Christians, X is frequently combined with the Greek *rho*, which has an "r" sound but appears in Greek as the symbol P, and together they form the "Chr" in Christ. But X also stands alone in denoting Christ, seen most commonly today with "Xmas," which is not blasphemy but merely a different way of writing Christmas.

What about T?[128] Yes, it has some similar Greek letter (*tau*) ties to Christianity as with X, and the symbol may also be referred to as a Saint Anthony's cross. But its real transgression lies in being the same shape as the wooden cross of the crucifixion of Jesus, which is the most recognized symbol of Christianity. Guilt by association is sufficient to have it banned from use.

The Left has taken down statues of Confederate generals because the Confederates fought for slavery. It is not enough that they may be thought reprehensible and unredeemable, it is that they are not to be thought of at all, and there shall thus be no reminders of any sort. History is to be erased, and if it is naturally assumed that they will not be featured in future history books to avoid reader hyperventilation, it is not a leap to imagine that current books may be subjected to librarians charged with eradicating those persons and their images one scissor cut at a time. It can be the same for letters of the alphabet thought reprehensible and unredeemable.

If you believe that Confederates deserve it, then puzzle through the removal of the statue of William McKinley in Arcata, California.[129] McKinley enlisted in the Union Army to *fight the Confederates* and served with distinction, later becoming the 25th President of the United States. Not worthy enough? *No.* The Left says McKinley was mean to *Native Americans*, something that could today also be said of all twenty-three Presidents preceding him. But wait, many of those were also slave owners, *or horror of all horrors, Christians.* Who does that leave, just Barack Obama? But didn't he put children on the border in cages before Donald Trump did? *Who or what is immune?*

The Left has also held that manger scenes may not be displayed for Christmas, and that the Ten Commandments may not be displayed at all, as part of their über strict ruse of the "constitutional" separation of church and state. Lest the Left be offended, ESPN removed their own *Asian* sportscaster named Robert Lee from broadcasting a University of Virginia football game on the chance he might trigger nauseating thoughts of

the leader of the Confederate forces, Robert E. Lee.[130] Was
ESPN overreacting? Probably not, given that the Left has had
people fired for even speaking one of their now-banned words.
"Niggardly" has zero racial content in its etymology or current
meaning. Its offense is to sound like the N-word. *From here on,
be very careful when using the word "bigger."*

So, do you doubt that the Left may seek to ban T and X?

Here's how that might look, repeating this section so far:

As menioned in **FORBIDDEN FRUI**, he Lef already bans saues,
displays, names, and houghs, so i can be no surprise ha leers
of he alphabe, if somehow deemed discriminaory or jus generally offensive, could be banned as well. For sarers, here are
wo leers conneced o Chrisianiy—and we know he Lef wans
o diminish religion broadly and Chrisianiy specifically as a
source of power in Americans' lives.

Chrisian principle is he foundaion for much of he Consi-
uion and is he faih of almos all he Founding Fahers, who he
Lef views as racis, whie supremacis, misogynisic, paernalisic,
self-dealing, landed genry seing down laws o preserve heir
places while diminishing all ohers'. ha was *hen*. Wha is *now* is
he Lef's deerminaion o esablish a secular sociey devoid of he
"discriminaory" beliefs of organized religion and he power
hose beliefs may insill in he believers. Once, family and church
provided he suppor for he poor and he sick. Oday, govern-
men seeks o provide ha safey ne, and families and churches
wih "backward" or "unscienific" beliefs are chasised as unfi
o serve in *all* ways if hey fail o mee *any* of he Lef's puriy ess.

Is a known symbol for Chris. I is he Greek symbol for leer

chi, and is wrien as . For Chrisians, is frequenly combined wih he Greek *rho*, which has an "r" sound bu appears in Greek as he symbol P, and ogeher hey form he "Chr" in Chris. Bu also sands alone in denoing Chris, seen mos commonly oday wih "mas," which is no blasphemy bu merely a differen way of wriing Chrismas.

Wha abou ? Yes, i has some similar Greek leer (*au*) ies o Chrisianiy as with , and he symbol may also be referred o as a Sain Anhony's cross. Bu is real ransgression lies in being he same shape as he wooden cross of he crucifiion of Jesus, which is he mos recognized symbol of Chrisianiy. Guil by associaion is sufficien o have i banned from use.

He Lef has aken down saues of Confederae generals because he Confederaes fough for slavery. I is no enough ha hey may be hough reprehensible and unredeemable, i is ha hey are no o be hough of a all, and here shall hus be no reminders of any sor. Hisory is o be erased, and if i is naurally assumed ha hey will no be feaured in fuure hisory books o avoid reader hypervenilaion, i is no a leap o imagine ha curren books may be subjeced o librarians charged wih eradicaing hose persons and heir images one scissor cu a a ime. I can be he same for leers of he alphabe hough reprehensible and unredeemable.

If you believe ha Confederaes deserve i, hen puzzle hrough he removal of he saue of William McKinley in Arcaa, California. McKinley enlised in he Union Army o *figh he Confederaes* and served wih disincion, laer becoming he 25[h] Presiden of he Unied Saes. No worhy enough? *No.* He Lef says McKinley was mean o *Naive Americans*, something ha could oday also be said of all weny-hree Presidens preceding him. Bu wai, many of hose were also slave owners, *or horror of all horrors, Chrisians.* Who does ha leave, jus Barack Obama? Bu didn' he pu children on he border in cages before Donald Rump did? *Who or wha is immune?*

He Lef has also held ha manger scenes may no be displayed for Chrismas, and ha he en Commandmens may no be displayed a all, as par of heir über sric ruse of he "consiuional" separaion of church and sae. Les he Lef be offended, ESPN removed heir own *Asian* sporscaser named Rober Lee from broadcasing a Universiy of Virginia fooball game on he chance he migh rigger nauseaing houghs of he leader of he Confederae forces, Rober E. Lee. Was ESPN overreacing? Probably no, given ha he Lef has had people fired for even speaking one of heir now-banned words. "Niggardly" has zero racial conen in is eymology or curren meaning. Is offense is o sound like he N-word. *From here on, be very careful when using he word "bigger."*

So, do you doub ha he Lef may seek o ban and ?

If you think that is ridiculous, please reread the prohibitions against statues, displays, and names just discussed above. They are all cut from the same cloth. It is just a matter of how far the Left can go and still receive your acquiescence. In the case of T and X, expect there will be Congressional hearings to get them banned, but that the Left will permit some unoffending placeholders to be substituted for T and X. These will function to remind readers of the sounds to pronounce in their heads and to make the visual tracking of words and sentences easier. Some university linguistics professors will get large grants to study that. *At least the sounds of T and X do not offend!*

Following that, here's a guess at what the written English language in America will look like, prospectively substituting the [symbol for T and the > sign for X in the first and last paragraphs of the previous passage as examples:

As men[ioned in **FORBIDDEN FRUI[**, [he Lef[already bans s[a[ues, displays, names, and [hough[s, so i[can be no surprise [ha[le[[ers of [he alphabe[, if somehow deemed discrimina[ory or jus[generally offensive, could be banned as well. For s[ar[ers, [here are [wo le[[ers connec[ed [o Chris[iani[y—and we know [he Lef[wan[s [o diminish religion broadly and Chris[iani[y specifically as a source of power in Americans' lives.

So, do you doub[[ha[[he Lef[may seek [o ban [and >?

NO ROCK AND ROLL–OR COUNTRY, OR RAP

VIOLATION:
Inequality, Politically Incorrect Thought

STEPHEN KING, THE PROLIFIC HORROR WRITER, and avowed Lefty, commenting on his voting role in the Oscars, said he would never consider *diversity* in voting, only the *quality* of the art itself. He was then murdered by his own on social media — *mauled,* just like one of Cujo's victims.[131] To be frank, it seems he had been revealing his disgusting, discriminatory views for decades. Why was the *villain* Cujo **black**, and the powerful *heroine* Carrie **white**? Why didn't he make the Jack Nicholson character in *The Shining* **transgender**, or at least insist on an all transgender film crew?

Feminists have already come up with scoring systems for films, looking at things like the proportion of non-hetero and non-male cast and crew roles to judge how worthy a film is. Pressure is on Hollywood to quit producing movies with straight white men as heroes.[132] No form of art is immune to this threat, but some will suffer more when it is their turn. Put popular music near the top of that list. Music is susceptible to being so image-driven that it can be manufactured almost at will—think The Monkees, the boy bands, and the Disney divas. So why not manufacture it to accommodate—nay, *promote*—political correctness?

The best rock and roll music has always been about challenging authority and has frequently been politically incorrect—Elvis's hips and Jagger's lips. Rock and roll—or country, or rap—will not escape the wrath of the authoritarian Left. It will be challenged *by* authority—first social media zealots, and then lawmakers—and it will *become* politically correct by decree, just like with affirmative action, or fair housing laws.

The Rolling Stones are all *white men*, so they are wrong from the start. How about a Muslim woman, a disabled Korean guy, a Mexican trans man, and a sassy black grandmother? Now that's *art*! *It's got a beat, and you can dance to it.* Why not require musical performers to get government licenses to perform, and just not grant any to artists and acts that are not diverse? After all, since so many young people idolize the top musical artists, why allow *bad* role models?

How can the Rolling Stones continue to get away with singing about black slave girls in "Brown Sugar"? Doesn't "Harlem Shuffle" brazenly appropriate black culture? Isn't it unacceptable to suggest "Let's Spend the Night Together" as a substitute for explicit informed consent for sexual activity? How can we permit them to sing "Honky Tonk *Women*" or "Street Fighting *Man*" only to reinforce binary gender stereotypes? And isn't "(I Can't Get No) Satisfaction" an unforgivable veiled taunt of the gender dysphoric?

Sure, the Rolling Stones are from another generation, and maybe are better just ignored. But then what about Ed Sheeran? He took "Shape of You" to #1 in 34 countries in 2017 but, for starters, his lyrics are highly problematic. "*Boy*" this, and "*girl*" that. Where are the *other* genders? You say you're in love with my body? *Excuse me, my eyes are up here! And what about my* **mind**? You may be "crazy"? *Do you know the pain you are causing the* **certifiably** *mentally ill?* Plus, has anybody noticed how *white* Ed Sheeran is? Fifty years after the Rolling Stones, and we are still stuck with *white* artists? *Ed Sheeran makes Casper the ghost look Nigerian.* In the video for the song, his love interest is *brown*, and he took so much of the song itself from the group TLC that he had to give them songwriting credit, and they are *black*. It looks like *virtue signaling*, and sounds like *cultural appropriation*. Guilty!

Country music is no better—it's also too white, even when the token black sings (*shout out* to Charley Pride, and Hootie).

It often glorifies patriotism and even religion. *Yecch!* It objectifies women, and never makes it clear that not all women actually have to have vaginas to be women and to be objectified—which, crazily enough, is a trait country *shares* with rap.

"Where's all my non-binary bitches, yo?" said no rapper ever. *The Left can fix that!*

NO UNDERWEAR

VIOLATION:
Carbon Emissions

DOUBLE BAGGING IS FROWNED UPON in the grocery store as wasteful, to be reserved for only the most extreme of loads. Why should it be permitted in your pants?

This is just one of many coming prohibitions on wasteful uses of resources—resources consumed that needlessly create carbon emissions. Needless creation of a carbon footprint will be used by the Left to shut down any number of things objectionable for that or any range of surreptitious reasons. Don't like guns? *Not only are they the source of gun violence, their manufacture is a crime against the earth.* Think horse racing is inhumane? *It's also a waste of carbon.* Repulsed by boxing? *Not only does it glorify violence and objectify the ring girls, the event irresponsibly expends carbon.* It's all bad!

Underwear, in too many instances, is a *redundant* piece of apparel—bringing a needless creation of carbon emissions.

The Left has already suggested that we need to cut down on clothing made of synthetic materials, and underwear stands *guilty*.[133] There is entirely too much stretchy, clingy underwear, and even the "good" 100% cotton variants require a needless tilling of the earth, and processing, and transportation, and eventual disposal. *And isn't cotton inextricably linked with slavery?* It's all bad!

It may be difficult up front to ban and regulate such a personal and often unseen commodity, but leave it to the Left to try. While an outright ban may one day succeed, in the interim, this may be a great opportunity for rationing, as for strategic materials during World War II. This could drastically reduce the amount of underwear without having to adjudicate one-by-one whether there are specific instances where underwear may be desirable. Citizens would receive either physical ration tokens or new electronic versions managed by an app. Underwear purchases would require the typical funds, along with the presentation of adequate tokens. Doctors may be consulted for medical excuses. Religious passes are, of course, unlikely. In contrast, perhaps people who don't need their tokens for underwear, maybe like a Harvey Weinstein, could sell or trade them. And reducing the number of tokens over time could effect a de facto ban before ever declaring the real thing.

Enforcement of a ban may present some interesting opportunities. As the Left veers more totalitarian on carbon emissions, it seems reasonable to expect that citizens would be encouraged to report one another for violations. Locker rooms in schools and clubs may be especially treacherous for those who may try to covertly pull on a bra or boxers. Watch out for medical personnel looking to collect their bounty after seeing patients undressed. Official government underwear checker enforcement agents seeking to uncover what you have covered may also linger in supermarket freezer aisles or gentlemen's club parking lots to gain advantage in their compliance monitoring.

NO ETHNIC RESTAURANTS

VIOLATION:
Politically Incorrect Thought, Inequality

THE POLITICALLY CORRECT HIJACKING of your experiences dining out is a big topic, and you can be assured you will soon be sorry you ever heard of it.

The classic 1984 heavy metal music send-up movie *Spinal Tap* has a famous exchange between two band members concerning their rejected cover art for their record, *Smell The Glove*. It was to have a man pushing a glove into the face of a greased naked woman wearing a dog collar. It went like this: David St. Hubbins: "They said the album cover is a bit sexist." Nigel Tufnel: "Well, so what? What's wrong with being *sexy*?" David St. Hubbins: "*Sexist*, Nigel."

In 1984, not many may have been familiar with the term, "sexist." Today, a similar mistake might be made between "culturally appropriate" and "culturally appropria*tive*." Be forewarned! The first is desirable, and the second is very, very bad. It is *racist!*

"Cultural appropriation" seems to have first surfaced in the Left's politically correct browbeating over children's Halloween costumes. Kids innocently donning a Pocahontas or Aladdin costume from their favorite Disney movie were suddenly derided for "stealing" the culture of a group to which they did not belong. Who knew that buying a physical copy of an animated picture—*a drawing*—of an item of clothing would so disrespect Indians and Arabs!

If stealing just an animated representation of a very small piece of someone's cultural environment was reprehensible, imagine how much worse it would be to steal a real piece of food of the same kind *that someone in another culture once cooked*. Now that is low. *Rogue! Reprobate! Rapscallion! RACIST!*

In this case, when we say "steal" we mean simply to "prepare it for eating"—no one is *actually* stealing anyone else's food away. In California, it is not even an enforced law to steal a piece (or cases!) of food of minimal value, but rest assured, *"stealing" the culture* of another gets the Left upset real fast. A big no-no is labeling food as "authentic" if it is not made by a person of the same culture. As bad or worse is trying to disguise that sin. *The white devil is trying to trick you into buying "his" food!*

An Asian *Los Angeles Times* columnist seemingly decided that Yamashiro needed to be investigated and outed. It is a fifty-year-old Japanese restaurant in a Hollywood hilltop mansion built by two German Jewish brothers in 1914 to lovingly display their Asian art collection.[134] The columnist's own small problem with authenticity—he is *Taiwanese* and from *Tennessee*—led him to declare himself only the jury and to recruit two Japanese "experts" as the judges to tear the place apart. He quickly determined "authenticity was a slippery concept." Along with an architect, they decided there to be *Chinese* and maybe even *Swiss* design elements. Some sign lettering was in the absolutely degrading Chinese "chop suey" font. Also, the *lighting* was gauche! Net, it was an "inauthentic fantasy of Japanese culture that has generated profits exclusively for non-Japanese people."[135] Verdict? Guilty of both sins: inauthentic authenticity, and making money for someone not of the Japanese culture. *Round eyes is raping you!*

Across town in Silver Lake, the White Guy Pad Thai food truck is pretty clear that this is pad thai, made by, *yes*, a white guy.[136] No disguise. Is that good enough? *No.* A food critic for Paste digital magazine believes that the problem is not cooking another culture's food, it is "the lack of examination of the complex power structure that surrounds that appropriation that's unsettling." So this white guy spent weeks in Thailand learning from vendors and chefs how to cook pad thai, thus gaining expertise as well as respect for the Thai culture, but he failed in thinking he could transplant it to America, where it will be defiled by the power and privilege culture stacked against brown people.[137] *Nice try, whitey!*

There's also a not-so-technical question about just what constitutes appropriation. If we take a Cuban sandwich, characterized by ham, pork, cheese, pickles, mustard, and Cuban bread pressed in a sandwich press, and it's not pressed, is it still a Cuban? How about if we replace the ham and pork with turkey? Is it a turkey Cuban, or just a turkey sandwich on Cuban bread? What if we substitute out the Cuban bread? Are we okay now as long as we *don't* call it a Cuban? But what if we *do*? Does calling something that is not a Cuban sandwich a Cuban risk appropriation even if none of the food has been used?

Another white guy has a food cart called White Boy Tacos in the Broadway section of Los Angeles. Except his tacos contain barbecue, or lime-ginger shrimp, or *scrambled eggs*. Are they "authentic"? No, not even trying. Is he disguising anything? No, he's the white guy, with his un-Mexican "tacos." *But he is using tortillas.* Is he disrespecting the *tortilla*? *No, he's disrespecting the entire Mexican culture and the powerless women who make tacos with simpler ingredients just for their families to survive! He is a person of privilege—he has a **cart**—who is profiting from the experience of an oppressed people! And he doesn't pay them a licensing fee or any portion of his profits.* Yes, but he does work to donate one free taco to the homeless just down the street when any customer buys three for $8.[138] [139] Not good enough? **No**. *It's not the homeless from whom he's appropriating tacos.* Try to follow and keep up.

Want to ratchet all this up to a new level? Replace "cultural appropriation" with "racial plagiarism."[140] Even though race is a narrower concept than culture, you needn't confine race to only describing *race*—use it as a *catchall* to get people's attention. Even *pictures* of food are racist! Ever notice how every picture of Chinese food has chopsticks in it? *That's racist!*[141] No one puts lederhosen in every picture of German sauerbraten. No one puts a surrender document in every picture of French quiche lorraine.

The upset with appropriation, or racism, or whatever word can sound most despicable seems to be a one-way street, however. Can Chinese people do no wrong? Does every Chinese-run restaurant in America actually prepare their food with respect for the culture and old ways? Do they need to go back to China every so often to get recertified? What's the standard? Are they making their noodles by hand or getting them in giant bags from a big bad manufacturer? Do they have a pond of free-range Peking ducks behind the shop?

Further, have you seen a Chinese takeout joint that doesn't sell Coca-Cola? That's not Chinese. They dishonor Dr. Pemberton and the great state of Georgia in the United States of America. Did rice pudding get invented in Thailand? It's served in Thai restaurants. What if it came from India? Shouldn't Thai owners be licensed by *someone* to sell it, for a fee? Should it be served with a disclaimer and an apology? And how can Indian owners of 7-Elevens get away with selling roller hot dogs? That food is from New *York*, not New *Delhi. Don't you just hate it when immigrants steal things?*

At least the Left's manufactured controversy cannot be accused of being *sexist*—all may suffer it. A white woman nutritionist who opened a Chinese restaurant in Manhattan found herself closing early one day—*for good.* She made the mistake of describing hers as "clean" Chinese food, and even contrasted her recipe for lo mein as not leaving diners feeling "bloated and icky." Of course, as a *white* woman she is unable to claim any improvement to this noble food regardless of whether it may be legitimate and objectively true. And her "bloated and icky" seemed a not-so-veiled reference to the use of MSG, which may result in dreaded "Chinese restaurant syndrome." That malady itself *thankfully* has been debunked as wanton racial bias.[142] It was designed to hatefully disparage the right classy Chinese for white gassy hineys. After social media raised a stink and *The New York Times* started reporting, the owner made the mistake of admitting wrong and apologizing. Perhaps the only positive was her explanation that the establishment name, Lucky Lee's, was more connected to her husband, Lee, than to any scheme to also *steal* a Chinese name for authenticity.[143] [144]

Unlike cold Manhattan, Portland, Oregon is real community, and people stick together. So it was only the first step to force a food truck named Kooks Burritos to roll out of town before sundown. The two women owners actually proudly admitted to courting or pestering Mexican "tortilla ladies" into giving them techniques and tips of the trade while on a trip to Mexico. Peering into kitchen windows helped too. Success back at home seemed to follow until the Left's alternative media got involved. Charges of appropriation and reprobation were so heady that one outlet was eventually forced to change its headline, and another had to pull down their post completely.[145] [146] Death threats to the two women ensued.[147]

But the damage was done, and kicked off a whole other effort to ensure *diners* could stay safe. An anonymous collaboration was released titled "(Alternatives To) White-Owned Appropriative Restaurants in Portland." It provided a list of "bad" restaurants, quick derogatory notes, and the "people of color" dining spots to replace them: "These white-owned businesses hamper the ability for POC to run successful businesses of their own (cooking their own cuisines) by either consuming market share with their attempt at authenticity or by modifying foods to market to white palates."[148] [149] Understand? Changing recipes to what people like is itself **racist**. *Quit Columbusing my food, bro!* Since this effort was necessary to "correct a power imbalance ... that is the result of centuries of institutionalized racism and unchecked capitalism," you should take comfort in knowing that *appropriation* was also charged for *"egregious" décor. Stay safe.*

Is anything immune to the race-baiting and capitalism-bashing? How about a nice mai tai (or two) in a cool tiki bar? *Yes, it will be a tiki bar owned and operated by real Polynesians, so not to worry.*

It's no good! We missed *colonialism* and *militarism*—and the tiki bar is their bastard child. First came the "religious" missionaries to stamp out the culture and then the imperial US to seize Hawaii for its geographic, military value! Just read a University of Hawaii professor's "Defiant Indigeneity: The Politics of Hawaiian Performance" to learn how *ignorant* you were when you bought the drink to keep the tiki mug you thought then was *cool*.[150] *You just dehumanized indigenous people, misused their symbols, and exploited the traditions they held sacred.* All for a lousy mug and a half a buzz. *Can you fall any lower?*

While we're being edified and lectured, we might as well turn to "Commodity Racism, Cultural Appropriation, and the Perpetuation of Oppressive Food Discourse," and head back to dreary Portland for another university paper, authored at Oregon Health and Science University. Here's the deal: since society is "racist, exploitative, and oppressive" our thinking and talking about food is as well. Stop saying "authentic." "Ethnic" is bad, and *inaccurate,* because white people may be ethnic to all the other people they marginalize. And never say "exotic!" It *others* people! Oh, and by the way, did you know *Aunt Jemima* and *Uncle Ben* may *not* actually be making money from *their* food?[151] Have racists appropriated them too, or have they actually been kidnapped and held against their will on Madison Avenue for decades? **Set them free!**

NO GENDER-BASED MEDICAL EXAMS

VIOLATION:
Gender Differentiation, Inequality

IN THE BEGINNING OF 2019 the headline read, "Gay man impregnates transgender partner who identifies as male."[152] *Okay, dude gets his male-identifying partner who is a biological female pregnant. Got it.* By the end of 2019 things got more complicated, with the latest headline reading, "Transgender man ... and his non-binary partner welcome a baby thanks to a sperm donor who was also transgender (and so was the doctor)." There, a biological woman who transitioned more than ten years ago stopped taking his testosterone to be able to get artificially inseminated by the donor sperm from a transgender woman. The transgender doctor assisted, and the non-binary partner cheered.[153] *Quick,* how many penises make appearances in this story? A) *1,* B) *2,* C) *3,* or D) *More information is needed.*

So things are happening fast. Democrat Julian Castro was still confused at a Democrat Presidential debate when he argued that with his brand of "reproductive justice" even a trans woman should not be denied the right to an abortion.[154] Except trans women don't have ovaries, though a *penis* may pop up here and there. Meanwhile, Planned Parenthood prides itself on getting it right that abortions are not just for women anymore. No longer does their intake form ask whether "you have sex with men, women, or both?" Now they wisely ask whether "your partners have vaginas, penises, or both?" They understand that trans men and non-binary persons may need abortions.[155] And since *men* do not appreciate being referred to as *women,* they have purged gendered language, and no web pages are pink or effeminate. Once again, the LGBTQ community is wresting control away from traditional feminists. *Everybody shopping for an abortion deserves respect.*

Trans people have reported many problems with the medical community, and it is trying to catch up.[156] Trans people get misgendered with prior names and inappropriate pronouns. Office personnel won't make OB/Gyn appointments for guys named Steve, uterus or not. Even doctors are squeamish and frequently don't know which end is up.[157]

In response, prominent organizations and facilities have tried to become more welcoming. In its Trans/Non-Binary/ Gender Nonconforming Health and Wellness effort, NYU trumpets that it follows the WPATH (World Professional Association for Transgender Healthcare guidelines). Their Gender & Sexuality Team works together to improve issues related to "SOGIE (sexual orientation, gender identity, and expression)." Even "non-heteronormative relationship structures (such as poly) and sexual practice (such as BDSM/kink)" do not faze them.[158] *Bring it on!*

The University of California-San Francisco (UCSF) has its Transgender Navigation Program, of which they are very proud. Nothing is missed—feminizing hormone therapy, masculinizing therapy, fertility options, vaginoplasty, phalloplasty, and binding/packing/tucking. Particular attention is paid to the physical examination. Personnel are directed to use a "gender-affirming approach," be careful with names and pronouns, and examine only "those body parts that pertain to the reason" for the visit. *No matter how curious,* "examination of the genitalia is not appropriate in the context of an acute visit for an upper respiratory infection."[159]

British Columbia produces a thirty-two-page manual dedicated exclusively to "Trans-Inclusive Abortion Services." It focuses on language before moving on to dispelling myths, like "Trans people cannot be pregnant." It advises, of course, don't out a trans person. Don't refer to "women and trans people" because that says they are mutually exclusive. Don't over-apologize for the mistake you have already apologized for.[160] *Don't stare or act surprised! Don't slouch. Eat a good breakfast.*

As fast as things in the no gender differentiation world are moving, it seems the medical community is *still* struggling. In a very short amount of time, activists have pressed the case that gender is not linked at all to physical characteristics, but to state of mind. That mental state may even change with the sunrise. Gender is now argued not to be objective and outwardly observable, but subjective and inwardly generated. UCSF still tells its providers that the "pelvic exam may be a traumatic and anxiety inducing procedure for transgender men," but it has no advice for those identifying as transgender *women*. To review, these are people who do not possess working female reproductive organs, though again, the pesky *penis* may appear.

Some time ago in England, a man appeared at a doctor's office insisting upon a pelvic exam to include a pap smear to test for cervical cancer. The doctor was tied up in paperwork for years when the man complained to the health service after the doctor told him he did know how to accommodate him.[161] This repeated itself in British Columbia the same month in late 2019 as the pregnant transgender man and his non-binary partner welcomed their new bundle of joy. In this case, a biological man identifying as a "lesbian" filed a Human Rights complaint for being refused his own gynecological examination. He claimed that the medical practice had abdicated its responsibility to aid in his pre-transition support for gynecological problems.[162]

Obamacare already requires men to pay for pregnancy coverage. Doctors in the US will want to avoid the publicity and liability that comes with complaints about denied medical care, and what was formerly objective and real is now moving to subjective and anything imagined. Put it all together, and gender-specific health care will have to give way to inclusive non-differentiated care from which people may opt out, but which doctors may not limit up front.

Mr. Chang, are you ready for your mammogram?

Ms. Anderson, would you please turn your head and cough? You are also due for your prostate exam, if you'd like it.

NO WOMEN'S SPORTS

VIOLATION:
Gender Differentiation, Inequality

NORMALLY WHEN SOMEONE ASKS for acceptance and coexistence, others nod in agreement based on the notion of "live and let live." Normally when someone asks for entry, others open the door. But normally those admitted don't walk in expecting to soon *displace* those extending the welcome. Not so in women's sports.

There is today a major rift in women's sports, and it's not between *men and women* — unless you count among the *men* those *transgender females* who disclaim their male biology to compete as *women*. The real rift is between women's rights feminists and LGBTQ activists. Or we could call it the Left and the Left-*er*. The feminists were quite happy with the federal government's Title IX, a civil rights law passed in 1972, banning discrimination in school programs and activities receiving federal funds. It had the effect to establish separate women's sports and to create extensive resources, including scholarships earmarked for women. That affected sports programs in K-12 and colleges directly, and the Olympics and professional sports indirectly as they benefitted from many more highly trained women athletes.

Increasingly, *trans* women, women who still possess the male DNA and many physical traits they were born and developed with, are competing not in *men's* sports ("excuse me, I am a *woman*"), but in *women's* sports. And per our expert spokes*trans*woman, "sport is a human right."[163] Trans women often dominate, leaving the biological women in their dust. At the collegiate level with the NCAA, and for the Olympics, these trans women may compete as women only if they take steps (usually *medicine*, a big step down from the Olympics formerly requiring *removal of the testes*) to suppress their testosterone production to meet a threshold level for the previous twelve months.

Even so, trans women typically retain the increased O_2 capacity, greater muscle mass, bone size, lower body fat, and increased joint stability of their birth sex.[164] That said, the Olympics and NCAA have nevertheless been pressured to relook the testosterone and other requirements in the name of "fairness." *How can women be **forced** into hormonal treatments?* Yet amazingly, the Olympics already allows the transgender women to have higher testosterone levels (up to 10 nmols/L) than some men (average range 7.7-29.4 nmols/L) and many, many times higher than birth-sex women (average range 0.12-1.70 nmol/L). "Transgender women after hormone therapy," maintains a trans woman academic advising the Olympics, "are taller, bigger and stronger on average than cisgender women. But that does not necessarily make it unfair." She cites "sociological disadvantages" the trans women may face as counterbalancing.[165] Others note cis-women may have parents that pay for the best training, and no one is trying to regulate that.

So women, who won their hard-fought crusade for equal opportunities, are now once again losing out to men. Except you can't call them *men*, because it's politically incorrect. An incensed trans opinion writer for LGBTQ website *Outsports* decried the thought of trans women being labeled "biological males" as transphobic "passive-aggressive misgendering."[166] The ACLU rejects transgender girls being told they are not girls, and then turns the whole argument on its head by arguing that discriminating against "girls" —just *transgender girls*, that is— in women's sports *is* what Title IX is supposed to protect.[167] If you believe otherwise, *you* are sadly *"misinformed"* about biology and gender.

However, it is the ACLU zealots who were misinformed, or perhaps knowingly misleading as part of their lobbying. Title IX prevents discrimination on the basis of **sex**. Back when nobody argued that gender was separate from sex or that gender was purely *subjective* while conceding that sex was *objective*, that was not expected to be a problem. Today, it's a mess. The Left wants an Equality Act from Congress that would add gender identity to civil rights protections. But at the same time, many voices also want an exception for women's sports for Title IX. Otherwise, the NCAA could not enforce the testosterone suppression—they would be *discriminating* by requiring it of some "women" (trans) and not other others (the cis-women majority).[168]

Can women's sports survive? Maybe not. At the high school level across the country there is a mishmash of regulations. Regulations about testosterone levels are not uniform— with eighteen or more states simply allowing competition among any self-identifying—and the problems anticipated by the Equality Act have already come true.[169] In Connecticut in 2019, the top two finishers in the women's indoor state championship for the 55-meter dash may each have had a not-so-little problem—a *penis*. Each self-identified as a trans women athlete.[170] The genesis of the problem was an enlightened new state law of 2011 that banned discrimination based on *gender identity*, which per that law is *100% subjective*.

A conservative Christian nonprofit—labeled a "hate group" by the Southern Poverty Law Center—filed a civil rights complaint on behalf of three of the bona fide female competitors, and those girls themselves ultimately filed a lawsuit against the Connecticut Interscholastic Athletic Conference (CIAC).[171] [172] They cite discrimination and resulting loss of honors, of opportunities to compete at higher levels, and of recognition leading to college recruitment and scholarships.[173] Do they have a point? Well, the two trans competitors also finished 1-2 at the *outdoor* state championship. One holds the all-time state record, was named the indoor track and field athlete of the year by the *Hartford Courant*, and shares the honor with the other of winning the state's sportswriters' "courage award."[174] That all-time record holder's response to the question of her physical advantage over girls? *"Run faster."*[175]

With all this fuss, at least six state legislatures have seen bills introduced to prevent trans females from competing in women's sports.[176] Multiple opinion surveys in 2019 found a majority of Americans favor that.[177] [178] Naturally, the LGBTQ activists reject even the *language* of the questions in the poll as "biased euphemisms and anti-trans code words that transphobes use."[179] A women's track and field coach in Connecticut says if the state is not willing to acknowledge the physiological advantage males—including *trans females*—have over females, "we could really save the CIAC a lot of money and just have one coed championship."[180] In other words, *abolish women's sports.* Proposals for adding slots for cisgender females in postseason competition to compensate for transgender domination themselves fall victim to concerns over a discrimination *tit for tat.* Same for creating classes within women's sport—as with weight for wrestlers. *Hmm, what would the classification be—testicular size?*

Leave it to academia to really solve it for all the rest of us dummies. Yes, our professors from New Zealand tell us, the

Olympics allows trans female competitors to have higher testosterone levels than even some males, and that and the enduring physical advantages of trans women is problematic for fair play. So shouldn't "the male/female binary should be reconsidered in favour of something more nuanced and useful?" Why not a *third* category of sports for trans and inter-sex women? Or, better, not unlike creating classes, how about as in golf, a *handicap*—for trans women, based on hormone levels? It could even be expanded to an *algorithm* that includes other physical characteristics, and that evergreen favorite of the Left, *socioeconomic status*.[181]

You grew up in a single-parent household on welfare and your mother could not afford a car? *Look how much faster the computer says you are. You are a winner!*

NO GREETING CARDS

VIOLATION:
Carbon Emissions

GIVING UP GREETING CARDS for Christmas, and birthdays, and anniversaries shouldn't seem like such a big deal after you come to understand that the Left really wishes you would just give up celebrating the occasions themselves. Greeting cards run afoul of all concerns about a ~~new ice age, global warming, climate change~~, *the weather*. All those needless greenhouse gases and carbon emissions!

Nothing seems to escape the scrutiny of the Carbon-busters. One set of calculations goes through the carbon footprint created by manufacturing a car, versus taking a flight from the equivalent of Boston to Baltimore, versus producing a gold necklace, versus *sending a greeting card.* Even though the greeting card has a claimed footprint about 3,000 times smaller than the flight and necklace, and more than 120,000 times smaller than the car, we are told that we should *skip the card.*[182] Ignore the occasion! Or at least just send an *e-card—* but *buy* one, *because sending a free one makes you look cheap and like you may not really care that much.* (Like admitting you love your tiny carbon footprint *more* than Grandma's big birthday!) More great advice from the Left!

Of course, there are noodges out there to figure even the carbon footprint of sending an e-card, so you can never be a carbon virgin in their eyes. But pray tell, doesn't a carbon footprint calculation create a *carbon footprint*? Oh, you did it in your *head*? Sure. *Well played.*

To be fair, Americans buy close to seven billion cards every year, so small numbers do add up quickly.[183] Could some not be sent? *Yes.* E-cards for some? *Yes.* Is the industry already going to considerable lengths to make cards more environmentally friendly?[184] [185] *Yes.* But the scolding and finger-wagging dismiss the very act itself as unnecessary and uncaring—for the *earth*. The Left is quick to detail all the ways the carbon is generated—harvesting trees, producing paper, printing, transport to stores and homes of senders and recipients, and disposal—but seems to miss the big picture:

people like sending and receiving cards. It makes them feel good. It may lift the spirit and contribute to good mental health. That's the countervailing calculation that is never done or even acknowledged. In a world that is increasingly reduced to fleeting electronic bits and bytes, cards provide a tangible lasting record that something that is cared about is happening. The Left may not like that some expenditure of carbon is required for that, but that's the way most people want it.

Short of putting a carbon tax on everything or outlawing greeting cards in particular, it seems that the Left begrudgingly will be subject to being wished happy birthdays and receiving valentines for the immediate future. *Let's hope they recycle!* Then again, don't underestimate their ability to steamroll over the will of the people. *In the meantime, send them your well wishes to let them know you care.*

NO MATHEMATICS

VIOLATION:
Inequality, Self-Reliance

Teacher: Heather, what is 2 to the 3rd power?
Heather: 8.
Teacher: No, I'm sorry. It is the erasure of the "historical contributions of people and communities of color."
Teacher: Craig, what is 6 minus 4?
Craig: Easy, 2.

Teacher: No, you failed to "identify individuals and organiza-tions that have reclaimed mathematical identity and agency."
Craig: But 2 is right!
Teacher: "What is right?" You must come to "see the mathe-matical value in making mistakes."

IF THE TEACHER'S RESPONSES SOUND CRAZY, well ... they are all taken *directly* from Seattle Public Schools' K-12 Math Ethnic Studies Framework. Its four themes are Origins, Identity, and Agency; Power and Oppression; History of Resistance and Liberation; and Reflection and Action.[186] That framework would replace time dedicated to teaching *math* with time teaching about the *racism that math brings*. That begs the question to come, which is why even teach a subject that is deemed *racist*? How can merely highlighting and explaining it be sufficient for the Left? *If mathematics is racist, there should be no mathematics.*

Seattle received much press and criticism in late 2019 for its proposed curriculum, but it didn't create it out of thin air.[187] In 2017, the Seattle school board welcomed the push from the NAACP to bring ethnic studies into multiple subjects, and in 2019 the Washington Legislature passed a law directing ethnic studies to be developed for grades 7-12. Oregon, California, and Vermont are reportedly setting down the same path.[188] Working with the NAACP was Black Lives Matters at School, an organization created by a man who was also the leader of Social Equity Educators and a member of the former International Socialist Organization. *See where this is going?*

Amazingly enough, there is a rift between the race-baiters and the socialists on just what *flavor* of inequality is most to blame on math: **race** or **capitalism**. *Economic class is the oppressor, not race!*[189] "No!" *Yes!* Lost in the argument are *algebra, geometry, and calculus.*

Similar to the concern over Seattle was the concern over a University of Illinois professor who wrote in 2017 "mathematics operates as whiteness." She said she was misconstrued, and that what she *really* said was that it was whiteness when it did not recognize the contributions of all cultures to mathematics, and when it was used to measure people—as with test scores. Defending herself in *the Journal of Urban Mathematics Education (JUME)*, she just digs deeper. She can't get past page one without first schooling the reader on the differences between "Indigenous" and "Aboriginal," "Latinx" and "Latino," and "Black" and "African American." Then she cites as warnings her prior works decrying "White supremacist capitalist patriarchy." It's absolutely systematic! She wonders about "decolonizing" and "rehumanizing" mathematics, too.[190] Wait, didn't you understand your twelve compulsory years of math as *dehumanizing*? *Figures.*

She is not alone. Also seeking to influence American education in *JUME* is a professor, from Brooklyn College, who seems to say that remedying the supposed objectivity and "meritocracy" of math is nearly an impossible task. First, she reports meritocracy "ignores systemic barriers and institutional structures that prevent opportunity and success," making it an insidious "tool of whiteness." Second, teachers who like to claim *not* to notice race are actually using their professed "color-blindness" to willfully dismiss "the impact of enduring racial stratification on students and their families." Finally, those that *do* notice racial differences most often cast them "in terms of deficit constructions about students, their places, and their families."[191] Bleak. *Who knew all that happened while reciting times tables?*

So the Left is worried about math and inequality—but not *just* inequality. There's also the issue of self-reliance, which they reject. Dependent people are more easily led, and dumbness facilitates and eases dependence. The Left notably includes teachers unions, who are among the biggest contributors to the Democrat party.[192] The unions lobby *for* teacher wages and *against* student test scores.[193] [194] Democrats like to count on black and minority votes, and they have a half-century of social programs to keep them comfortable. *No, smart and educated is not at the top of the list.* That half-century coincidentally has seen little progress in improved educational outcomes. Test scores did not go up.[195] What did go up? *Teachers' salaries!*[196] The US ranks well below other developed countries for reading and math proficiency, while at the top in expenditure per pupil.[197] In math, the US scores on par with Hungary, Belarus, and Malta, and below China, Russia, Canada, the United Kingdom, and even the Slovak Republic.[198]

Is it a surprise then that Seattle Public Schools, which sees some of the worst achievement gaps in standardized testing in the US between blacks and whites, in 2019 *stopped* measuring and reporting that statistic?[199] No, instead, they have a new department of *African American Male Achievement*—and the promise of the Ethnic Studies Framework to teach that getting the right answer isn't even the objective![200]

Remember, it is not the low achievement that is the problem for these students, it is the racist belief that to even measure is helpful. Or as our "mathematics operates as whiteness" professor likes to say: "We cannot claim as our goal to decolonize mathematics for students who are Black, Latinx, and Aboriginal while also seeking to measure their 'achievement' with the very tools that colonized them in the first place."[201] Does Seattle Public Schools' K-12 Math Ethnic Studies Framework advocate *anything* be measured? Of course, *stupid*—**activism!**[202]

Dumb is beautiful!

NO PETS

VIOLATION:
Animal Use, Inequality

SOMEWHERE BETWEEN THE TIME of the cavemen throwing rocks and when Fred Flintstone was able to saddle up a tame brontosaurus to do his work for him at Mr. Slate's quarry, humans decided cruelty to animals was a no-no. No abuse! Today, animal *abuse* is to be replaced with animal *use*. Groups like In Defense of Animals, United Poultry Concerns, Vegan Outreach, Mercy For Animals, Compassion Over Killing,

Showing Animals Respect and Kindness, and the Farm Animal Rights Movement debate such things as whether they should call for a Species Equality Act that would transform the "commodity status" of animals and break from using animals for food and clothing—and entertainment, and property.[203] [204]

Protests against using animals for food are long-standing, but usually get little day-to-day notice. *Soy for some, but burgers for most.* Clothing may get attention if it's a red carpet event flaunting *fur*, but thus far not many are willing to give up *wool sweaters* or *leather shoes*. Banning animals for entertainment sounds more extreme, but has had sobering success. Want to see the killer whale show at SeaWorld? Too late, it was flushed away in 2019.[205] Wouldn't the little ones in the family enjoy seeing the elephants at the circus? Ringling Bros. and Barnum & Bailey succumbed to bogus lawsuits spanning two decades and retired the elephants in 2016.[206] Okay, how about at least a trip to the dog track? Nope, banned in Florida—where it started in the US—effective 2021. Now the only animal entertainment choices on a Florida vacation may be the mouse and duck families of Mickey and Donald—and their culture has been *appropriated* by humans dressed in costumes, with cartoon heads. *That must stop, now!*

How tame and insignificant does it have to be before it's permissible to be entertained by an animal? Do hairy brothers-in-law count? Is a bird show too much? Will the birds be mistreated? Will their wings be clipped? Will interactions with humans make them neurotic, as was claimed for the killer whales? Or is it just interactions with *some* humans? Should there be a personality test for the *handlers*? Video clips of animals doing something cute are favorites on YouTube. Should clips of dogs turning doorknobs and kittens playing with each other be *banned*? Should it be up to YouTube, or do we need a *law*? Is it okay to *smile* while walking your dog? What if someone sees and reports you to the Animal Welfare Institute, or to your local sheriff?

Treating animals as property raises the dander of the militant animal rights Lefties real fast. *Who made humans superior to other life forms?* That's the kind of topic to generate a doctoral thesis and endless academic chatter. Didn't God give Adam dominion over the animals? *Oh yeah, whose god? Isn't that god guilty of speciesism, which suggests that animal suffering is less significant than human suffering? How can there be true justice for farm animals when the end result is being eaten by the oppressor, no matter how well treated while alive? Why can't animals be granted equal rights? When will they be returned to their land? Why can't they own that land? Shouldn't there be reparations?*

Crazy? How about the Animal Legal Defense Fund naming Justice, a *horse*, as a plaintiff to recover financial compensation for the medical care he required as a result of his "owner's" neglect. That same organization would seek recognition for farm animals as *crime victims*. How about court-appointed guardians paid for by taxpayers?[207] Now, who's the *master? Will Mr. Ed finally be emancipated from Wilbur when he is granted his legal "personhood"?*

Do you really think you will be able to own a pet ten or

twenty years from now? Animal activists could work for an outright ban on owning another sentient being. *It's like* **slavery**. An alternative would be an upfront payment to go to compensate animals for their suffering and servitude. $2,000 for a puppy sounds right, to be accounted for under penalty of the law on your annual tax filing. The government will send $200 on to the animal fund and spend the rest to build the size of government and create more dependency, just for *humans*—for now, at least, until each species is identified as *a new identity politics group to be courted and controlled by Democrats.*

NO CASKETS AND BURIALS

VIOLATION:
Carbon Emissions, Religion, Inequality

LOTS OF STUBBORN, OLD-SCHOOL FOLKS will do all they can in their *lifetimes* to resist and even fight the assaults of the Left. So what worse way to win the battle and lose the war than to be disposed of in *death* by the way the Left directs?

There is no environmentally defensible rationale for you being buried in a casket, or being buried at all. The Left knows that. There may be religious, spiritual, decorum, and personal reasons that are all very good, but they are easily drowned out by the Left's shouts, which will come. It's just a fight they haven't gotten to yet.

Municipalities confronted with how to maximize precious

acreage will land the first blow. Who can justify setting aside room for cemeteries that could be used instead for a strip mall that generates tax revenue, or *better*, affordable government housing that generates *dependency*? Government in the US has already demolished cemeteries in favor of public works like highways, but previously they had most all been relocated elsewhere. In Europe, the land issues are centuries old, and there are varying traditions ranging from mass stacking of bones in underground catacombs to "renting" burial plots that require additional payment every twenty-five years under penalty of having your bones dug up to make way for new money. If you want to be buried in the US in an urban area, you may be forced instead to make one final one-way trip out to the country—until the woke officials there come to the same decision. Don't forget, the Left's reach is *everywhere*—above ground and below, *this world and the one beyond*.

Caskets are easily derided as plush private planes without the wings and engine needed to fly you where you'd like to go. *Copper, bronze, chrome, and stainless!* Prices can range from $1,000 to 5,000 and more—all to briefly shine in the light of day before heading underground for eternity.[208] The Left will highlight this as needless production of a carbon footprint for someone who will gain absolutely no advantage from it. It may produce the worst cost-benefit calculation ever attempted. Of course, religion will not be valued in that calculation, and any protestation will be met with accusations of selfishness even in death. How could *religion* justify carbon emissions? *Caskets will have to go to save the planet.* There exist the equivalent of cardboard boxes, and they can be placed into pedestrian concrete burial vaults or grave liners—but they still take up valuable space even if they don't consume precious resources. Instead, the Left will insist on *cremation for all*. That eliminates caskets *and* burials. And it works to fight *inequality*—with finality! *You may have had a big house or even a mansion in life, but you will inhabit the same little vase as everyone else in death.*

IN EVERYTHING, FIGHT CLIMATE CHANGE

NO DISPOSABLE ITEMS

VIOLATION:
Carbon Emissions

DON'T USE PLASTIC WATER BOTTLES to stay hydrated. *Get a reusable container.* Don't use plastic straws, and don't expect them to be replaced with paper ones. Both create needless waste. *Drink from the water glass*—the one the server handed you while holding it by the rim you are to drink from. Please, don't ask for those plastic takeout trays. *Could you bring your own casserole dish or foil tray instead?* Will Tupperware do? *What? No, idiot, that's **plastic**!*

The new Gospel According to Carbon Emissions is just too easy for the Left to beat you over the head with. It has Inquisition-like power for persecution. Anything and everything you may use or do that requires something to be made or transported—including *you*—creates *carbon emissions*! Carbon emissions are *bad*! If you do not agree, *you are bad*!

California, naturally, was first to ban plastic bags in 2014 for paper or reusable.[209] By 2019, it had halted the handing out of plastic straws without a customer request.[210] Then San Francisco International Airport declared it would no longer allow the sale of commonplace bottles of water.[211] The city of Berkeley topped that by mandating that coffee shops and restaurants charge a surcharge of twenty-five cents for every disposable cup starting in 2020.[212] *Bring your own or rent a real mug!*[213] What city will be first to require that customers bring *seashells* to have their liquids served in? Seashells from the sea require no manufacture and generate no new carbon footprint. Plus, every seashell on land alleviates plastic crowding in the sea!

Of course, all the latest legislative fury overlooks the underlying realities of the business systems that brought us fast food and beverages. The whole output is designed to be one-way. McDonald's does not include dishwasher as one of its coveted career opportunities. Everything used to serve the food is made of paper or plastic. Starbucks kiosks and even full stores have no room for storing reusable ceramic plates, glassware, and metal utensils, much less big industrial dishwashing machines for it all. Then there are the inescapable health issues: the same government working to stamp out disposables may have very strict conflicting rules about even handling customer-supplied containers.[214] Customer containers too often make the same trip into bathroom stalls that cell phones do. Bottle deposit laws do exist in ten states, but the returns often drip with the former contents and attract pests.

That's not to minimize the problem of America tossing over 100 *billion* disposable cups every year.[215] That is the product of a mobile consumer society that also has big benefits, like wealth, safety, and freedom. Instead, the Left skips past the embedded realities and starts touting tote-along metal containers and "mug exchanges," which will be managed by an *app!*[216] [217] *Call it i-mug!* One naïve do-gooder suggests that Americans drink espressos rather than grande lattes to cut down on the *size* of the containers needed. *Oh, and how about just stay and drink your coffee here? We will rent you a table!* In their ideal world, everyone would set out in the morning loaded as if they were summiting Everest, packing in and out with them all their durable containers.

Somehow, much of the packaged food industry has escaped what the restaurant industry is being saddled with. But why should you be able to buy a bag of potato chips in a *disposable* bag? *Bring your cloth sack.* Breakfast cereal in a *cardboard* box? *Why not a reusable wooden crate?* Campbell's tomato soup? *No need for a can—bring your bowl, and we'll dip some of ours into yours!* The Left actually longs for the return of the pioneer general store.

There is no reason to stop at food when our society uses

disposables in so many other places. Why do hospitals have to be so fussy? There's too much medical waste. Needles needn't be shared between patients—that would be *gross*—but surely, the same patient should get *several* uses out of one. Bandages and wound dressings seem to get pitched too fast. *Turn them over or send them to the laundry.*

Hotels may be finally getting the message and discontinuing the toiletry miniatures, but when will they return to the common sense of the *family* bar of soap? *A quick rinse between guests is so much better for the environment than breaking out a new bar.* Speaking of bathrooms—not just at hotels and public restrooms, but at home—why flush so much *toilet paper*? Why not repurpose some of those *facecloths*? Before disposable diapers, moms *washed out* cloth diapers, so who needs toilet paper? Please, make your guests feel right at home, and set out a few extra facecloths *just for them*! *Or maybe, soon, they will be toilet trained by the Left to carry their own.*

NO SYNTHETIC FIBER CLOTHING

VIOLATION:
Carbon Emissions

BAD NEWS FOR THOSE COMPANIES that make a living at organizing your closets to turn up more storage space: you will not need nearly as much space once all your synthetic fiber clothing is **banned**. Worse news for you: all those functional fabrics will be gone. Moisture-wicking athletic wear? No-wrinkle shirts? Sexy, slinky club wear? Stretchy pants for comfort? Clingy, warm winter clothes? Stain-resistant work clothes? *Don't think so!* But check out the new fall line of *burlap sack sweats.*

You see, all those synthetic fibers are derived from *petroleum*—gas and oil, for the slow-to-learn. Yes, your favorite clothes are actually *plastic.* Just like the shopping bags. Just like the drinking straws. Just like the disposable cups. Aren't all those getting **banned**? Your clothes create carbon *emissions.* They leave a carbon *footprint.* They destroy the *planet*! *You are a very bad person! You should be shamed!* No longer shall the worst playground insult be "your mother dresses you *funny,*" but instead, "your mother dresses you *environmentally irresponsibly.*"

Your clothing should also be **banned**, just like the bags. Sometime about twenty years ago, polyester, acrylic, nylon, and other synthetic fibers moved past natural fibers like cotton, wool, and burlap as the predominant content in clothing worldwide. Today, it's about 60% for synthetics. *Ignorant and irresponsible narcissists like you are to blame! You need to pay attention to science.* Not only does making synthetic fiber clothing propel climate change, those plastics actually break down and shed fibers to *pollute the oceans,* per a 2016 study from the UK. Washing a load of clothes can throw off over 700,000 microfibers! Even walking around wearing these clothes can throw off fibers.[218] *Don't you watch CSI?*

It's hard to argue for wearing polyester stretch slacks based on *that* study. Another study from 2018 found that 73%

of certain fish caught in the Atlantic 750 miles off the coast of Newfoundland had plastic microfibers in their stomachs.[219]

So what should be done? The professor authoring the washing study suggested "filtration of effluent" and "changes in textile design."[220] Perhaps washing machines could just add filters, like the lint screens in clothes dryers. Or consumers could wash all their synthetic clothes inside the equivalent of a sealed cotton pillowcase. Easy! Chemists could also reengineer the fibers to reduce the breakdown. Or consumers could choose the fewer-shedding fibers, like polyester and blends, over acrylics. Almost as easy! Maybe do a *second* study as well, before relying on just *one* to redirect resources and public policies.

What has the Left said so far? Not surprisingly, another university researcher says just don't buy so many clothes, and don't wash them until they are *filthy. Finally, a great excuse not to do wash!* Of course, facts and science and reason have not played much of a part in the ban of plastic bags, so don't expect them to reign over matters of clothing, either. Expect a ban, or at least taxes or fines.

Bans are easy to understand: here today, gone tomorrow. Certainly, it could easily happen with the Left lobbying similarly crazed legislators. There is ample precedent, and not just for plastic bags—think of guns, and gun magazines. Taxes or fees could be *very* punitive, and that too has been a favorite of the Left for penalizing sales of ammunition. It's worth a try here. The washing study found polyester released about four times the number of microfibers as polyester-cotton blends and that acrylic measured in at six times. So take a jacket that's wholly made of cotton and available for twenty-five dollars. Next, make it punitive by taking the similar polyester-cotton blend jacket that may also be available for twenty-five dollars and *double* the price to fifty dollars. It's not *natural*! Now require that a pure polyester jacket must be sold for *four times* that, at $200. Finally, legislate that the irresponsible acrylic jacket must be sold for no less than *six times* the cotton, at $300. Let the government keep the difference to fight pollution or racism, or to fund office parties. Still need a jacket made of *acrylic*?

Suggestion: *while there's time before this plays out, start searching on the internet for early 1950s Sears and Montgomery catalogs so that you may view your coming selection of natural fiber government-approved clothing.*

NO FLORISTS

VIOLATION:
Carbon Emissions

HOW DO YOU SEND YOUR LOVE? Candy? Romantic dinner? Teddy bears or pajamas? Or do you prefer to destroy the earth with your *flowers against humanity*?

What's your excuse? Just *thick*? Think a carbon footprint is something to call Stanley Steemer to have removed? Or are you more the "let them eat carbon" climate change *denier*?

Whatever your issue, if you will just shut your mouth and

open your eyes and ears, you can be lectured on why your dozen roses are killing the planet.

Here's the first problem: the flowers came from somewhere far away, so they have to be transported. About 80% of the roses sold in the US come from South America. They are shipped via carbon belching planes. They arrive, probably in Miami, where they are put on refrigerated trucks to be driven to flower distribution centers or individual florists. When they are sold, they are driven again in a refrigerated truck to the one you want to show your "love."[221] *Carbon, carbon, carbon.*

Why not get *local* flowers? It's a great idea on paper, but South America has the sunshine and heat Massachusetts usually lacks. *Lighting and heating* a greenhouse instead of growing *outside? Carbon and carbon!* Plus, in Ecuador, where the flowers were shipped in from, the workers were walking or biking to work.[222] Not in Massachusetts. *Carbon.* If we are really keeping score, we also have to add the carbon released from producing and transporting the fertilizer and the pesticide used in growing the flowers. *Carbon carbon, carbon carbon.*

There are also environmental concerns beyond carbon. Not only can water be polluted with runoff from the chemicals, the water itself may be depleted from the locale and exported within the flowers.[223] Then there's the waste. Of course, the flowers will eventually be thrown out, travel to fill a landfill, and give up their final fragrance of polluting methane. Don't forget the gaudy plastic wrap, which will also head to the landfill, and maybe that weird chunk of foam that the flower stems may be sunk into.

Since much of the flowers for Europe may be coming from Africa, and those for the US from South America, the Left also wants you to look out for exploitation in the floral supply chain. In Kenya, the minimum wage is €1.25 per day. Tanzania and Ethiopia are lower, and Uganda has none at all. Colombia has problems with pesticide exposure and sexual harassment for women laborers. India seems to like to force young boys to work twelve-hour days watering flowers and loading trucks.[224] To overcome all this to allow a flower purchase with a minimum of guilt, Colombia created a certification program that monitors everything from composting, to pollution, to labor standards including day care centers and accessible health care.[225] *Anything less in a daffodil would be irresponsible.*

Still want to send flowers? If the lecture hasn't yet taken all the joy out of the thought of sending flowers, it should be plainly noted that the whole floriculture is a needless expenditure of precious resources. *Florists are the devil.* Why not put your energy into building eco-friendly yurts for Pakistani villagers? Just send your sweetheart a notice that you made the donation in his or her name. Or take a pledge to *exhale less and emit less carbon dioxide yourself.* You can rope in your significant other and do it *together* on Valentine's Day rather than buy flowers and go out to dinner and whatever else. No heavy breathing. *Do it for the planet!*

NO CHRISTMAS TREES AND LIGHTS

VIOLATION:
Carbon Emissions, Religion

THERE IS A MEMORABLE SCENE in *National Lampoon's Christmas Vacation* where Chevy Chase's character excitedly first turns on 25,000 Christmas lights on his home. The lights gloriously come on for just a second or two before the entire cityscape blacks out owing to his power consumption. In years to come, no one will understand that scene because they will never have experienced outdoor Christmas lights before they were outlawed.

Carbon emissions, as reported, are a convenient excuse to remove *anything* troubling to the Left. If it may consume any resource during or even after its lifetime, it may be vilified, dismissed, and banned at will. So it is with Christmas trees and Christmas lights. The special bonus here is that banning Christmas trees and lights also curtails a key celebration of the Christian faith. Halting carbon emissions *and* religion? ~~Heavenly! Divine!~~ Well deserved!

Certainly the lights do consume energy, but so did lighting the exterior of the White House during the Obama administration to celebrate same-sex marriage. It used to be that people were allowed to make personal choices as long as they paid their bills. The First Amendment is supposed to guarantee the right to celebrate your religion of choice, and it does not carve out twinkling lights. But increasingly, religion is portrayed as discrimination in disguise. Christmas trees and lights are where that trend intersects with the growing momentum on the Left to do something—*anything, everything*—about climate change. Christmas lights will not survive the confluence of those trends.

Christmas displays have long been on the ropes on *public* property. Preserving displays of nativity scenes there may turn on whether Jesus, Mary, Joseph, and the Three Wise Men are joined by Santa, Rudolph, and a menorah, as then there are not exclusively Christian images shown. Christmas lights on *private* property may be assailed on multiple other grounds—*bah humbug* homeowners associations may regulate them, as may municipal zoning ordinances.[226] The Supreme Court of Arkansas ordered homeowners to limit their Christmas display based on the legal principle of nuisance.[227] All of this has happened prior to today's woke era, where environmental impact and climate change bring new fuel to the war on Christmas.

Even if Christmas lights may have some fight with the Left still in them, Christmas trees do not. Wait, aren't *artificial* Christmas trees okay? Hardly, they are a crazy combination of metal and plastic(!) that seems less environmentally friendly than nuclear waste. "Real" Christmas trees, even though renewable and typically sustainably farmed, are dogged by the images of dead trees at the curb and fields full of stumps. The earth grows them, then man takes them and abuses them as stolen holders for gaudy tinsel, baubles, garlands, and (*gasp!*) electric lights—possibly to glorify an old-timey white guy from church—while co-opting the trees to help deceive kids about the truth about *another* old-timey white guy in a creepy red suit. Easy to defend? *Christmas trees and lights need OJ's legal team, fast.*

NO CELEBRATIONS

VIOLATION:
Carbon Emissions, Family Sanctity, Religion

IF YOU WOULD BOW TO GIVING UP greeting cards as needless wastes of carbon for Christmas and birthdays and anniversaries, you are not going to turn around and be successful in arguing to celebrate the events at all. People celebrate by *buying* things like cards ... and gifts, and cakes, and party supplies. They arrange dinners and get-togethers. They *drive* to get there. For Thanksgiving and Christmas, many *fly* to get there. The carbon effect is multiplied hundreds of times over. And what's the difference between going to church to celebrate Christmas and going *any* Sunday? It's just too much, and it must *all* be shut down.

The climate change crazies will be pleased to quote just how much carbon footprint is generated for any of your activities. For now, much of it is little more than shaming— *you shouldn't do this, you shouldn't do that.* Celebrities on Facebook will preach that you should use just one square of toilet tissue, or drink from reusable water bottles, or buy only hybrid cars, or purchase "carbon offsets." But lawmakers are already busy passing laws restricting your freedom to live as you choose. Lightbulbs, appliances, and HVAC units are already regulated. The European Union (EU) banned vacuum cleaners that were *too* powerful.[228] *A dirtier planet is acceptable, but not a warmer one.* The $2 trillion coronavirus relief act in the US was nearly derailed by the Left insisting on incentives for solar and wind power while punishing the devastated airline industry for using fuel and flying people. *Things* are more readily regulated than *people* and their activities, but controlling and limiting celebratory *events* is clearly doable. Just look to all those events quickly cancelled to feel good about fighting the virus.

Given the Left's success to date at convincing a wide swath of the population that humankind should mount its largest undertaking in history to fight nature's own continuing changes in climate, the pace of mobilization will only accelerate. Our Democrat leaders like to say climate change is the greatest existential threat facing the world.[229] [230] A convergence of the Left's desires will see *celebrations* battled with certainty. Banning celebrations also serves to diminish family sanctity and religion, two of their most hated competing sources of power for those whom they wish to control.

Celebrations of birthdays and anniversaries are nothing if not celebrations of family. But even patriotic holidays are. President's Day provides the occasion for spring break and countless family trips to Disney. Memorial Day and Labor Day are celebrated, starting with family. Fourth of July typically sees piling into the family car to go watch fireworks.

Thanksgiving creates the largest travel day of the year, with families rendezvousing from far and wide to celebrate together. How doubly effective for the Left to restrict or ban all these celebrations in the name of battling climate change while benefitting from limiting family bonding and influence! The same goes for religion and religious celebration, but this one is more obvious and likely to draw resistance. The Left has worked ceaselessly to remove religion from society to limit the power people take from it. They focus on K-12 schools, because they can influence the children for a lifetime, but also because it is so easily done, with the majority of administrators and teachers liberals who want to purvey the politically correct messages of the Left. Schools have already gone out of their ways to abolish most celebrations other than Martin Luther King, Jr. Day, especially religious ones. They hide behind spurious and convenient misinterpretations of the law to deny even *recognition*—not *celebration*—of religious holidays. Christmas Break is *Winter Break*. Easter Break is *Spring Break*. Schools are careful to note they close at these times *not* to recognize any religion, but merely to respond to the "operational" matter of otherwise high absenteeism.[231]

Whether for celebrations, or decorations, or the religious doctrine itself, the Left is too smart to picket churches directly. They instead concentrate on winning their points in the courts, and attacking the schools, where virtually all children may be found, rather than the fewer found in the pews. Not-so-rogue teachers find ways to take the "no celebrations" even further, banning from classrooms even reindeer, candy canes (*their*

"J" shape may be imagined to stand for Jesus, the red a symbol for the blood of Christ, and the white for resurrection!), and even the colors red and green.[232] *It seems "J" may really signify the joy that the Left removes from all elements of life they seek to conquer and control.*

NO VACATIONS

VIOLATION:
Carbon Emissions

Says you: "I'm going to Disney World!"
Says the Left: "Actually, you're not."

YOU CANNOT JUSTIFY THE CARBON EMISSIONS created by a vacation to Disney World. Regardless of driving or flying to get there, a huge carbon footprint will be generated. *You are also responsible for your part in having thousands of acres of native land in Florida cleared and developed and asphalted.* All that energy consumed to build the parks! To run it, a gargantuan electric bill every day … every day *since* … and every day *into the future.*[233] *All for your amusement,* **while the earth cries.**

Naturally, when you arrive, you'll rent a car to burn some more carbon. Then, you'll want to eat, and use the bathroom, and buy single-use plastic bottles of water, before you use the bathroom *again. You are a human tornado of swirling carbon emissions.* You'll probably leave lights on unnecessarily in the hotel room, and take extra long showers and set the air conditioning extra low to splurge on someone else's dime. You'll generate lots of trash, and finally, thankfully, go home without demanding that the Everglades also be drained and paved over at your whim.

Do you really think there *won't* be efforts to shut places like Disney World down? In the meantime, why not require each attraction to post its carbon footprint per participant? Perhaps guest passes can be scanned for each attraction and a cap put on energy consumed. *If the kids want to do the Tomorrowland Speedway with those carbon-powered cars, we can only still walk up the Swiss Family Treehouse without exceeding our energy limit today.* Or, guests could pay at the *end* of the day, after being assessed for each ride's footprint—and each meal's, and each drink's, and each flush's. Maybe, instead of person by person, Disney could just have a daily energy use cap, and shut down at like 4:45 or 6:09 when it's reached. Maybe they could still stay open as long as they choose any given day, but the Left can reduce the operating days from 365 to about 320 ... or 220 ... or just 120. *Be reasonable. It's for a good cause.*

There may be vacations that create less carbon emissions than Disney World, but in every case, *you have to get there.* Just camping in a national park or even on your brother-in-law's land in the other end of the county leaves a carbon footprint: what about the *smoke* from your *campfire*? Or the *fumes* from your *cookstove*? Plus, now you are leaving an actual physical footprint—dragging your big feet across the face of Mother Nature. It's inexcusable. **Stay home.**

Luckily, you have been provided technology to take the place of these now primitive vacation experiences. Instead of buying the Disney vacation, you will buy the Disney vacation virtual reality glasses. Don't worry—*it won't cost any more.* In fact, it will be priced just like the Disney vacation, with the bulk of the cost going to fight climate change. The government will collect and administer those funds to battle climate change at the Left's insistence. Remember how the vacation to Disney World with three kids cost about $6,500 all-in last time? *It will be the same.* The reality glasses and software license rentals will cost about $1,500, and the other $5,000 will start to make up for your past transgressions against the earth and your fellow man. Used to go camping for a long weekend mini-vacation for only about $600? That could be a little tough to match since the VR glasses and software alone will run over $1,000 before the carbon offset charges. *Maybe you shouldn't go "camping" as much.* Or we could offer you some very nice *pictures* and even some *gifs* you could view on your mobile device or computer. *Look, the **clouds** move in this one!*

NO SPORTING, ARTS, OR CONCERT EVENTS

VIOLATION:
Carbon Emissions

THE DAY IS NOT FAR OFF WHEN ANY HUMAN ACTIVITY will be evaluated for its carbon footprint.[234] Need to go to the hospital?

Do you really *need* to make the trip? Couldn't you wait and combine it with going to the supermarket? Couldn't you book a rideshare rather than take that big gas-guzzling ambulance? Any *necessary* expenditure of carbon will be examined for mediation or reduction, as with the hospital ride, and any *discretionary* expenditure of carbon will be argued for elimination.

Events are very hard to justify because the alternative—everyone stays home instead—is a very low bar that is impossible to match.[235] Naturally, the biggest events, like the Super Bowl and the Olympics, are the biggest targets. Much is made of the carbon footprint of the Super Bowl. The National Football League knows it is under the microscope and has been linking to some sort of green initiative for each of its Super Bowls for over twenty-five years. In 2007, it launched into buying carbon offsets and planting trees to "equalize" the carbon emissions of the Super Bowl.[236] A recent addition has been to toss plastic beverage cups in favor of much more resource-intensive and costly aluminum ones (that are "greenest" only if they are reused *and* recycled).[237] [238] Other organizations have been more ham-handed in their political correctness: NASCAR took until 2008 to switch to fuel without lead, three decades after the US government pressed it for passenger cars.[239]

There are a lot more sporting events than the Super Bowl, however.[240] Major League Baseball schedules nearly 2,500 games annually. But there are many other sports, and often they occur at many other levels: semi-pro, collegiate, high school, grade school, community, workplace, and more. That's hundreds of thousands of events, maybe *millions*. The NFL has staff paid to massage their image and thus even claims student book donation drives in their *green* efforts. They also tout reusing water, food waste collection or composting, and recycling bins among their efforts. Even stadiums with access to public transport or eliminating parking lots get bragged about.[241] Will *your* local school or community sports organizer have the same resources to defend its carbon footprint?

Do you even understand the carbon footprint of a high school football game? First, there is the footprint of the stadium and grounds. Carbon belching machinery was used to level the field, and to put up the stands, and to erect the lights. Electric now flows to the lights, and water flows to the toilets. It must be generated and pumped, and in the case of the water, also disposed of. Indoor venues must also be heated or air conditioned. Food will also be trucked in, to generate trash, waste, and, eventually, sewage. That sets the table, and then people show up. Buses and many cars bring athletes and fans to the location. This produces a large amount of carbon emissions, to be doubled on the return trip home. The people consume things and throw away what's not wanted while there. They go to the bathroom. The players have had to have all their clothing and equipment manufactured—and cleaned. The teams also held many practices, with many of the same carbon emissions, including from the necessary transportation for that. *Has your community bought any carbon offsets or planted any trees to compensate for all this? No?*

Many spaghetti-limbed Leftists may have little care for athletic events, but what about *their* art in the park or LGBTQ film series? Those events are open to the same criticism. Will the patrons stand for a doubling of ticket prices to cover the price of carbon offsets or "social licenses" sold to compensate for such *irresponsible* events?[242] Would it be enough to promise to only walk or take public transportation, and then not buy anything, throw away anything, or use the bathroom while there? Is there really *any* benefit to gatherings of people? Couldn't it just be streamed on a mobile device? *Isn't that why we need 5G?*

The Oscars, Emmys, Tonys, MTV Video Music Awards, People's Choice Awards and all the others—none is justified in its carbon footprint. Fans already stay home and watch on television or on the internet. Most in attendance are guests, not nominees. There's no good reason for them to fly in at the *earth's expense*. They could stay home too. And don't even talk about the Cannes Film Festival. Private jets—and *yachts*?

Old enough to know about the Rolling Stones tours of 1969, 1972, 1975, or 1978? It's not old age that will prevent them from touring in their doddering 80s. *It's carbon.* Ever drive 300 miles to see Led Zeppelin, or AC/DC, or Madonna? *That won't happen again.* What about your crazy roommate that followed the Grateful Dead two different years in his camper van with four other Deadheads? *It's a moment frozen in time from a different era.* Don't be selfish. *"Truckin'"? No, it seems you will be sitting at home.*

NO RETAIL SHOPPING   125

NO RETAIL SHOPPING

VIOLATION:
Carbon Emissions

YOU DON'T REALLY BELIEVE THE LEFT would allow you the expenditure of energy and the corresponding creation of carbon emissions for a trip to the mall when you could just order online, do you? What you are doing is *anti-Earth!* You love *yourself* more than you love the *planet!* You are not *green!* You can never be one of *us!* Never mind that there are some things that you like to see before you buy, or that you can never seem to get a pair of shoes online that fit. *And no, checking out the hottie working at the bookstore is never an excuse to burn carbon!*

Retail locations are already closing at a record pace. 9,300 stores closed in 2019, up nearly 60% over the prior year and the highest since it seemed like a number to start tracking in 2012.[243] Amazon, which started out as a bookseller and has crushed its brick-and-mortar competition, is now a $280 billion company, is valued higher than Walmart, and has produced the world's richest man. It is doable! Perhaps most impressively, they now sell everything from jewelry to furniture to groceries. But even partners are wary—FedEx stopped delivering Amazon packages because it was unprofitable in the short-term but a threat long-term that Amazon's own growing delivery system would be a competitor.[244] The occasional concerns of the Left with Big Business Amazon—as with Alexandria Ocasio-Cortez blocking their expansion in

New York—will fall to the thrall of their greater passion for their Green New Deal. *Every family has a favorite.*

Not that they are ever good with math, but this is a case where the numbers support the Left. Let's say we have one million packages of toilet paper to distribute. How do we minimize the cost of getting them from the manufacturer to one million households? Through retail locations, we would have to send manufacturer trucks to distribution centers to serve all fifty states, then have the retailer send them to individual stores in their trucks, and finally, wait for consumers to drive, one car at a time, to shop for them. In contrast, the Amazon model has seventy-five fulfillment centers, and increasingly it is their own trucks that deliver directly to consumers upon demand. That one delivery truck may replace fifty consumer trips to stores, and there are additional efficiencies with managing fewer inventories, and with end-to-end system optimization.

What would it take for the Left to pull the trigger and stop you from retail shopping? Not much—just elect *any Democrat* as President. All have embraced the Green New Deal in some fashion, and the continuing sweep to the Left by their party makes every new day more ripe than the last for radical change. Candidate Andrew Yang was ahead of the curve in touting his American Mall Act to repurpose dead shopping malls. He was unclear on for what, but the leading answer seems to be a perennial cause for Democrats: *affordable housing.*[245] [246] All the necessary ingredients seem to be coming together for a tasty Leftist stew: carbon emissions, the ill health of retail, a plausible economic argument, and affordable housing. How better to limit carbon emissions than to have people live where they would shop? Maybe the Amazon pickup point can be the Borders they put out of business. Maybe an Auntie Anne's can be saved to provide nutritious food. Maybe another storefront can be reserved for selling carbon offsets. *Maybe the affordable housing can be subsidized, or even free, to build dependence!*

NO LAND DEVELOPMENT

VIOLATION:
Carbon Emissions, Inequality

THE LEFT HAS OPPOSED LAND USE for a long time. They don't want timber harvesting or even road construction on fifty-eight million acres of land without roads in the National Forest System.[247] They don't want hunting on public lands. They don't want pipelines. They don't want new coal mines. They don't want drilling for oil, whether in Alaska or out in the water off the coast of California. They don't want the fracking that has made America energy independent and less susceptible to Middle East politics and economic ransom. They don't even want *dead* trees used or even removed—California has 100-150 million dead trees to fuel their catastrophic forest fires.[248]

Land *development* far surpasses land *use*. Use is maybe only hiking and hunting, or a dirt access road, or a hidden underground pipeline. Development is understood to add value by clearing natural obstructions, constructing roads, installing utilities, and building anything from blacktop parking lots to homes to skyscrapers. The Left doesn't like land development either. Certainly, anything that goes from *no* land use to land use to land development is rejected as much worse than land use alone. But even where there is already use, development is decried. Knocking down low-income or minority neighborhoods to build a road or stadium is protested; knocking them down for gentrification is excoriated. This is despite the centuries-old doctrine that society benefits when land is raised to its highest purpose. As another example, many liberal municipal governments not only guide but greatly limit development through zoning that insists upon high-density housing as a way to conserve open land—*and maintain some affordability in the face of government overregulation.* Some of these same governments are happy to welcome illegal immigrants, who apparently create *no* impact upon housing needs.

The EPA, a Deep State haven for Leftists embedded in government, is infamous for halting development, one regulation at a time. And states have their own environmental agencies in addition to the EPA. Stories of farmers, builders, and homeowners told they may not use or develop portions of their own land because the EPA has declared a seasonal puddle a body of water abound. Trump has eased that somewhat, and if he had not, his own border wall would be subject to year- or decade-long delay to study its effect upon migratory sparrows, or lizards not even seen in those areas. Still, for many, the EPA is just *one* regulatory agency standing in the way of development and progress. A housing development, a strip mall, or even an individual home carved out of a family tract of land may take months or years of planning approvals through multiple regulators to get a green light, with inspections and even possible reversals proceeding through the duration of the project.

The takeaway should be that there exists a baseline of resistance to land development that climate change and its carbon reduction clarion call can now only push higher. This supercharges the prior environmental concerns and provides new cover for any other social or political objectives. Development and carbon reduction run in opposite directions, and development cannot win.

What will happen? Development will slow. Redevelopment will be a main source for housing, warehousing, and light manufacturing, but it will be subject to the expected political battles of who wins and loses. For housing, high density will be the norm. This could be accomplished in a variety of ugly ways. A 50s ranch home sited on a half acre could be required to be knocked down and redeveloped as an eight-unit apartment. If not knocked down, the existing structure could be forced to be modified to accommodate two or three families instead in order to be sold or rented. With the Democrat's enchantment with socialism, there's always *confiscation*—but no one says you have to move out of your home just because it's turned into multiunit housing—*maybe you can stay in one of the units.* Or don't allow homes with more than three bedrooms to be inherited—they become the property of the state, to be converted. If the Left chooses, it can progress faster by taking all private homes in America and putting them under government control so that each can be divided to house between two and eight times more people. Housing needs would thus be covered so that development could be suspended for at least forty or fifty years.

Finally, there is tremendous potential for the Left to use carbon emissions as the catalyst to steer development to cure what they claim as America's *other* existential threat: inequality. High density, subsidized housing mandated by Democrat legislators, liberal judges, or a new socialistic regime can serve the Green New Deal while greatly redistributing wealth. The Green New Deal represents such a mouthwatering opportunity for the Left to grow government while bamboozling the public that it can only be stopped if they are kept from power. Republicans cannot control the Presidency and one or both houses of Congress forever, *so it is an inevitable reality.*

NO HOME MEALS OR KITCHENS

VIOLATION:
Carbon Emissions, Self-Reliance

WHY DOESN'T THE ARMY HOUSE SOLDIERS in private apartments with nice kitchenettes, or just pay for their stay at a Residence

Inn? *Haha.* They don't call it being *in the service* for nothing. Soldiers are in the service of their country. For everyone else, the government is supposed to be in the service of them. But that's not how the Left sees it. The Left likes big government, and control, and dependence—for *you.*

How about *fancy printed menus* in the Army mess halls? *Are you kidding? Get in line!* Expediency and efficiency dictate one mess hall ... one meal ... one big pot. That expediency and efficiency dictate the same for you. You can't justify the carbon emissions of driving to the supermarket once or twice a week. You can't justify the carbon emissions of buying food packaged in such small quantities that the packaging nearly outweighs the product. You can't justify the carbon emissions of cooking just for you or your family. You can't justify the carbon emissions of *manufacturing* your refrigerator, microwave, range, and oven for you. You can't justify the carbon emissions of *using* your refrigerator, microwave, range, and oven.

The Left has the answer for all that. *You should eat at a mess hall or wait at your doorstep for the same delivery as your neighbors.*[249] If you can walk there or take public transportation, you go to the mess hall. If not, the mess hall will come to you. No trips to the supermarket. *(Wait, do we even need supermarkets now?)* No packaged food. No energy use for cooking. No appliances.

But ... *government soup kitchens for all?* Yes, either eat-in or delivered. Especially to get started, though, private industry may be contracted as feeders. Little Caesars sells a large cheese or pepperoni pizza for five dollars. It may be the most food per dollar anywhere, save for perhaps a bag of raw turnips.

Certainly, if there are not other private concerns ready to supply, there will be plenty of Left-, liberal-, and Democrat-connected family members, friends, and toadies hungering to step up to the plate to profit. Down the road, after extensive, expensive studies farmed out to universities and more friends and family, it will be desirable that your rations be reduced to pellets or powders that just need a little water added. Amazon Prime will have the government contract to deliver you a month's supply of breakfast, lunch, and dinner in three shoebox-size cartons. *Save the planet! It's for the children!*

The Left also likes the idea of you being dependent. It's a double win: *climate change* and *dependency*! Consider their dominion over African Americans since the Great Society programs as a mere dalliance on the way to the *real* triumph. And as dependence goes, it's tough to beat *eating*. Controlling health care is desirable, but it really only controls the *unhealthy*. That leaves a lot of healthy and potentially rowdy opponents poised to push back. Controlling education smartly seeks to control the mind, but that doesn't work against either end of the bell curve: the smartest still think what they want, and the dumbest just can't be educated to reliably go along. *No, control food.*

Withholding food is *awesome*. It really works: Mr. Robertson has a concealed carry permit and is a member of the NRA. *Lose his food deliveries off and on for the next six months and see if he wises up.* Little Miss Maria is a member of the College Republicans. *Wipe out the balance on her university meal card.* Grace, Danielle, and Pat, along with four hundred others, were identified via facial recognition technology as attending a Right To Life rally. Put them on the *dissident meal plan,* which cuts their calories by 55% but otherwise appears the same as the regular food. *Haha! We will turn them into unwitting patriots by reducing the size of their carbon footprints—and their shadows!*

NO MEAT

VIOLATION:
Animal Use, Carbon Emissions

Q: Why did the chicken cross the road?
A: I dream of a world where chickens can cross the road without having their motives questioned.

THAT ANSWER TO THE CLASSIC HUMOROUS QUESTION may sum up the position of animal rights activists: do not reduce the noble chicken to the punch line of your insensitive jokes! Carnist! Speciesist! *Misogynist-turning-your-same-abuse-to-animals-ist!*[250]

There is no defense of inhumane practices for treating animals, whether cattle, pigs, or chickens. Once maltreatment is exposed, those conditions are difficult to continue for long, as they are bad public relations and bad business. Even then, there are *always* exceptions to good practices.[251] [252] Still, for many in the animal rights movement, even one exception is one too many, and any macro changes always seem to come too slowly. They have plenty of remedies for that.

Human activists may not eat animals, but they are not reticent to eat their own. Senator Bernie Sanders got protested by the group Direct Action Everywhere (DxE). Why? He is viewed as *pro*-hunting and *pro*-agribusiness. He supported the Farm Bill of 2014 that had a goal of *helping* his state's dairy farmers. Worse, back in 2006, he was so bold and misguided as to support the Animal Enterprise Terrorist Act—an unforgivable piece of legislation that made it illegal to break in and release lab or farm animals.[253] *Who will free the lab rats? Power to the rodents, right on!*

DxE doesn't agree with other activists (like the Reducetarians—yes, *really*) who would "settle" for Americans giving up meat for veganism.[254] *There are **people** to be punished!* No, DxE wants you to refuse to eat animals and to even refuse to sit where *other* people are eating animals. DxE likes to go into restaurants and yell at diners, or tell the life story of an exploited *hen* named Susan, or stage "die-ins" where activists cover each other in fake blood and pretend to eat each other.[255] [256] That's when they are not executing their "open rescues" that are the same criminal operations targeted by the Animal Enterprise Terrorist Act. They view that law itself a crime against *species equality*.[257] "We are trying to destroy animal agriculture," says the DxE co-founder, making it plain and clear.[258]

If that sounds so extreme as to be dismissed by voters and their lawmakers, there is an alternative path. That path draws its inspiration from the tactics of the climate change purveyors. They want the costs of the "negative externalities" of carbon generation to be made up and assessed to all energy users, like by taxing carbon, or through "cap and trade" schemes. Energy prices for home heating and transportation would soar overnight. Some animal activists urge the same, and not only would they charge for the *environmental costs* of raising animals—land use, feed, water, waste disposal, and more— they would charge for *general public health issues* from eating animal products, for *"damage" to farm and processor personnel wellbeing,* and certainly for *animal suffering.*[259] Think a thirty-dollar steak is expensive now? How about using that thirty dollars for a gallon of milk and saving up **$200** for your steak?

Short of any such grand scheme, increased government regulation alone may raise costs as the Left desires. Even consumer demands for improved conditions giving chickens and pigs more room cannot help but raise prices when fewer animals fit under the same roof. California has already legislated such.[260] *Free-range chickens are not free.* Some of the same activists seeking to increase the footprint of operations to provide the animals more space would then use the same increased footprint to set the trap to argue increased damage to the environment. Taking a different tack, In Defense of Animals instead promotes "veganism as a spiritual practice."[261] *Don't have religion yet?* Then try this for the ultimate Lefty *kumbaya*: eliminate animals as food, make people eat plants, and take all that feed used for chickens, pigs, and cattle and *feed it to people instead* to SOLVE WORLD HUNGER!

CONTROL YOUR BELIEFS

NO POLITICAL PARTIES

VIOLATION:
Politically Incorrect Thought

TO BE CLEAR, WHILE THE LEFT WILL ENSURE there are no more political parties, there *will* be **one** party: the Democrats, or the Democratic Socialists, or the Social Justice League, or whatever Alexandria Ocasio-Cortez and her allies want to name it.

Aiding her and the Democrats is the media, plainly taking their side and demonizing any other. Fifty years ago, the political affiliations of America's top newscasters were not obvious. Chet Huntley may have been liberal, but if he was, it did not resonate in his reporting. David Brinkley may have been liberal, but it also didn't come across, and he was thought as much libertarian as anything.[262] Walter Cronkite *was* a liberal, but he could be accused of not much more than a grumpy tone in his professional regard of Republicans.[263] Then came Cronkite's twenty-four-year successor, Dan Rather. Rather *was* obvious, from an ambush interview of Vice President George H. W. Bush in 1988, to headlining a Democrat fundraiser in 2001, to reporting that President George W. Bush's military service was a sham in 2004, for which he was pushed aside at

CBS News and unsuccessfully sued them.[264] [265] Now with no limitations in his dotage as a respected voice of the Left, he has tweeted continually to criticize President Trump and appeared on CNN to urge, "Everyone try as best we can to contain this president and the damage he's doing to this country."[266]

The current mainstream media vilifies President Trump so much and so widely that to list even a sampling of representative examples would produce a book of its own. Capturing the essence of all that however is the *Washington Post*. It produces a report that pins on Trump an average of over 400 "false or misleading claims" monthly.[267] A claim later repeated seems to count as a new one. Many are Trump's opinions, but if they disagree, they cast them as *falsehoods*. Then Democrats and other Lefties shorthand the measure to a kind of "lie-meter" and simply refer to his "thousands of lies" or to him as the "most lying President ever." *See how it's done?*

Echoing all this is every sad-faced celebrity or Hollywood hack or whatever that can tap on a computer or mobile device. Check in with Barbra Streisand, Bette Midler, Debra Messing, Rob Reiner, Ron Howard, Patricia Arquette, Don Cheadle, Rose McGowan, and John Leguizamo for a taste of *"Hitler Pathological Liar Morally Bankrupt Terrorist Regime"* gumbo.[268] [269] [270]

Academia follows close behind. How about the "More Than Five Hundred Law Professors Write A Letter Favoring Impeachment" headline by *Forbes*?[271] And don't forget the Washington establishment Deep State. Check out their "More than 2,000 former DOJ officials call on Attorney General

William Barr to resign," as headlined by ABC News.[272] *Are you ready to cast off your views and accept theirs?*

All work in concert to convince the American people that Trump, Republicans, and Republican values like limited government and self-reliance are out of touch, outmoded, and even outrageous. *They are wrong! They are dangerous!*

With Trump having proven quite capable of defending himself again and again, the Left is happier to turn to easier marks, like sixteen-year-olds wearing Trump's Make America Great Again hats. Nicholas Sandmann was libeled by numerous liberal media outlets and celebrities for standing still and looking into the face of a Native American who walked up to him, beating a drum and chanting.[273] Given the "guilty" hat, it was he that was reported as the harasser. It was even declared that his face was "punchable" by a CNN personality.[274] From there, death threats flowed to Sandmann and his fellow students, and his high school had to close for a day. Jim Carrey literally painted them, with a "Baby snakes" title.[275] Kathy Griffin was one to portray them as Nazis.[276]

Of course, the initial reporting was a preordained story just waiting for the right video clip, and it was all inaccurate. In a rare case of justice meted out to Leftist tormentors, Sandmann has sued multiple news organizations for $275 million each and individuals ranging from members of Congress to celebrities for amounts ranging from $1-5 million. CNN has already settled.[277] Sandmann's hat and good behavior may have secured his fortune.

It can be no surprise that with all the vitriol and persecution, many Republicans are reluctant to advertise their political preferences. As a teenager with little to lose, Sandmann wore the hat. Many adults with careers and community standing — *and mortgages* — do not feel they have that luxury. The hat stays in the closet, but behind the curtain, they vote their beliefs. Trump's 2016 win was so unexpected because his support was so underreported.[278] That seems to continue to this day. Through early 2020 in the run-up to the next election, poll after poll again reported that about any of ten Democratic challengers could beat Trump handily, even if they could not appeal to more than 10% of their own base.

So if the American people will not be easily *convinced*, then they should be *coerced*. Despite sixty-three million supporting Trump with their votes in 2016, and the likelihood that the number may have risen higher with credit for an expanded economy, no new wars, and key terrorists dead, the Left's effort to coerce proceeded with the impeachment and failed removal of Trump. Those sixty-three million were to be disregarded by just 230 Democrats in the House of Representatives as they passed their articles of impeachment. The media, Hollywood, academia, and the Deep State cheered them on.

Speaking of Hitler — *thank you, Rosanna Arquette, Louis C.K., Patton Oswalt, Saturday Night Live, Robert De Niro, and Cher, all of whom have related Trump to him* — it was Nazi Germany that had only one legal political party.[279 280 281 282 283] In 1928, the Nazi party received less than 3% of the federal election vote. In 1933, Hitler grew his power by blaming the arson attack on the German parliament building, the *Reichstag*, on his communist party opponents. The term "Reichstag fire" came to be the general label used to describe the staging of an inflammatory event by a political movement to vilify opponents and shut down liberties. The day after the fire, Hitler caused the suspension of extensive civil rights: freedom of expression, association, public assembly, and the press; habeas corpus, and privacy of mail and phone communications. They were never restored. In the 1933 election, just four months after the last, the Nazis gained another 10% of the vote. By 1938, after banning other parties, they received 99%.[284]

Impeachment was the Democrats' failed Reichstag fire. If successful, they would have bypassed all the Nazi civil rights bans to go straight for stripping the vote from half the population. *Republicans, you can stand with the Jews. Independents, go over there with the Gypsies and mentally ill, unless you are ready to* **change** *your affiliation.* **Last chance!**

When is the next Reichstag fire?

NO ACTUAL HISTORY

VIOLATION:
Politically Incorrect Thought

HISTORY IS INCONVENIENT. And very messy. Increasingly, everyone wants to pick a side. Male vs. female. Binary vs. non-binary. Black vs. white. Colonial vs. indigenous. Religious vs. *other* religious. Religious vs. *non*religious. While it may have been nice—or even a matter of life and death—to have been part of the winning side at the time, today it seems better to claim being on the losing side, to be seen as more *righteous* to have endured any hardship or injustice.

Statues are coming down, and holidays are being renamed. We know what the Left wants done with Christopher Columbus and Robert E. Lee—they are to be removed from modern-day life, and all traces should be removed from history as well. History books are already written to color and twist history to the views of the Left. US Founding Fathers are downgraded not just for some owning slaves, not just for allowing slavery to continue for a time, but for supposedly setting up a system that subjugates blacks to this day to such a degree that the slavery still exists, though without the label. In another revision, the US had no moral authority to end World War II with atomic bombs in Japan because Japanese people were human too, and arguably much more worthy than the hundreds of thousands of Americans who might have died in a traditional invasion. Or hear that Bill Clinton was impeached after being charged with multiple felonies committed while in office, but that's surely not to say he *deserved* it. Blah blah blah.

The easiest form of history revision is just to not report what does not fit the desired narrative. Christopher Columbus is today reviled for himself taking Caribbean islanders as slaves, as if it was theft of innocence of the New World. Those that he took as slaves had already experienced the unsavory practices of warring indigenous tribes—taking the men of neighboring tribes they fought and *torturing and reportedly eating* them, and keeping the women—as *slaves*.[285] [286] [287] Similarly, many American Indian tribes took as slaves the people of the *other* American Indians they defeated.[288] By that measure, how is it acceptable to participate in Indigenous People's Day? After we sanitize history to remove the aggressors, is there any history left to report? That may exclude all humankind. Perhaps history worth reporting will be limited to some fairy-tale jungle somewhere where no animal has ever fed on another, and all the creatures live in harmony.

How do you talk about or study the US Civil War if you must not speak of Robert E. Lee and the rest of his generals and the entire Confederacy? Maybe the Left can approach it as they deal with the discussion of rape law in law schools. That has already been curtailed because some on the Left find the dialogue upsetting, or even "triggering." Is slavery *less* upsetting? Why not agree that it can never be discussed at all, or at least not initiated by anyone not an actual descendant of slaves, or until recently a slave themselves? There is no need to discuss the actual disturbing historical details of slavery when all will concede that the concept alone is disgusting. But how *do* we fill the chapters about the Civil War if the generals and slavery are forbidden topics? Should we write in evil extraterrestrials in place of the Confederates? Absent slavery, does the North simply go to war against the South in a power grab of their means of production and to steal their wealth? Or do we just report only the values, objectives, and victories of the *good* side to avoid any lurid descriptions and sickening rhetoric of the *bad* side? *Tell us about burning down the bad plantation, but not about the bad people who defended mistreating the slaves who worked there.*

Lately, there has been a move not to report names of those who commit heinous crimes, as with mass murders committed with firearms. The idea is not to glorify the miscreant. They are not to even enter the annals of history. Why not go back to apply that to the murder of Rev. Martin Luther King, Jr.? But is it enough simply not to *name* James Earl Ray as the assassin? He still has to be discussed and acknowledged, even if just as "John Doe," or "Bad Man 1." Why not take the opportunity to rewrite the history in a way to have King tragically perish that eliminates the distressing bloody death in a motel entirely—and in a way that can be *celebrated*? Perhaps he can have a heart attack while serving others in a soup kitchen. Maybe it's that he shared a prison cell with Nelson Mandela, but only Mandela survived the ordeal. Or maybe he just turns into atoms of light when he reaches the mountaintop. Why not take a good man with a good life story and make it *better* whenever you can? Turn it into a lesson. Do it *for the children*! They need to inherit a better world not burdened with all this awful history.

NO JOURNALISM

VIOLATION:
Politically Incorrect Thought

THERE ARE ACCEPTED PRINCIPLES OF JOURNALISM. The American Press Institute is a nonprofit dating to 1946 that is dedicated to sustaining a free press in the public interest. In 1997, after either *four* or *ten* years, depending upon the account, the august body named the Committee of Concerned Journalists produced a Statement of Shared Purpose that put forth nine principles. They include: *Journalism's first obligation is to the truth, Its first loyalty is to citizens, Its essence is a discipline of verification, Its practitioners must maintain an independence from those they cover, and It must serve as an independent monitor of power.*[289] [290] Do *any* of these describe the biased fake news that we have come to know all too well?

Is it CNN's anchor Anderson Cooper injecting his own judgments into a 2020 Democrat Debate, saying to former Vice President Joe Biden, "President Trump has falsely accused your son of doing something wrong while serving on a company board in Ukraine. I want to point out there is no evidence of wrongdoing by either one of you"?[291] Is it ABC News' Chief Global Affairs Correspondent and debate moderator Martha Raddatz choking up and appearing to cry while reporting the implications of the election of Donald Trump on election night 2016?[292] Is it *The Washington Post*, that blindly reported Nicholas Sandmann, the high schooler wearing a

Trump hat in Washington, DC, "blocked" Native American Nathan Phillips, and "would not allow him to retreat," accepting the lies concerning Phillips without any verification, thus painting Sandmann as a racist?[293]

The examples could go on and on. Fawning coverage of Hillary Clinton. Disinterest in investigating the charges of Hunter and Joe Biden's corruption with the Ukraine. Indifference to allegations that Democrat Rep. Ilhan Omar has committed bigamy, tax fraud, immigration fraud, and campaign finance violations. Any given day, the reporting is *colored* by the biases of the major news outlets, and on too many days bona fide fake news is *passed off as serious journalism* that is supposed to be following those principles of truth, verification, and independence. If journalism is to adhere to those fundamental principles so laboriously produced, then today we may declare there really is **no** journalism. In reality, the news is more like an "Opposite Day" episode of *The Twilight Zone*, similarly scripted for dramatic effect and a moral lesson.

Perhaps journalists just can't help it. They self identify as Democrats over Republicans at a ratio of 4:1, according to a 2013 Indiana University study. There is more evidence the ratio has risen greatly over time. Very few journalists today claim to be Republicans.[294] And thus it is that the liberal bias in the news is real and, unfortunately, accepted as normal.[295]

Until now, you may have generously concluded that "Opposite Day"—however badly journalism does the opposite of what its principles call for—is somehow arrived at *innocently* as a by-product of the biases of journalists. *They are only human!* A trip to Harvard University busts that myth and exposes how the sausage is actually made. Bias is deliberate and demanded. In October 2019, their student newspaper, *The Harvard Crimson,* ran a story headlined "Harvard Affiliates Rally for Abolish ICE Movement," giving publicity to the movement to wipe away the US law enforcement agency. In doing so they attempted to honor those fundamental journalistic principles, which they believed obligated them to provide subject individuals and institutions they report on to have the opportunity to respond.[296]

WRONG, said a student-led immigration advocacy group, who started an online petition that quickly gathered hundreds of student signatures. By just reaching out to ICE for comment, the paper was declared reckless and charged with "cultural insensitivity" and "blatantly endangering undocumented students."[297] Before long, the student government backed the protestors, accepting the "validity of their expressed fear and feelings of unsafety." They urged the paper to *change their ethics* "to commit to journalistic practices that do not put students at risk."[298] The Harvard College Democrats agreed, as did the Harvard Graduate Students Union-UAW.[299] In other words, *simply tell one side of the story if it is demanded by the Left.*

"Opposite Day" is real with the fake news media, but rarely and only reluctantly admitted. Harvard shows that the lack of transparency is now no longer even required—the word is out, and the Left demands the news only the way they see it.

NO TOY GUNS

VIOLATION:
Guns

WHAT SOCIETY COULD BE SO CALLOUS, UNCARING, AND DEPRAVED so as to fail to protect its own youth from danger? Labor laws protect children from exploitation, as do sexual consent laws. Those under age are forbidden from engaging in contracts and marriages. Minors may not be served alcohol or sold cigarettes. When this society determined even that was not sufficient protection, the drinking age was raised and cigarette vending machines were banned.

More recently, without changes in the law, private businesses have merged boys' and girls' merchandise and merchandising to fight gender stereotyping and protect the gender-shapable from being railroaded into either dolls or toy guns *against their will*. At the same time, private businesses rarely even stock toy guns. Again, when this society determines these protections insufficient, the law will have to be invoked to effect greater uniform safeguards for the children. In the case of toy guns, the Left wants the law to ban *toy* guns, presumably to ban *toy gun violence*.

Interestingly, no one seeks to ban *dolls* because of the harm they may be imagined to do. Can it be denied that Barbie dolls clearly objectify young women? The fashionable outfits promote consumerism and materialism. Barbie also imposes unattainable body imagery upon girls—the company admitted as much by changing Barbie's proportions to those more humanly possible.[300] [301] Who can ever quantify the pain that has been forced on girls, looking back and forth between Barbie and their own images in the mirror? It is incalculably cruel. And for how long will we tolerate Barbie advertising just picturing *girls* enjoying Barbie? Aren't they reinforcing outmoded gender stereotypes? Can't that delay a young boy coming to terms with *his/her/zyr* true gender identity? Finally, and heretofore unspoken in polite company, is the effect on the many boys who have seen a Barbie undressed and may have gone on to become sexual predators and offenders. It is concerning that such a potentially malevolent force in American life has been elevated to that of a cultural icon.

Applying the same critique to toy guns, it is nigh impossible to build as strong a case for harm. What is the *positive* of playing with a Barbie? An argument might be made that playing with a doll in the image of an infant builds valuable empathy and nurturing skills in children, but Barbie is neither life-size nor lifelike. If all Barbie does is provide an object to play with or socialize over, she could just as easily be a stuffed animal—or a *beanbag*. If she was a chess set or even a deck of cards, the play might at least build some thinking skills, but she is just an articulated piece of plastic with hair—*plastic* hair.

Toy guns are images of real guns. What do real guns do? They are issued to every country's military and police for defending national security and maintaining law and order. Playing with a likeness that promotes that seems to be very admirable. If even a small proportion of those playing with toy guns gained some inspiration to protect and serve their country, it would be a positive for society. It's the same for those whose enjoyment of toy guns lead to advancing to training with air guns and then, when of age, with real guns. Marksmanship is a valued skill. Hunting skills may put food on the table and afford self-reliance. Further, self-reliance established through taking responsibility for self-defense builds the confidence of the individual while taking a burden of protection off of society. The country has benefitted by the millions from those with guns defending the country or themselves and their families.

Of course, the Left would not even hear this argument. They take the opposite side and choose to cite only the *negative* of real guns—that they facilitate only crime and violence. Since guns are inanimate objects, what they are really arguing is that a gun in the hand has an innate and unalterable effect on the human mind that leaves the person incapable of doing good over evil. If Barbie fell victim to the same reasoning, and was attributed an equivalent power, she could do *only* what was imagined above—cause body shaming, gender dysphoria, and sexual crimes. *She should be banned.*

Looking at toy catalogs and toy advertising post World War II and continuing into the golden age of TV and movie Westerns, toy guns were continually promoted to children. This was with good reason—guns were the tools of the good guys, whether American GIs or Roy Rogers. No parent would refrain from giving a child a toy gun because they were concerned that its image would overpower the child's better judgment to birth a budding Nazi or outlaw. That toy gun has not increased in professed fake power in the last fifty years—it is still a tool for good and remains just as inanimate as its real counterpart.

Given the mythical power that the Left believes guns have over humans, perhaps it is not surprising that the madness can be extended even further. A nonprofit calling itself the Empire State Consumer Project contacted Hasbro with its dire concerns over their Nerf Ultra One Blaster. (For the Nerf-illiterate, these Nerf devices expel lightweight foam cylinders tipped with soft rubber.) In calling for the toy's removal they questioned "promoting play with huge automatic weapons." "Who would this child be shooting with his cache of assault weapons?" Again, they imagine the toy may only turn the child into an evil psychopath: why not instead "spark the peace-filled imaginations of children?" they blindly wonder.[302] Apparently the kids would never imagine themselves as peace-filled soldiers, police, or guardians of their loved ones, or even as just having fun with a toy that builds eye-hand coordination, and enables target shooting with foam darts, or safe interactive play with a friend.

If kids are only imagining themselves as drug dealers, gang members, and murdering thugs, perhaps it is the mental pathology of the children themselves or the moral teachings of the family that are at fault, not the Nerf gun. *The gun does not bring the evil to the person, the person brings the evil to the gun.*

NO HALLOWEEN

VIOLATION:
Politically Incorrect Thought

THE LEFT IS OUT TO REGULATE every possible human behavior as either "good" or "bad" —according to the standards that they alone declare. Halloween is going down, fast. *It encourages bad behavior.* From the basic prohibitions on racism and sexism, the Left has expanded to every possible characteristic and decided each good or bad for Halloween costumes. (Fat is bad, but skinny is apparently still fair game—unless *eating disorders* are invoked; prisoners are bad, but the non-incarcerated are okay as long as another forbidden characteristic is not depicted.) The multiplier on all this prescriptivist tail chasing is cultural appropriation, a relatively new creation of the Left to further enforce only the behavior they approve.

Cultural appropriation, for those not woke or even awake to the world, is the purported "taking" of elements of a culture that is not your own.[303] [304] That "taking" is to be taken literally, even though in the case of Halloween, "taking" means just "wearing something for a few hours that I bought or made." The Left also likes to ascribe bad motives, like desiring to appear superior, cool, edgy, or carefree. Even worse is a *profit* motive. Clearly, eight-year-olds have no profit motive in dressing up for Halloween, and who is to say that eight-year-olds wanting to appear cool is bad—*other than the Left*?

All of the "-isms" include a value judgment that treating,

or even reacting to, one group or group member differently than another group/group member is bad. Yet human behavior and even biology can run counter to that value judgment— said another way, the value judgment may not be a truth to be blindly applied in all cases. The Left insists otherwise.

Human brains are wired to find affinity with people and things with which they are familiar. If two young Polish couples meet at a hotel pool in Las Vegas they will likely be more comfortable hanging out together than with others. Even two mismatched Polish couples would have an affinity not shared with others in the pool. Are they, therefore, racists, or ethnicists, or nationalists, or whatever else the Left may assert? Similar people often enjoy being together. That accounts for Black Student Unions, women's tennis leagues, and senior centers. Are the blacks racist, the women sexist, and the seniors ageist? The Left seems to violate their own rules when they find no problem with the black students wanting to be only with each other. Babies react favorably to familiar faces. If a month-old Asian baby cries when held by a black nurse, is the baby *racist*? What about a four-year-old? *Better check with the Left.*

Cultural appropriation relies on these same debatable value judgments, not on facts. There is no man-made law that says that someone of German descent "owns" the German culture. Is it different for blacks or Hispanics? Don't think so. There is also no natural, or higher, law that a member of a culture has a lock on owning their culture. How does one Filipino own all of today's culture in the Philippines? Does a Filipino bricklayer own the university professor culture? And if that is impossible, how does one Filipino own all of *yesterday's* culture in the Philippines—all that has preceded him or her there since the beginning of time? What if the Filipino is only half Filipino and the other half Malaysian? Does he or she now own *two* cultures, or only *half of each*? Yet the Left would have you believe that any and all Mexicans "own" sombreros, and Native Americans, tomahawks. Even seen a Mexican in a multicolored, embroidered, and tasseled sombrero lately? How about Native Americans walking around with rubber tomahawks?

If cultural appropriation is legitimate, why waste it on a ridiculous thing like Halloween costumes? Why not get serious? The Wright brothers, two white Christian American guys of English, Dutch, German, and Swiss ancestry, invented powered flight. Why should blacks or Mexicans or women or Muslims be allowed to fly? *It's cultural appropriation! It's outrageous!* But let's make an exception. Let's just be magnanimous, and truly hope that somewhere in time one of those peoples' ancestors invented donkey carts, so they don't have to walk everywhere.

The whole concept of cultural appropriation seems far-fetched, like a game designed for penalties instead of smooth play. Further, *and perhaps you may have noticed*, it is not at all *inclusive*, which the Left tells us is one of their gospel truths. It is as *exclusive* as it gets. *You are not from here, so you can't do that!* It is also interesting that cultural appropriation is always portrayed as a forced *taking*, and never as a withheld *sharing*. What happened to *share, and share alike*? Or *treat others as you would like them to treat you?* Clearly, these were not rules taught to the Left.

So all the Left's Halloween prohibitions may be viewed in the context of just them saying so. Comply at your own peril and compromise to your self-respect. LSPIRG, an advocacy group at Wilfrid Laurier University in Ontario, has a #IAmNotACostume campaign dedicated to policing hurtful Halloween costumes. Here is their list, verbatim:

- An Egyptian person
- A Mexican person
- Day of the Dead
- A Geisha
- A G*psy
- An Indigenous person or a person of colour (though it is okay to dress as a particular individual e.g. Obama or Snoop Dog - as long as you do not try to embody their racial identity by doing black face, brown face, wearing cultural garments or wigs representing Black hair like dreadlocks)
- A Ninja
- A prison inmate
- A mentally ill person in a psychiatric facility
- A transgender person (there's a difference between dressing as a trans person as a joke/mockery and dressing in drag. Many folks use Halloween as a safe opportunity to play with their own gender and drag has a long history of being connected to Halloween)

- A Hula Dancer
- A homeless person
- Fat suits
- Costumes that make fun of sexual and gendered violence (e.g., "flasher")
- Costumes that degrade or dehumanize sex workers, dancers etc.[305]

While taking the advice of advocacy groups is optional, taking the direction from many teachers and school administrators is not. Many now dictate similar costume rules under penalty of students being un-costumed or sent home. Others simply grab the broom from the retired witch's costume to sweep Halloween out the door, which is, of course, masked in fake *inclusivity*. From Illinois: "[W]e are focused on building community and creating inclusive, welcoming environments for all. While we recognize that Halloween is a fun tradition for many families, it is not a holiday that is celebrated by all members of our school community."[306] *CANCELLED*. From Wisconsin: "The reality is that the celebration of Halloween at school leads to student exclusion."[307] *CANCELLED*.

*Tell us again how those kids **wanting** to celebrate Halloween are **included**?*

Perhaps the thought police on the Left should instead choke down some of their own medicine and admit that they are now illicitly cancelling what they themselves had largely *appropriated* to begin with. Halloween comes from the Celtic festival of Samhain, which was celebrated in Ireland, parts of the United Kingdom, and northern France.[308] By the Left's own rules, none but descendants of those people can celebrate or permit others to celebrate—*or cancel*—Halloween.

NO COMEDY SHOWS

VIOLATION:
Politically Incorrect Thought

Q. What's the difference between a person on the Left and a puppy?
A. When the puppy grows up, it will stop whining.

IF YOU DON'T THINK THE LEFT WANTS TO KILL COMEDY, hear it first-hand from one of their highest ranks: the university professor. One from University of Iowa sums it up like this: "Bill Maher had a show ... called *Politically Incorrect*. He took pride in saying the things he's not supposed to say. But the reason he's not supposed to say it is because of the successful advocacy of basic human rights."[309] And there you have it: *jokes violate **human rights***. Killing comedy is *self-defense*. Preventing *comedy genocide* justifies striking first. Yes, some innocents may be caught up in the collateral damage, but that may happen in any *good* war.

Comedian Shane Gillen made it as a new *Saturday Night Live* cast member in 2019 for all of five days—a long weekend, in on a Thursday, and out by Monday. What did he do? NBC decided he was more "offensive, hurtful and unacceptable" than funny after they became aware of prior comedy routines deemed racist and homophobic.[310] Along the way, he had used the words "chinks" and "faggots" and apparently, he wasn't referring to weak spots or bundles of sticks. A Philadelphia comedy club owned chimed in that she had already banned him and was compelled to say, "[a]s a queer female-bodied comedian, a man using the language he did and got so much recognition for was really disheartening."[311]

Comedian and movie star Kevin Hart made it only four days as host of the 2019 Oscars. He also ran into problems with the LGBTQ community for past (nearly a decade-old) tweets and comedy bits. He had crudely and arguably comedically talked about how he would react to his son being gay. Hart had the Academy of Motion Pictures Arts and Sciences announce him as host on Tuesday only to get a follow-up call on Thursday requiring him to issue an apology, which he refused. On Friday, he did apologize—and step down in the same statement.[312] [313] The Oscars simply went without a host for the televised ceremony.

But neither Gillen nor Hart were *collateral* damage; they were targeted *directly* from the moment of recognition of their human rights violations. Writing for *the body is not an apology*, "an independent, queer, Black woman run digital media and education organization," a "cis het white woman" contributor comes to terms with her own "learned racism" and the problem with comedy all in a single column. Comedy misused by the "empowered to belittle the disempowered ... is a form of oppression." It "undermines the legitimacy of suffering, removes accountability from those in power, and reinforces stigma."[314] *Gillen and Hart are just the domestic incarnations of Soleimani and Al-Baghdadi.*

Another woman comedy club owner in suburban Boston went beyond banning one of her declared offending comedians from *future* appearances—she stopped the act mid-show and offered refunds. What was the trigger? The comedian joked that as an Uber driver, he made all his female passengers *ride in the trunk.* She defended her action by saying "no woman in the world would have felt safe in that room"—except that the room was a comedy club, and *it was a joke,* not a threat.[315] At Columbia University the students themselves stopped a show when the comedian told a joke about a gay black guy. The set was deemed "counter to the inclusive spirit and integrity" expected, and declared "unproductive in this space."[316]

There may be times when just stopping a show in progress is not enough. In a Florida comedy club, a Muslim comedian joked about terrorists. He finished the show, but following a 911 call that reported his joke, he got a visit from police to make sure it was only his sense of humor that was a threat.[317]

In response to all this, Dave Chappelle has prohibited fans from sharing his live material without written permission. Louis C.K. forbids cell phone use at his shows. Pete Davidson, the *Saturday Night Live* cast member who seems to take his comedy very seriously, has decided to have all attendees of his shows sign non-disclosure agreements with a $1 million penalty for even discussing the material or offering opinions "by any means."[318] What is the *confidential information* not to be disclosed? *Anything he says or does at the show.*

Overall, comedians themselves have been lamenting the political correctness and "cancel culture" for some time: John Cleese, Dennis Miller, Patton Oswalt, Jim Norton, and Lisa Lampanelli among them. Gilbert Gottfried reasons that today Charlie Chaplin would have to apologize to the homeless for his Little Tramp character; and W.C. Fields and Dean Martin, the same to alcoholics and their families. Larry the Cable Guy makes his point with his politically correct version of "The Night Before Christmas." Chris Rock says he no longer plays colleges because the audiences are too easily offended.[319] Jerry Seinfeld agrees: "They just want to use these words: 'That's racist, that's sexist, that's prejudice.' They don't even know what the hell they're talking about."[320] There is a National Association for Campus Activities that works to match talent with entertainment opportunities, including comedy, on the established college circuit. That organization is dedicated to "eliminating" any language that is "discriminatory or culturally insensitive," so Rock and Seinfeld are hardly joking about the hostile environment for comedy on campuses.[321]

Of course, comedy is not confined to clubs. Mel Brooks has said that he could never make *Blazing Saddles* today, though that movie comedy is coming up to a half-century old.[322] But *Borat*, about an awkward Muslim, is from only 2006 and it could likely also not be made. Seth Rogen agrees with his creative partner when he says, "[b]y the time my kids are grown, all of our work will be deemed unwatchable."[323]

That work includes *The 40-Year-Old Virgin, Knocked Up,* and *Superbad*—all iconic movies of just the last decade. As a final word, consider *Snow White and the Seven Dwarfs,* Disney's first feature-length animated film of a mere fairy tale. Snow White is too white to be cast as a sympathetic character today. The "dwarfs" are not to be marginalized with an offensive label; they are proud *persons of alternative stature!* And why not just say what is really stigmatized with *Bashful* and *Dopey?* Couldn't they really be named *Autistic* and *Developmentally Different? Can't the script be reworked to make them the heroes?*

NO FEMININE PRODUCTS

VIOLATION:
Gender Differentiation

TO BE POLITICALLY CORRECT, there can be no more "gendered" products of any kind. You can *have* men's and women's shoes, and they can look different, and they can fit differently to accommodate different sized feet, but you just can't *call* them men's and women's shoes. Same for men's and women's hair color. And shavers. And on and on.

Why? *It's offensive!* Take a transgender woman. *Please.* That transgender woman may have been born—excuse us, *been assigned*—a man. She may have much larger feet than most all females. How will she feel when she is forced to return to the shoe department of her former gender? Who does Shoe Carnival think they are dealing with? *Rubes and suckers?* How cruel! Take that sign down that says, "Men's." And what does Famous Footwear want to be famous for? *Tears and humiliation?*

Now take an even greater humiliation. What about products for which it isn't just fit and color that may vary for the sexes, but actual *function?* What about "feminine" menstrual pads? What about our transgender woman, who may not get periods, but will be tortured by the sight of the product proclaiming that she is not yet a "real" woman? Perhaps worse, what about transgender men? Transgender men may get periods and be forced to use "feminine" products. How can you feel like a man when you are forced to tape a feminine pad on your boxers to catch your menstrual flow? Do you want to be responsible for needless *gender dysphoria?*

Always feminine sanitary products does not! Parent company Procter & Gamble has announced that they will take the universal feminine gender symbol, the one with a circle on top of a cross, *off* of the Always products.[324] *Presto chango! It's not just for women anymore!* Procter & Gamble is one of the world's largest makers of personal care products, so it seems that there could be another gender-neutral shoe to drop. What about the blue and pink versions of Huggies baby diapers? *Isn't that an impermissible gender stereotyping—and at such a formative and impressionable age?* Just who is Mr. Clean supposed to clean up for? That dude looks to be straight—he wears an earring, though in the *left* ear—but isn't it time he declared his preferred pronouns to clear up the matter? *Could he be transgender, please?* And what about all those slogans? "Gillette. The best a man can get." *Really, what about transgender* **women** *who need to shave? Don't they deserve the best, too?*

For now, transgender *women* will just have to deal with it. Procter & Gamble is starting with transgender *men*. On the Gillette Facebook page, they posted an ad showing a transgender man getting his first shave under the watchful eye of his father.[325] But will changing the slogan to "The best a humyn can get" risk angering animal rights activists? Don't *pigs* also deserve "the best *they* can get" to get rid of those undesirable bristles? *Billy goats* and those unkempt and dirty beards? *Is there no end to exclusion and inequality?*

NO MEN'S-OR WOMEN'S-CLOTHING OR STORES

VIOLATION:
Gender Differentiation, Inequality

TO AVOID MISGENDERING a small segment of the population, there can be no men's rooms and women's rooms for public bathrooms. "Feminine products" aren't just for women anymore because that may upset the trans men users who lack any acknowledgment and are thus experiencing *erasure*. The rolls of women's sports are being opened to people with male body types and male DNA to avoid offending these athletes who *believe* they are women. How long will Hollywood persist in its *Superman* and *Wonder* **Woman** *gender* *stereotyping?* Isn't the time for *Batqueer* long overdue? *To the Batcave, Robyn!*

You know it's coming. How can there continue to be men's and women's clothing? *That's discriminating!* If there can be no more men's and women's clothing, how can there be men's and women's departments or webpages for stores? How can there be men's and women's sections in jewelry stores? Or separate skin care, shaving, and hair care products? *That's offensive and objectifying! Wasn't this all a plot by cis-men in business to make more money anyway?*

Victoria's Secret—*owned by a cis-man*—can't just get away with hiring one transgender model and hope to sidestep the new reality.[326] Why are there not more teddies that accommodate breasts *and* a penis? If they will not be Victor/Victoria's Secret, maybe they should stick to the truth and rebrand as *Victoria's Secret Bias!*

Target, along with eliminating gendered bathrooms in its stores, has already taken the boys and girls signs down from its kids bedding and toy sections.[327] Selfridges, a British department store not suffering from the same Midwest mores preventing Target from going all-in, added new lines of gender-neutral clothing. *And* filled three floors with unisex apparel. *And* added gender-neutral mannequins.[328] *No more ten-year-old boys titillated when the mannequins are being changed!* Now maybe they will be replaced by *drooling ten-year-old **non-binary** kids.*

The rapper Young Thug wore a ruffled dress on the cover of his album. Kanye West wears a leather skirt to perform, though he still appears more modest and maybe self-conscious about his booty than wife Kim Kardashian—he wears his over pants and covers the whole affair with a too-long t-shirt. Celine Dion makes her statement with what she sells: her own line of gender-neutral children's clothing. The Council of Fashion Designers of America added a unisex and non-binary category to their New York Fashion Week in 2018, *finally*.[329]

Many cities now have gender-neutral clothing stores. In New York City, perhaps the most famous was The Phluid Project. While it closed after two years for the same reason as other brick-and-mortar stores, it is expanding into fragrances, education, and alliances. The fragrances combine feminine and masculine notes and use bi-phase technology (*which sounds like a medical breakthrough for the gender dysphoric*) that maintains two colors until shaken. The founder says the store successfully brought attention to "a dated construct, which is around this binary way of being."[330]

Even secondhand stores, like Shop Take Care in Canada, are working to eliminate men's and women's clothing. Yes, it may have been *made* with a gender in mind, but you wouldn't know it from their merchandising. In-store, there are no gender labels. There are no *size* labels. Instead, racks are arranged by *color*.[331] *Let's get matching outfits! David, you look amazing in that sheer salmon silk top with your dark chest hair peeking over. Look, I found matching shorty shorts with room to tuck!*

REDEFINE "FAIRNESS"

NO DEGREES, DIPLOMAS, OR EXIT EXAMS

VIOLATION:
Inequality, Politically Incorrect Thought

THERE'S GOOD NEWS if you never got that college degree, or even a high school diploma. *You are still special!* Despite universal agreement that American workers need to be highly educated to fare best in an increasingly competitive global workplace, many on the Left insist that high school exit exams and the proficiency-based diplomas they produce, along with college degrees, have no place in today's world.

What? Yes, degrees are really not much more than spurious "credentials." Proficiency-based diplomas are much worse. If you guessed that could be because they are *racist,* you have demonstrated a proficiency in fast learning. But the Left doesn't think much of proficiencies—especially *yours.*

Here's what one think tank tells you what you should think about degrees: "The upshot is that credentials can actually create barriers to entry that inhibit people with fewer economic and social advantages from moving up."[332] Translation: if you are black or brown and not rich, you may not get the "credential" that white people get, and that's not fair.

It's racist. Oh, you didn't ever go to college, or try to get financial assistance or a scholarship, and you never liked school, might have a bit of a drug problem, and may or may not have a criminal record? *It's still unfair! Those damn white people and their "credentials"! Get rid of them!*

The hoo-ha is louder for diplomas, if for no other reason than that it's easier for the Left to control the high school environment. Teachers' unions are notoriously Democrat— they are some of America's largest political donors, and 95% of those donations typically go to Democrats.[333] In addition, here, the argument is about *kids,* and, at least legally, kids are more easily corralled and controlled than adult college students. But don't worry, all the froth and folly that flows from Leftist academia in the collegiate ranks quickly dribbles down to the secondary education system. The idea that there may be a diploma for some, a mere "completion certificate" for others, and nothing at all for those who lack proficiency or even participation to get to graduation makes their heads explode. It makes people who achieve look unfairly better than those who don't, and that is not only politically incorrect—it is degrading, debilitating, and *discriminatory.*

In a nutshell, high school diplomas can be awarded by two means, credit and proficiency. With the credit method, you simply take and pass courses to amass enough credits to hit the minimum required. With the proficiency method, there may still be credit qualifications, but the proficiency is mostly demonstrated by taking an exit exam in one or more subjects. The rationale provided by proficiency proponents is that it forces schools to come up with multiple ways of effective instruction—even personalized—to ensure that the most students achieve mastery in the areas deemed most important to prepare for college, the workforce, and life.[334] Desirable accountability naturally follows.

Detractors cite mostly social issues in their opposition. Yes, grades are very important in rounding out the picture. Yes, instruction is directed to those subjects mandating proficiency. Yes, any test may have measurement error. But then the argument turns to the failing of exit exams resulting in *excluding* those who flunk, which these supposedly smart advocates fail to distinguish as a tautology while touting it instead as deep thinking. Of course, they can name in advance who will fail at differential rates—"English language learners, African American, Latino, American Indian, and low-income students"—but they never seem to consider whether that may be because the tests *validly* identify more students among these groups as lacking proficiency. Then their fundamental failure to understand their own tautology advances to yet another: mistaking association with causality—*racist causality*, at that. Their argument would not be complete without their warning that failing proficiency tests surely leads to jail, right after dropping out and failing to find a job, except for those who shortcut it all and *go directly to jail* via the "school-to-prison-pipeline."[335]

The detractors also like to ignore inconvenient facts. For instance, a review of many exams shows they do not require particularly high levels of proficiency. California's now vanquished test was set to sixth- and seventh-grade standards for math, and eighth-, ninth-, and tenth-grade standards for English.[336] State officials in Florida figured 40% of those not passing their exit exams would not have graduated anyway, because they had not completed their required coursework. Further, states allow second, third, and even *sixth* and *seventh* chances to pass the exams, with new help often provided between testings. Finally, it is not even clear that exit exams produce higher dropout and lower graduation rates—recall that the whole design relies on directing instruction to subjects and students to achieve at higher levels! As a result, *many do.*[337]

Apparently, those findings are no match for those lobbying against proficiency diplomas. Not so long ago, those states with exit exams topped out at twenty-seven. For the graduating class of 2020, only eleven states remained.[338] This comes as Leftist educators have refocused on diploma *quantity* versus diploma *quality*. The new, politically correct focus is on high school *graduation rates*. In the 1990s, NYC Schools Chancellor Ramon Cortines led the effort to push all students to take only the *highest-level* Regents exit exam.[339] A generation later, in 2015, as Los Angeles Unified School District Superintendent, the same man instead touted his graduation rates (*all-time high!*) against the backdrop of Democrat Governor Jerry "Moonbeam" Brown having signed the bill to *eliminate* California's exit exams.

So is that all it takes for social injustice and racism to be remedied—just eliminate the meaningfulness and quality of diplomas? *Haha.* No! With a new measure of *success*, there is a new measure to *manipulate*. Gov. Moonbeam also allowed students who had previously failed the exit exam to receive a diploma *retroactively*—going back about ten years.[340] Instant increase! Even Republican Gov. Haley of South Carolina did the same, going back one year. [341] Six other states have methods to do the same.[342] Chicago plays the game of shifting students who are "trouble" out of the mainstream into alternative schools. That exited student no longer counts against mainstream graduation rates—unless he or she *graduates* from the alternative school, in which case the *mainstream* school gets the credit. Some operate as online alternative learning centers that consume only a few hours daily. [343] Texas broadly employs the same "off the books" strategy. Schools all over the country allow students who fail courses to take online "recovery" versions that are less rigorous.[344] *Dumb it down and go to town!*

All of this is in the name of *better education*, as seen by these impressive and manipulated higher graduation rates, which in fact hit a historical high of 84.6% in 2017, up nearly six percentage points in just six years.[345] Unfortunately, two other key indicators of high school achievement do not corroborate this "success." The National Assessment of Educational Progress has measured reading and math achievement in three grade years, going back to 1992. For 2011-17, there's no real discernible increase in the measures.[346] The Scholastic Aptitude Test, unfortunately, showed consistent *decreases* in reading, math, and writing scores from 2011-16, at which time it was retooled, and the math, reading, and writing scores *magically all recalibrated* **higher**.[347] That is a great victory for American education! Not to mention, *manipulation and Leftist talking points!*[348]

Let's get America's new scholars graduated and succeeding!

NO MALE ARTISTS

VIOLATION:
Inequality

Girl Power!

IT WAS NOT SO LONG AGO that answering the door to let the little girl down the street go through her spiel before buying several boxes of Girl Scout cookies was considered supporting women. Then government got involved. In the 1960s, affirmative action sprang from Executive Orders and then court decisions to protect women against discrimination in employment and college admissions. They also created resources and incentives for women-owned small businesses. In 1972, Title IX in the US made it federal law that nobody on the basis of their sex could be denied benefits or subjected to discrimination under any education program or activity receiving Federal assistance. Today, many businesses tout their female ownership as a basis for being patronized over other businesses—presumably owned by men, or the nominal "majority." But the person buying the product or service gets to decide. In work that doesn't have lots of participation from women—auto mechanics, plumbing, landscaping—no one gets fussed about "supporting" men.

Interestingly, women are also underrepresented in the arts. Much of that is historical—women just didn't (or couldn't) participate. *Is there a Top Ten of women Impressionist painters?* It's true for the art world, and less so in the music and film industries, which do not have the same historical weight of inertia. Today there are few or no formal barriers to women in the arts. *So we're all good, right?*

Actually, *no*. Things must be set right, *now*. But how to kick against an entrenched male hegemony that keeps women under the bootheel? *Start counting.* There are multiple systems for rating films on the number of women portrayed. The Bechdel test counts whether the work has at least two women in it that talk to each other about something other than a man.[349] Another system literally called Diversity Scoring scans the character list of the work, and counts those that are not straight white human males as a percentage of the total characters. By that system, many women and Lefty apologists may take some comfort that at least the *Star Wars* franchise is really progressing from its backwards 70s roots.[350] A third system would actually tally the gender and racial makeup of both cast and crew as well as compute the percentage of female dialogue to feed algorithms to produce "objective" scores. Naturally, rating is the prelude to *protesting*. Even with all of this furor, there are reliably stories *every* new year about the too-low inclusion of women in the Academy Awards.[351]

The Baltimore Museum of Art is not content with rating and

protesting. It has decided to "rectify centuries of imbalance" in 2020 by quadrupling its acquisition budget and then *buying no art created by men*. The action is "reflective of the systemic sexism" they feel they must combat. Of course, they are still quite happy to accept *gifts* of art created by men.[352] *Got any?*

The museum wisely stopped short of also barring men from *admission*. Not in California, where Girl Power struck again when comedian Iliza Shlesinger performed her "Girls Night In With Iliza—No Boys Allowed." Of course, as the only performer, this was a "no male artist" showcase, but she further made it clear men were not welcome in the audience. It was supposed to be an "interactive discussion … aimed at giving women a place to vent" and to raise money for Planned Parenthood. She got sued by a man who was told he could enter the theater only if he sat in the *back ~~of the bus~~*.[353] Shlesinger, a comedian and not a lawyer, seemed ignorant that the same laws that protect her from discrimination on account of her sex protect that other category of human beings—*men*—as well. Much the same occurred in Austin, Texas, when the Drafthouse theater chain decided to hold *no men allowed* screenings of *Wonder Woman*.[354]

Gaining more notoriety was the Statement Festival, in Sweden, which accepts "women, non-binary and transgender only" as both performers *and* attendees. Staged in 2018 and inspired in reaction to sexual assaults at other festivals, it told "cis-men" to stay away so the others could have "a safe space … without feeling scared for their personal safety." The festival was cited for discrimination by a government ombudsman, but not penalized as they did not enforce the man-free rule at the gate.[355] *And how could they, since the Left tells us gender is just a state of mind?* Even a dedicated *Show Us Your Junk* security queue would not work.

After a year off, the festival planned a comeback for 2020, which was pushed to 2021 for the Covid virus. While the performers must identify as women, non-binary, or trans persons, not *all* supporting band members have to. Then there is the little issue of who lugs the gear to and from the stage. For that, cis-men will do as a type of over-muscled subhuman gorilla. To ensure crowd safety, however, the organizers insist that they be confined to a backstage *man-pen*: they "will under no circumstances have access to the public area." Organizers state that they do *not* believe "all cis-men are rapists," but during these two days, cis-men will just have to "find something else."[356]

And afterwards they will be welcome to do their jobs picking up the trash—if they are not too scary. Subhuman Power!

NO BEAUTY PAGEANTS

VIOLATION:
Inequality, Gender Differentiation

NOT EVERY WOMAN CAN BE BEAUTIFUL, but according to the Miss America pageant, they *can* win a scholarship—if they are single and never married, no more than twenty-five years old, have talent, and have a compelling social platform to champion. Don't worry about appearance—*we are sure you are beautiful on the inside!* No more evening gown competition—just wear something *comfortable*. Swimsuits? *No, you are not to be objectified! You are safe here.*

No longer is Miss America a *beauty pageant*—and it is most certainly **not** a *beauty contest*—it is a *scholarship competition*! As the feminists who took control of the organization tell us, it is Miss America 2.0.[357] [358] The women are not *contestants*—they are *candidates*!

But shouldn't those in a *competition* be **competitors**? *Don't be silly! They are here to support and cheer for each other. We are also Woke 3000 and #MeToo Squared!*

But just how woke *is* the new feminist-directed Miss America pageant? Well, you have to be a United States citizen.[359] No illegal aliens, or even "undocumented residents." *Ouch*, says the Left, *we need to get on that.* Oh, and you can't be pregnant, and for much of the pageant's history could *never* have been—which somehow seems to shame miscarriages, but of course, the real target was *abortions.*[360] *How could they!* exclaims the Left, *that is disempowering to women!* And—*wait for it*—isn't there still that little "natural born female" rule?[361] *Why, that's anti-LGBTQQIAAP!* sputters the Left. *Are you really saying that Maria, the Honduran transgender person here illegally since 2007 who had a pretend real abortion last year to affirm her right as a woman, cannot win your scholarship?* **Boycott!**

It seems the Miss America competition is straddling two worlds unsuccessfully. The 2019 event was held not in

Atlantic City, nor in Las Vegas, but in the Mohegan Sun casino in *Connecticut*. Even Atlantic City made it clear a few years ago that they no longer wanted to be associated with the affair. Recall how the contest was reliably around Labor Day every year in September? In 2019, it was held in the dead of winter, the week of Christmas—*you know, when everyone is thinking about watching television.*[362] And the TV ratings? 3.6 million viewers, down 16% from the prior year, and off a full one-third from the last telecast to feature the swimsuit competition, in 2017.[363]

From a branding standpoint, anyone familiar with the Miss America pageant thinks of swimsuits, gowns, talent, Atlantic City, and September. Miss America 2.0 is virtually unrecognizable. Every pole has been kicked out from under the tent except the talent competition. Talent—ah, yes, the singing, musicianship, dancing, twirling, and ventriloquism? *No, the competition now prefers it a bit more substantial.* The 2019 winner, a doctoral candidate in pharmacy, demonstrated the "catalytic decomposition of hydrogen peroxide" with drugstore components, including dish soap and food coloring.[364] Again, with one foot in each world—*self-aggrandizement* and *entertainment*—the brainy "talent" was on the level of a junior high school science fair demonstration and barely a step removed from swishing your own mouth or cut with the foaming action of hydrogen peroxide.

There are other beauty pageants, or scholarship competitions, or televised ogle-fests, or whatever you want to call them. Miss Universe is best known, but there are also Miss

World, Miss International, and Miss Earth. As yet, no others have cast off the physical appearance components while attempting to maintain some reason to watch or attend. Spelling bees and speech contests have never been ratings hits. Even the Miss Earth pageant, which promotes environmental awareness and is supported by the United Nations, assigns a majority of its judging criteria to *beauty, form, and figure*.[365] Miss Universe in 2018 attracted a transgender woman as Miss Spain, but she still had to be damn hot and work a runway in heels and a pink bikini.[366] *Everybody must stick to the rules!*

So Miss America has jettisoned the obvious physical beauty components while still maintaining a puritanical lock on pure, virtuous women who aren't pregnant, ideally have never gotten pregnant, and haven't appeared nude in a magazine or on the internet. *Two worlds.* It won't work. The next two worlds conflict will be between the feminists and trans advocates. The feminists won't be able to keep biological men—trans or otherwise—out. A trans woman recently sued to be eligible for the Miss United States of America pageant.[367] When Miss Universe went through the same controversy, beginning in 2012, they allowed trans and non-binary women to compete. But Miss Universe still judges physical appearance, and Miss America does not, so Miss Universe's contestants are easily sorted out on looks by *losing* preliminary competitions. When Miss America is forced down the same path, a trans woman *who still looks like a man* would be able to advance. The winning science fair project could put her over the top. At that point, why not *all* biological males? Anything less would be discrimination.

Why can't Miss America be a pimply, pudgy accountant named Fred who supports troubled hoarders and whose talent is multiplying large numbers in his head?

NO DATING FREEDOM

VIOLATION:
Inequality, Politically Incorrect Thought

CAN YOU REFUSE to seat someone in a restaurant because they are Muslim? *No.* Can you refuse to rent an apartment to someone because they are female? *No.* Can you refuse to fill a prescription for someone because they are gay? *No.* Can you refuse to provide someone physical therapy because they are black? *No.*

So how is it that you can refuse to *date* someone who is Muslim, female, gay, or black? And while we are at it, how can you refuse to date a *trans man* or a *trans woman*?

Who gave you the right to *discriminate*? As punishment, the Left, through the courts and the laws to come, *could* require you to date trans men and women, but *let's let bygones be bygones. Let's just get you started on a proactive, mandatory, diverse dating regimen.* Just think of it as another form of *personal service*—one not to be denied. It's just like the physical therapy example, though both of you may have to take your pants off to meet the mandate. *Hey, it's the 2020s—join the modern age—and bring condoms, just in case!*

Listen to the words of a trans man, Lee, on the difficulties of dating, and understand that the government will have to step in to remedy the reluctance (the "polite" word) and the discrimination (the "real" word) of would-be dates: "Internet dating when I was a lesbian was infinitely easier than how it is now as a trans man." "As a trans guy," Lee continued, "the majority don't seem to know what to make of me, so they run away. I've played around with the big reveal, and I know the two are linked." Lee poignantly confided that it is unfair that he is somehow expected to reveal the status of his genitalia and fertility as a condition of kicking off a relationship.[368] His experience cannot be denied, and the only question is when will the government step in and how much will it require to overcome the discrimination levied against Lee—and *all* those who have not enjoyed dating success. It is a *public health* issue to have so many so unfulfilled. *It's bad for the prostate, or whatever you may have.*

The Left will posit societies have benefitted from inter-marriage between disparate parties for centuries, and forced dating could aid that. Royalty has often encouraged or arranged marriage to partners from different countries to forge alliances and prevent conflicts. Colonizing countries see the increased interaction with the colonized peoples result in marriages and other relationships that strengthen bonds, and that eventually may equalize the hierarchical colonizer/colonized power dynamic. So why not dating in the United States of America, *right here, right now*?

By age fourteen, every person in the US could be issued the equivalent of a diversity dance card. The number of dates required would increase every year up until age twenty-one, when it would level off at six per annum, which would continue until age fifty, with exceptions for periods when engaged or married. Each year a designated array of sex, sexual orientation, gender-identity, race, ethnicity/national origin, or religion representatives would have to be dated. That form would be filed annually with the U.S. Department of Health and Human Services. *How better to promote love and understanding!*

Never had a dinner conversation with an Iranian woman? Curious what's under a Sikh turban? Ever cuddled with someone of your own sex? Always wondered what intersex genitalia might look like? Want to hear what it's like to be an illegal immigrant firsthand? Need to find out if what they say about black men is true? All of this *and more* will be revealed.

Thank you, equality experts! Thank you, rabid Left! Thank you, Big Government! Thank you caseworker at HHS, who pointed out a Jewish lesbian might check either box!

NO MARRIAGES LIMITED TO ONLY TWO PEOPLE

VIOLATION:
Inequality, Family Sanctity, Religion

NO, THERE'S NO MISPRINT AND NO MISUNDERSTANDING. This isn't about marriages limited to two *opposite-sex* persons—one man, one woman. It isn't even about marriages between two *same-sex* persons—that's been legitimized since 2015. No, it's about not limiting marriage to just *two* people. Surely you are not so blind, so jaded, so shallow to not understand marriage in its current form *discriminates against single people!* Not only does it hurt their feelings with this *exclusion*, it strips them of the over *1,000 benefits, rights, and privileges* conferred by marriage that the U.S. Government Accountability Office cataloged in 2004.[369]

The Defense of Marriage Act of 1996 that limited marriage to one man and one woman was struck down by the Supreme Court in 2013 for violating the Due Process Clause of the Fifth Amendment. *Obergefell v. Hodges*, wherein the Supreme Court in 2015 extended marriage benefits to same-sex couples, cited the same violation, and another to the Equal Protection Clause of the Fourteenth Amendment.[370] The Supreme Court has yet to hear a case from a single challenging the denial of the benefits of marriage. *It will, just wait.* It plays to so many things that the Left rails against: inequality, sexism, white supremacy, wealth, and family sanctity. *Who knew marriage remains so evil and oppressive?*

Societies find ways to encourage and incentivize behaviors deemed beneficial—even *critical*—to the health and welfare of their citizens. Weak societies fall to strong societies. Strong societies survive and prosper. Strong is better! Government tax policy, for example, is a very effective tool, whether to steer energy-efficient purchases or to facilitate family formation and procreation. Married people have the option to file a joint income tax return, which can save money. They can create family partnerships to divide income among family members. They get to create life estate trusts. Surviving spouses may inherit the deceased's estate, and also get an exemption from both estate and gift taxes. Many more of those 1,000 benefits, rights, and privileges differentially profit married people. Spouses may collect on Social Security, Medicare, and veterans' benefits. In divorce, spouses get their share of marital property and have a case for child custody or visitation.

Employers get in the game, too. Employer-paid health care insurance and family leave are made available to spouses, as often are death and bereavement provisions. Retirement plans pay spouses as default beneficiaries. Hospitals allow spouses access and decision-making denied to others. Death arrangements, from funerals to autopsies, are the first right of spouses. Businesses offer special family rates for insurance coverage. Universities extend tuition discounts to family members. Adoption agencies favor married people in many ways. Courts give spouses privileges in everything from immigration to crime victims' benefits to visitation. They also allow suits for the wrongful death of a spouse, and famously permit one spouse not to be forced to testify against the other. Yes, there are many, many advantages.[371] *How can this inequality be allowed to continue?*

The Left will soon argue that singles are being denied the same due process and equal protection so notoriously withheld from same-sex couples. Singles are frequently stigmatized as weirdos, loners, and losers by our society, *and they deserve respect!* If so many changes have already been made to accommodate the *transgender* population that accounts for less than 1% of the population, just think of the case to be made for *adult singles*, who account for 45% of the adult population! They are the new oppressed! *Why is there no Equal Rights Amendment for singles? Where is the National Organization for Singles?* Singles, rise up!

Just as free health care, free tuition, and student loan forgiveness is offered by the Left *to curry favor and votes* with promises of free stuff, handing all the benefits of marriage to singles can be a massive ploy to create a new identity group. The question that follows is, if *all* are to receive the benefits of marriage as a universal entitlement, what is the utility of continuing to recognize marriage as anything but an arcane religious ritual? Why should it endure to hold any civil and legal sway?

The Left would be perfectly happy with that outcome. They say marriage has been traditionally *sexist*, with the man viewed as the dominant party. Weren't women considered the men's property? *Shouldn't we be tearing down statues somewhere over that loathsome history?* Oh, and wasn't marriage used to propagate *white supremacy*? Slaves couldn't legally marry, and the white master could violate the "marital" bed at his will anyway. *Take that, Thomas Jefferson, you pig!* How about *wealth*? Rich white men bent and shaped marriage from a religious ritual to a civil entitlement meant to protect wealth and pass it from generation to generation, ensuring the poor stay poor and the rich get richer. Meanwhile, the poor in America get married at lower rates than the rich, perpetuating this injustice. *Shouldn't this be a talking point for Rep. Alexandria Ocasio-Cortez?* One trusty journalist makes the case marriage should be replaced with "a more robust welfare state" and "a redistributive tax system that reverses wealth consolidation."[372]

And family sanctity? *Don't get the Left started!* A University of Oregon professor tells us that society has it all wrong: "marriage is sort of like welfare. The state expects that families take care of each other rather than the state taking care of people."[373] Yes, let the government take care of you, because it is the *family* that has failed to provide wealth and health care and college education for all people equally. Our journalist sums it up: we need "a resistance to the privatization scheme of marriage as substitute for more universal structures around mutual care and providing for our material needs." Government is stronger than the family. *Step aside, and invite government in to save the day!*

Indeed, in the extremes where everyone or no one can be married, the power of the family takes a blow. Family exerts an outsized influence on family members, and the Left knows it competes for power with the government they control. So family must be *diminished*; ideally, it must go. And if we acknowledge that family is indeed the strongest bond ever to unite humans, then for the religious religion ranks right up there as well. Whether diminishing marriage is an assault on the family, or on religion, or on both, the Left wins. *Let **government** be your husband, your wife, your father, your mother, **your God.***

NO POLICE

VIOLATION:
Inequality

HOW ABOUT THOSE OLD HIPPIE CULTURE MOVIES where the kids all refer to police as "pigs"? Then there's that 1967 picture of teens protesting the Vietnam War, where a guy sticks a flower in the muzzle of the rifle of a soldier "defending" the Pentagon. He was variously identified as either "Hibiscus," who was a founding member of the drag troupe, the Cockettes, or as "Super-Joel" who became a leader of the Youth International Party—the *Yippies*.[374] Man, those cats had no use for the police! That's *far out!*

Well, not anymore. Should it come as a surprise that those sentiments have had over fifty years to develop and spread? Some of those hippies grew up to become social justice advocates that took positions of power and influence in academia and government. And the blacks that in 1967 were still wondering how to claim the civil rights just legislated for them had not progressed straight to defying the police. That took years, and for a Barack Obama to say that it was ok— *necessary*, in many cases—to think of police across the nation as racist or homicidal.

For activists, shaming is a good first step. Olympia, Washington celebrated Trans Remembrance Day—the day that honors lives lost to "acts of anti-transgender violence"—with a lighting of their city hall. *Problem!* Security was provided by, yes, *police*. One protestor: "You're gonna light-up a city hall that has police, and police are part of the problem." "They kill my families. They make it unsafe to live," was also registered. And another: "Protected by people who are meant to eliminate us. How dare you!"[375]

If shaming can kick things off, maybe next could be the call for police to be disarmed. At the University of Minnesota, Students for a Democratic Society demonstrated for the disarmament of the campus police. Last time campus police fired a weapon? In 2012, to put a dying raccoon out of its misery.[376] *Really.* Multiple campuses have heard the call to disarm. At the University of California-Davis, the student Senate passed such a resolution, which included, "despite not needing deadly weapons in the course of their job, nationwide campus police departments continue to utilize a culture of fear."[377] At the University of Chicago, students calling for "immediate disarmament" marched with a "U of C Kills" banner after its first shooting by campus police in over thirty years.[378] There, during a spree breaking building and car windows with a large metal pole, a policeman fired a single shot at a manic student, wounding his shoulder. The student was seen on camera repeatedly refusing to drop the pole and charging the officer instead. One student who was *not* present saw it differently: "they've always been here to do things like f*cking shoot people with mental illnesses, and people of color."[379]

The third step? Perhaps you did not know there is a "three Ds" of police abolition: *disempower, disarm, and disband.* The abolition movement has taken hold following Obama's pronouncements and prosecutions of police departments following very public cases of minority deaths at the hands of law enforcement authorities from 2012 through 2016, starting with Trayvon Martin and on through Alton Sterling and Philando Castile. In all cases, those in authority accused were cleared of criminal wrongdoing, but that was not what Obama or social justice advocates wanted to hear. Instead, the narrative was and is that the police are racist, the criminal justice system is racist, and the country itself is racist. What to do? *Abolish the police.*[380]

In the midst of those publicized deaths, *Rolling Stone* in 2014 published "6 Ideas for a Cop-Free World," which includes the range of answers most all activists endorse to arrive at abolition: decriminalization of most crimes, with its resultant release of most current prisoners as well, mediation or intervention teams trying to counsel offenders not to offend, and "restorative justice"—*more* talking and counseling—for those that still do.[381] The activists also call for more mental health care, more jobs, more education, more understanding, and more love. Some concede they don't know just what a world without police will look like. *But still, we need a* **peace** *presence, and not a* **police** *presence.*

So who *do* you call when your car gets stolen, or Aunt Mary gets beaten up for her Social Security proceeds? Of course, many minorities argue they already have no one to call. It is a long-held belief that police are designed to serve the interest of whites and to keep everyone else in line—with police brutality and corruption part of that formula.[382] *Reform* is rejected because the system is thought to be too broken to fix. Only *overthrow* is acceptable. A socialist candidate for Seattle City Council, who campaigned on police abolition, came up less than 1,500 votes short of winning the seat. But in Philadelphia and San Francisco, progressive district attorneys like Larry Krasner and Chesa Boudin, who simply refuse to prosecute many crimes, *were* elected. The Left stands and applauds.[383]

The Black Panther Party in 1972 made ten demands in its platform. Half are directly relevant to this topic and others discussed in these pages:

- We want an immediate end to police brutality and murder of Black people, other people of color, all oppressed people inside the United States.
- We want freedom for all Black and poor oppressed people now held in U.S. … prisons and jails.
- We want freedom. We want power to determine the destiny of our Black and oppressed communities.
- We want completely free health care for all Black and oppressed people.
- We want education that teaches us our true history and our role in the present-day society.[384]

Police abolition has grown from the Black Panthers and the Left's *Rolling Stone* mouthpiece to the pages of the *Harvard Law Review* and prominent news outlets, and to the minds of District Attorneys in major US cities. Listening to the 2020

Democrat Presidential candidates, it was striking that many of the Black Panther mantras are now mainstream: America is racist, cops are too, laws should not be enforced, crimes should be decriminalized, prisoners should be released, health care should be free, and history should be rewritten.

One day soon, the Democrats may have the power to legislate all this. Let's hope they have the same success in legislating away all *evil*, so the police don't have to be called back from exile. Otherwise, they will create a police-free world where the whites hire their own private police, and the minorities finally *do* have their freedom—to negotiate "mediations and interventions" with the gangs who are left to fill the power vacuum.

In speaking here of the Left's push to be rid of police, why has there been no mention of the ~~riots~~, ~~protests~~, *largely peaceful gatherings* that resulted in American cities on fire in the summer of 2020 following the reprehensible death of George Floyd? All the calls to *defund* the police?

Because this chapter was written before all that. Nevertheless, it predicted exactly where things have now headed. For those wondering how all the mistrust, hate, and anarchy seem to have sprung out of nowhere, it didn't. It's been there, being fanned and stoked as this chapter has just detailed above. Still wonder whether the Left *really* is taking things away from you? Wake up and smell the smoke coming from your own neighborhood.

Oh, and don't forget, the government will protect you!

NO PRISONS

VIOLATION:
Inequality

JUST THE HEADLINES you'd expect from a publication like *Teen Vogue*:

- ✔ "Kim Kardashian's Hairstylist Is Launching a Super Affordable Haircare Line"
- ✔ "9 Pearl Necklaces That Harry Styles Would Approve of"
- ✔ "Lil Nas X Crashed a Wedding at Disney World"
- ✔ "Sarah Hyland Defended Ariel Winter's Dress From Internet Trolls"
- ✔ "What the Prison-Abolition Movement Wants"

Hmm, which one does not belong?

The problem is, *Teen Vogue* has decided it *does* belong. They describe their writer as a "radical organizer" who supplies a continuing political "op-ed column"—*as if their Kim Kardashian-worshipping crowd knows the supposed press distinction between fact and opinion.* Other titles have included "Appalachia's Long, Proud Tradition of Labor Militancy," "Meet the Rock Star Who Created A Guide for Protecting Marginalized People at Concerts," "America's Workplaces Aren't Often Safe for LGBTQ Employees," and "Climate Disaster Is a Labor Issue. Here's Why."[385] Another, titled

"What You Need to Know About the MOVE Bombing" brings the news of 1985 to today's teens to note that despite the legal system injustices to MOVE, they are still active with their "anarcho-primitivist gospel."[386]

The *Teen Vogue* writer introduces the teens to "esteemed" Angela Davis, the 70s radical, twice Communist party candidate for Vice President of the United States, and co-founder of the Critical Resistance organization dedicated to abolishing the "prison-industrial complex." Teens read that the US capitalist system (which "has to go") is a "major cause" of the "crisis of mass incarceration" and that imprisonment, a "form of punitive torture," is obsolete. Perhaps this is the first they have been let in on the secret that the US criminal justice system was indeed designed "as an instrument of racist terror," while the vaunted "abolition movement operates from an explicitly intersectional, racial-justice-focused perspective."[387] *There, doesn't that sound better already?*

Attentive teens will now be able to name the three pillars of the Left's prison abolition: *moratorium, decarceration, and excarceration*. The No New Jails moratorium campaign was thrilled that New York City's Rikers Island would be closed — until the city announced *four* new jails would replace it.[388] Decarceration is literally the removal of those jailed, though it is often blurred with excarceration, which seeks to divert people from ever going to prison to begin with. These come through efforts like criminal justice reform releasing inmates, or reducing sentences, or decriminalizing crimes, or just actively *counseling people not to commit crimes.*

Yes, the Left would have you believe that they can infiltrate gangs with counselors and mediators who would hear of potential upcoming criminal activity and then quickly and conclusively intervene to convince those involved to adopt an acceptable lawful solution. No more drive-bys. *You'll just have to "agree to disagree" on how your brother ended up with 112 stab wounds.*

The Left's plan goes like this: Close the prisons. Release the inmates. Counsel them and get them jobs. Put all the savings from closing prisons into initiatives like education, economic support, mental health services, and conflict counseling and mediation, so no one goes to prison again.[389]

Of course, this should be done at a community level; run by the community. In other words, no "whitesplaining" to minorities and marginalized peoples, and no using European standards of conduct and discipline and morality. After all, that's how we got the whole "school-to-prison pipeline" — *expecting black youth to behave to white standards,* like staying silent while the teacher speaks, or not assaulting others, or not disrupting classes. Oh, and getting rid of crimes and police especially would help ensure the cycle is ended for good. *No big thing.*

While a major predictor of success in life, including staying out of jail and prison, is growing up in a two-parent household, there is no mention in the Left's plan how all that diverted money will work to fix the underlying problem of over five times as many black than white youth growing up with just an unmarried mother.[390] *Can we cut the social programs* *that have actually **increased** that statistic?* How about those murderers and violent rapists no longer in prison? *Where is it they go again?* More than one Lefty has proposed that they wear GPS trackers so they may be *monitored.*[391] *Hey, don't be killing and raping with that on! And don't take it off, or you will be in trouble with the **community**!*

If the principles of prison abolition sound out of place in the pages of *Teen Vogue*, what about on Democrat Bernie Sanders' platform? Surely a hoped-for President of the United States would not call for prisons to go away? Think again.

On his website, Bernie called for cutting the prison population in half by abolishing the death penalty, three strikes laws, mandatory minimum sentencing, and other "excessive" sentencing; expanding release programs; ending cash bail; decriminalizing illegal immigration; decriminalizing marijuana and expunging previous convictions; giving intravenous drug abusers free needles; banning for-profit prisons; preventing black and brown children from being charged with misdemeanor crimes; and sending criminals into community supervision rather than prison, per Leftist "restorative justice" designs.[392] In total, sent back as "new good neighbors" would be one million criminals, and there's the "up-and-comers" who would never go in the first place. Not on his website, but promised in one of the Democrat 2020 candidate debates: on marijuana decriminalization, Bernie would actually have taxpayers *bankroll blacks* in the community to sell the marijuana rather than let "a few corporations control" it.[393] *What a wonderful world!*

Back at *Teen Vogue*, there is good news and bad news. First, the radical columnist is not sure that it is really teens who are reading her. But unfortunately, she reports, "I've had a lot of teachers hit me up and tell me like, 'Hey, I'm taking this piece you wrote and I'm bringing it to my classroom and we're discussing it.'"[394] *Prison abolition.*

Ah yes, schoolteachers, the stalwarts of the Left, shaping and perverting young minds. *Guess what, Bernie campaigns on giving* **them** *a raise.*[395]

ATTACK YOUR FOUNDATION

NO PARENTAL RIGHTS

VIOLATION:
Family Sanctity

THE LEFT HATES FAMILIES because they can't bank on all parents believing and slinging their BS for them. Some parents believe they don't need Planned Parenthood or LGBTQ advocacy groups or race-baiting consultants to substitute their values for their own in raising their children. They think they know what's best for their own children. They don't need cops or schoolteachers or new certified child abuse pediatricians working secretly with child welfare agencies to take their children away from them to be raised and educated per the government's agenda. Yes, not all parents can be anywhere close to being politically correct enough for the Left, *and that must be remedied.*

The K-12 school system may be America's biggest threat to parental authority. Few parents would teach their young children gender extends well beyond two sexes and is fluid day-to-day, that America is thoroughly racist, and that they are already halfway to prison in the school-to-prison pipeline if they are other than rich and white. Yet American schoolchildren are taught this *daily* by their own teachers, as *mandated* by legislators, or simply as *suggested* by lobbying groups and curriculum consultants.

In the State of Washington, the Office of the Superintendent of Public Instruction issued mandates to teach kindergarten and first-grade students there are "many ways to express gender," and by third-grade to teach that gender roles "can vary considerably." In California, a teacher read her young students two books on gender fluidity. The first was a "children's book" written by a transgender reality TV star. The second was entitled *Red: A Crayon's Story,* about a blue crayon that *identifies* as a red crayon. The reading was at a boy's parents' request. After the stories, the boy left the classroom and returned in girl's clothing, with the teacher reintroducing him to his kindergarten classmates as a *girl.* In response to parent protests, the school noted that while parents have a legal right to have their children opted out of sex education, "diversity and tolerance curriculas" are *not* sex education. The school additionally responded that its educational actions were appropriate, pointing to state law prohibiting discrimination on the basis of gender identity.[396]

The leftwing Southern Poverty Law Center political advocacy group has its own classroom curriculum arm, Teaching Tolerance.[397] A recommended book for first graders, *All the Colors of the Earth*, teaches self-love and knowledge while featuring biracial couples.[398] Another uses a wronged dinosaur family to start teaching the Six Elements of Social Justice Curriculum Design for Elementary Education, per the *International Journal of Multicultural Education*.[399] Rather than using these type books to teach vocabulary or plot elements, suggested classroom activities range from creating self-portraits that include skin tone identification to studying police brutality. Teachers are to progress from merely celebrating diversity to moving to an examination of the oppression seen in racism, sexism, homophobia, and religious intolerance.[400]

Pacific Educational Group (PEG) provides consulting with a goal of "transforming education" to K-12 school systems at a cost of hundreds of thousands of dollars each. Their driving belief is that "systemic racism is the most devastating factor contributing to the diminished capacity of all people, and especially people of color."[401] PEG claims to have trained hundreds of thousands of teachers and administrators. Other sources tally their reach to over 200 US school districts serving over **ten million** students, or *one in every five* students in the nation.[402]

PEG dogma trades in the realm of white supremacy, white privilege, and black nationalism while going on to declare micro-aggressions and vilify even task orientation and individualism as *racist*. A typical course, "Leading While White," claims to work to end racism by, among other things, "identifying and interrupting Whiteness when it prevents working in authentic partnership."[403] Seattle Public Schools hired PEG in 2002 and after adopting the doctrine had to pull down a webpage that listed **five** types of racism (*cultural, active, passive, individual, and institutional*) that defined individualism, future time orientation (planning ahead, or even being on time), and one single standard form of English as examples of racism. Race itself was characterized there as a "pseudobiological category."[404 405]

Those schools wanting a broader perspective, to include gender, race, and "systems of privilege and oppression" so as to school against not only *white* privilege but *heterosexual* privilege, *class* privilege, and *Christian* privilege may hire instead the National SEED Project.[406] Teachers will confront their own "feelings of fraudulence" on the way to teaching their students "to become multicultural world citizens as well as understanding their own privileges."[407 408] Through their seminars, SEED claims to have reached 30,000 teachers who have pushed their messages of bias on **three million** students.[409]

Concerned yet?

Sex education bridges education and health care institutions. Following up on a 2013 law that required Colorado schools to teach LGBTQ perspectives, Planned Parenthood and One Colorado, an LGBTQ lobbying group, worked to add measures to expand their influence on the law. This included banning opposing religious perspectives on chastity, monogamy, and two-parent families, which ultimately failed. However, following California's lead, another bill did pass that prevents counselors from advising the *gender?-I'm-not-sure-just-yet* kids to do anything but embrace transgenderism. Similarly, children as young as twelve may now get unlimited mental health care not only without the consent of parents, but without any information sharing with them.[410] Want to know what's troubling your pre-teen? Better hope they open up to you before it's too late, because the government says the therapist must *never* tell you.

Left holding the bag for the Washington state legislature, insurers got to inform policyholders of the *real* effect of the law allowing their children to get secret abortions: the parents would no longer have the right to know of "sensitive conditions" of their children's health care. *Anything* regarding mental health, substance abuse, reproductive health, sexually transmitted diseases, gender dysphoria, and even the squishy "gender-affirming care" would now be off-limits to parents.[411] This is not limited to counseling, but extends to prescription drugs and medical procedures. For substance abuse, the abusing child could be prescribed more drugs—now to be taken *responsibly*—as treatment. For gender dysphoria—the current term covering even "immature" and "confused"—the treatment could include counseling advocating "gender reassignment" along with hormone therapy in preparation for surgery on the eighteenth birthday. If the child is so trusting as to actually inform the parents of this covert plan, they may finally exercise a parental right — to allow the surgery *earlier*.

It doesn't take a law to limit the influence of parents over their children. Special interest groups have special interests in exactly this. The American Civil Liberties Union insists that abortion is as much a right for *children* as it is for women and so supports children receiving abortions without parental knowledge or intervention.[412] Planned Parenthood has a webpage for teens detailing laws for all fifty states and the District of Columbia to advise whether parents can be legally excluded, and additionally asserts, "You may be able to get a judge's permission to have an abortion without telling your parents." On that same webpage, teens who are pregnant and want an abortion are urged to call Planned Parenthood, so that they can be provided tips on any talking with parents. That page also offers one online chat link, *two* places to search for a clinic to book an appointment, and *five* social media links to encourage teens to turn to Planned Parenthood.[413] Their preceding web page is so helpful as to even explain to these supposedly mature children how to know if they are pregnant, starting with "pregnancy can only happen if semen (cum) gets in your vagina or on your vulva."

While Democrats thus far have not been so bold to take a national platform position advocating children's abortion rights without parental notification, the fight is already happening along party lines, state by state. But in a bit of a Freudian slip, the Democrat platform does advocate for abortion under the heading, "Women and *Girls*" (emphasis sadly added).[414]

To effect the ultimate restriction of parental rights, the children themselves must be removed. Democrats and the Left's Deep State have good models in history's most notorious totalitarian regimes. Soviet Russia took children from their parents' homes for a "good" reason—Olympic training, with national interest far outweighing parental rights and humanitarian considerations.[415] Nazi Germany likewise had good reason to create the Hitler Youth for boys and the League of German Girls to give up family and individual identity in support of Aryan ideals. Boys started at age six and progressed through after-school meetings, weekend trips, and summer camps to train to be warriors.[416] [417] China gave up their "one-child" intrusion into the family in just 2015 only to turn to forced removals and child brainwashing in their Muslim Uighur population for new punitive sport.[418]

Can't happen in America? Sorry, wrong. *Very wrong.* Government may declare children victims of their parents, with the ultimate penalty being temporary or even permanent termination of parental rights. The U.S. Department of Health & Human Services (HHS) publishes this data annually. They display a funnel chart that shows that in 2018 of 4.3 million referrals (somebody notifying child protective services of alleged harm to one or more children) covering 7.8 million children, 2.4 million of the referrals proceeded to full investigation, with 678,000 children declared victims. HHS uses a census estimate of 74 million children in the US in 2018. It's a big country, so many children are protected, but taken from a different perspective, 7.8 million children referred means **every tenth child** in America is up for protection and removal **every year**. And it is only every tenth of those every tenth children for whom the state determines protection is warranted.[419] Said another way, the government creates upheaval for **nine out of ten** families where the referrals result in no sufficient legal finding for maltreatment.

It seems a sloppy and overzealous system, fraught with needless family heartache. Who fuels the suspicion for government to investigate? **Government!** Legal/law enforcement personnel and social services personnel are among the three largest sources of those referrals that proceeded. However, the *largest* source is from education personnel—chiefly teachers, that politically correct group that overwhelmingly follows and promotes the Democrat dogma that says government knows better than you do. Worse, for the last year (2012) HHS reported the source of the great majority of referrals that turn out to be *unsubstantiated* after investigation, it was again educators that were the largest source—including 8% of all referrals determined to be *intentionally false*.[420]

Do you think a parent has to hurt, starve, or emotionally or sexually abuse a child to get a referral? *Think again.* Parents are threatened with the taking of their children—or their own *arrest*, another way of fracturing the family—for any reason the Left can imagine. In one school case, it happened for *protesting* a son's classroom exposure to the *My Two Dads* book normalizing homosexuality without being extended parental notice to opt out. The child was *five*.[421] In another, a seventh-grader was threatened with disciplinary action when a classmate said he *spun a pencil like a gun*. His father initially resisted taking him for an evaluation, which included disrobing, being confined to a bed, and providing blood and urine samples. Naturally, that found no connection to spinning a pencil or any problem with the child. But the father received notice from the New Jersey Department of Children and Families Division of Child Protection and Permanency (DCPP), advising it would investigate child abuse or neglect for his *lack of cooperation* in getting his son "cared" for. After the father's exchange of words with a caseworker, DCPP filed a court motion regarding his care of his child and outlining procedures to follow, at the peril of the boy (and his sibling) being *taken* and *offered for adoption*.[422]

Any other cases to note? Unfortunately, *plenty*, with these highlighted:

- For a single mom, being jailed *and* the child removed to foster care: the nine-year-old daughter asked to be dropped off (with a cell phone) to play with several dozen other kids at a nearby park rather than sit at the mother's work, but authorities declared the child abandoned.[423]

- For a widow with four kids, ages five to ten, who left them at home one day while she attended her college course, removal of all the children to foster care. The children were separated, moved frequently, sent to different schools, and reported they were physically and sexually abused while in state care. They were returned after a long fight that included a final home inspection in which the mother was told to be sure to clean her oven.[424]

- For a married mom, threatened at her door with an emergency custody removal order by a child protective services worker and sheriff demanding entry without a warrant. She had been observed by police leaving her six children inside her van (locked, running, air circulating) for ten minutes while getting them a snack. On this second visit, she allowed the officials in, and they isolated and interrogated her oldest—a five-year-old—before the social worker forcibly stripped all six naked to perform an examination. Her state also has an illicit practice of using *preprinted* court orders for removals.[425]

Of course, the authorities will still take your kids for the old-fashioned bump-and-bruise reasons. In one instance, a pediatric emergency room doctor had his newly adopted newborn removed from his home on the findings of a team in his own hospital. He fell asleep and rolled onto the infant, and then got her checked out of an abundance of caution. Birthmarks were mistaken for bruises, and a child abuse pediatrician misinterpreted a blood test. Even a prick mark from the hospital's own surreptitious procedure was attributed to the father.[426]

At this writing, the baby has spent nearly its entire life in state custody, and the case is scheduled for trial. Based on the endless litany of these stories, in a yearlong investigation NBC News talked to 300 families across the nation with reports of similar assaults on the family by government agencies and operatives. In one, a child abuse pediatrician accused a married couple of abuse of their six-week-old. The child and a sibling were then taken. Seven months and $50,000 later, a judge ordered the children returned and apologized. The mother is now pushing for policy reforms and legislative relief.[427]

The Constitution's Bill of Rights guarantees freedom of speech, to worship, and to bear arms, but offers no protection for parental authority—likely because it seemed so obvious. The Supreme Court has held that parental rights are protected by the Due Process Clause of the Fourteenth Amendment, but in a case in 2000 it broke with a long history of holding the parental care, custody, and control of children sacrosanct by failing to come to a majority ruling and instead inviting judges and states to come to their own decisions.[428] It is exasperatingly easy for Leftist judges and Democrat politicians to reduce parental rights.

Now the abuses have risen to such a level that parents have begun to endeavor to push back to reclaim God-given rights. A bill to amend the Constitution was introduced to do that in 2019, but has little chance of ever effecting the change.[429] With little success so far, the group Conservative Coloradans resisted the LGBTQ initiatives and also introduced their own bills, including a Parent's Bill of Rights to establish "parental rights related to directing the upbringing, education, and health care of a minor child."[430] Parents in Utah in 2018 did get at least a narrow protection with the nation's first "free-range parenting" law, codifying that kids can be reasonably unsupervised without their parents facing neglect charges, a proposition for a law that would have appeared utterly ridiculous just a generation ago.[431] In the meantime, while the Left risks America's attention taking children *bodily*, it unfailingly *takes their minds largely unnoticed*. It's a great strategy, advancing both fronts.

NO FAMILIES

VIOLATION:
Family Sanctity, Wealth

FOR TIME IMMEMORIAL, family members have banded together to weather life's challenges: war, disasters, sickness, poverty, crime, and everything else under the sun. Against the odds, mankind has survived, and no one can show that familial love has somehow diminished over time. Family continues to serve as the first backstop of support for its members, especially with parents for their children. Families are also granted special legal status. Parents serve as guardians and decision-makers for their minor children, and their influence typically extends for a lifetime. Spouses have many of the same rights between them. Even the minor children are granted an important right—to inherit the money and estate of the parents. In the family, the law recognizes those ties that bind.

If the law recognizes that blood is thicker than water, then the Left wants the law watered down or discarded. The Left really, *really* wants to substitute government for family. To do that the lynchpin family members, the *parents*, must be diminished in role and influence. And the left has multiple strategies for that, from the macro level of providing free stuff to transfer dependence from parents to government, to reducing the significance and incidence of marriage, to taking decision-making for children out of parents' hands, to physically separating children from parents for trumped-up reasons, household by household. That all takes place year in, year out with a host of tactics to overcome the sanctity and power of the family.

For the black community, Democrat and Left programs have reduced the formation of traditional families drastically. Today, just 31% of black children are born to two parents, and in 1965, about 76% were.[432] [433] Going back to the Democrat Great Society welfare programs of the 60s, black mothers receive living and housing assistance to be able to get by to raise kids without a father. Welfare assistance can *go away* if the mother is married.[434] Are blacks better off? The continuing disparities say no, but they and many of their children *are* more dependent.[435] Don't forget that blacks vote overwhelmingly for Democrats.[436] *What a happy outcome—for Democrats!* It all seems to add up.

It's not limited to the black community. Under Obama, middle-class wealth declined, and student debt soared.[437][438][439] Not surprisingly, family formation was pushed off to attempt to first establish financial health. Rather than cutting taxes and regulation to grow the economy for all as Trump did, the Democrat answer is to leave people poor and offer free stuff to their targeted identity groups. More food stamps. More assistance.[440][441][442][443] Students are to get from the government complete loan forgiveness and free tuition. Thirty million— typically minorities and young people—without health insurance are to get it, subsidized by the government through a new design that has those who had insurance now paying significantly more.[444][445] Government will provide what your hopelessly poor family cannot, and be grateful for that! *Oh, and vote Democrat!* There is no need for taking comfort and security at your mother's breast when the teat of government is always poking out and ready for another suck.

Marriage trends are already to the Left's liking. Given their social intervention into destabilizing that community, blacks have the lowest marriage rate of all major racial or ethnic groups in the US, standing at just 30%, versus 46% for Hispanics, 54% for whites, and 62% for Asians. Further, marriage is down from its all-time peak of 72% of all adults in 1960 to just 50% today.[446] Those Great Society programs appear to be far-reaching. Clearly, they also were supplemented by the Left's feminists, many of whom see no need for men beyond sperm content and the occasional pleasant dinner out. Legal relationships are unnecessary. The Left also attacks the religion that many see as the foundation of their marital bonds. Religion is unnecessary, discriminatory, and dangerous.

Yet another assault on the foundational elements of the family is the Left's war on men and boys. Girls get special curriculum and Bring Your Daughter to Work Day. Boys get declining academic achievement and accusations of toxic masculinity. Women get #MeToo uncritical belief and declared as victims of misogyny, and men get accused of rape without due process and have declining life expectancies. Even graduation rates and incomes see men losing ground to women.[447][448][449][450] The ultimate result will be men being judged less attractive as spouses and potential family patriarchs.

Covered separately, we have detailed the Left's efforts to decouple marriage from its purpose of family formation. Once the advantages and rights of marriage were reserved for one woman and one man. In just the past decade, the Left has gotten the centuries of tradition and law behind that kicked to the curb to provide the same benefits to any two people. And the pivotal case that struck down the Defense of Marriage Act had nothing to do with family formation or children, but the ability of one lesbian to claim the marital estate tax exemption following the death of her lesbian partner.[451] The purpose of marriage is now to facilitate the exchange of money and to fight discrimination. Many on the Left have decried marriage as a white supremacist tool used to ensure wealth stayed in the family. Now rather than beating them, they have fought to join them instead. Power is great for most, but money talks for the rest.

In sum, the Left systematically seeks to reduce the power and influence of the family so that government may take its place. Marriage is for anyone, and to overcome inequality. Men aren't fit to marry. The middle class is too financially insecure to marry. Marriage rates have declined with more government assistance to singles, an increase in feminism, and a decrease in religious belief. Free stuff, targeted first—and *successfully*—to the black community to gain their dependence, is now sought to be expanded to college students, other minorities, and anyone else who will reliably provide their vote in return.

How does the Left respond? *"You can call me daddy!"*

NO RELIGION

VIOLATION:
Religion, Politically Incorrect Thought, Carbon Emissions

THE LEFT'S CHIEF STRATEGY to diminish organized religion for eighty years has been to get the courts to rule to do their work for them. Most people rightly believe that the checks and balances of the Constitution produce a level playing field across most all topics, so they may question how the courts can be swayed to be anything but objective with that starting point. *Aren't they just enforcing the Constitution's call for* *separation of church and state?* Well, the Constitution had **no** such language and prohibited only the *federal* government from *limiting* the people's religious freedom.[452] That didn't apply to the states, and some states actually endorsed and supported specific religions, then and for years to come. It was a Supreme Court stacked with liberals appointed by Democrats Roosevelt and Truman that in 1947 solidified the "separation" notion and extended it to the states to greatly multiply its effect.[453] [454]

Since then, the Supreme Court has ruled on over three-dozen significant cases concerning religion — on average, one every other year.[455] There have been many decided by a 5-4 vote, with one person affecting the practice of faith in America for the many millions. To ensure that Democrats control who that singular person is, the Left is willing to fabricate stories of alcoholism and even gang rape, as seen with the confirmation hearing of Justice Kavanaugh.[456] *If that wasn't enough, what will it be next time?* Democrats routinely apply their own religion test for government service for presidential appointees to the judicial and executive branches — in total disregard to the Constitution. This is explicitly forbidden in Article VI, Section 1, Clause 3, reading "no religious test shall ever be required as a qualification to any office." Senators Durbin, Feinstein, and Booker have all made appointees answer for their religious beliefs during their questioning.[457] [458]

Targeting religion in schools is key, because it can affect knowledge and belief of the youth there for a long life to follow. For the singular topic of school prayer alone there is a continuing stream of court fights. Taken away was school prayer in 1962, a moment for *silent* (*don't you* **think** *that thought in your head!*) prayer or meditation in 1985, a singular prayer at the commencement ceremonies culminating thirteen years of schooling in 1992, and student-led prayer at football games in 2000. Apart from prayer itself, in schools Bible reading was banned in 1963 and the Ten Commandments in 1980.[459] You can clearly discern a pattern of eliminating the most visible and widespread practices first, and then working down a list to banish ever more limited ones for total eradication. At every step, schools must grapple with concern for liability for the ripple effect of the rulings. Ruling against prayer at *football* games does not mean the baseball or volleyball players are still free to do as they wish. School officials held responsible for *any* student religious expression is another contested area. Lower courts have found schools may also regulate the religious expression of *teachers* in school. The school and teacher may teach religion, but may not promote or celebrate or even critique it.

Reading the tea leaves of a 1989 Supreme Court decision and subsequent corollary lower court decisions informs how much government may permit community celebrations of Christmas, especially with nativity displays. The overriding answer is that government may no longer allow the celebration of the Judeo-Christian doctrine that was the basis of America's Constitution, and thus America itself. Does the nativity scene get included with symbols of other religions, like Jewish menorahs, or fake wrapped packages? Can secular symbols, like Santa Claus and the reindeer, be included with the Wise Men and the camels? These truly are the considerations for whether religion is being unconstitutionally promoted. The Christmas Winter Concert? It better have a lot of "Rudolph, The Red Nosed Reindeer," "Santa Claus Is Coming To Town," and "Frosty The Snowman" before "Hark The Herald" and "Silent Night" show up. Is a Christmas tree a forbidden religious symbol? A *naked* fir tree is not. But a *decorated* tree might be. What are the decorations? Candy canes and plain red glass balls? *Good!* Angels and crosses? *Bad! Mainly* candy canes and plain red glass balls, but with an angel on top? Your local court will answer that for you as part of the process of getting sued by the Left. *Are you sure you don't want to substitute the likeness of a trans woman for the angel?*

The Left has added a new successful set of tactics in their overarching strategy to eliminate the power of religion: *rebrand religion as **discrimination**.* Could a nun be a bisexual who frequently goes out of the convent to drink and party, gets pregnant, has an abortion, then has a series of sexual relationships with women in her convent bed when she is supposed to be serving God? If you answer "no," you are evil and dangerous, judging by groups like the Human Rights Campaign and many prominent Democrats. In this case, they shall argue that the Catholic Church's standards for conduct are discriminatory. They will say any judgment of the nun is governed by secular discrimination protections, not by religious doctrine. *Yes, the Catholic Church does have the freedom of religious beliefs guaranteed by our Constitution, but only if it does not impact any claimed LGBTQ rights.*

In embracing, most prominently, abortion and LGBTQ issues and constituencies, Democrats have aligned themselves into an axis against religion. In the remaining emails released by the State Department after Hillary Clinton deleted 33,000 of her choosing, it was related that she supported including contraception in health care plans to draw out religious "extremists" to create a wedge issue to inflame the base. In the emails reportedly hacked from John Podesta, the Clinton campaign manager, it was revealed that he started two groups, "Catholics in Alliance for the Common Good" and "Catholics United," to start a "Catholic Spring" to "plant the seeds of revolution" to bring "respect for gender equality" to the Catholic Church. Jennifer Palmieri, the campaign director of communications, engaged in email exchanges that charged that the beliefs of socially conservative Catholics were "an amazing bastardization of the faith" that evidenced "severely backwards gender relations."[460]

The head of the Democratic National Committee (DNC), Tom Perez, *demands* ideological rigidity of Democrat candidates, under penalty of receiving no party support. They must support the Democrat position on abortion—it is "not negotiable." "Every Democrat, like every American, should support a woman's right to [choose]."[461] However, unbending Democrat candidates will likely have an easier time with the DNC than dissenting Americans will—candidates may be denied funds, but at least they won't be labeled evil and dangerous and vilified for eternity. Democrats will go to all ends to diminish the power of religion in favor of the power of the state, which they always seek to control. They totally disregard moral and religious rules in favor of secular rules that they can create.

No matter if for religious beliefs regarding abortion, or for LGBTQ issues (or gun control, or illegal immigration), once an opposing voice is labeled evil and dangerous it seems Constitutional protections go out the window. Christian groups on campuses are denounced as prejudiced for wanting their organizations led only by Christians, as protected by the First Amendment freedom of association. Politically correct Democrat administrators and opposing students insist that making faith a requirement for a faith-based organization is tantamount to favoring one race or one gender. Therefore, to them, Christians are no better than the KKK—both groups make up their own *discriminatory* rules—and *everyone* agrees there should be no regard or concessions for the Klan.[462]

What could be worse than the Left's new tack to convince America that to embrace religion is to embrace *discrimination*? The Supreme Court **agreeing**, *which it did in 2010*. In *Christian Legal Society v. Martinez*, by a 5-4 decision, the court held that a Christian organization could not require that its members and leaders hold Christian beliefs, or even be Christians.[463] So now the Left's Supreme Court and discrimination efforts have powerfully united. While the decision only has legal precedence for state universities, its chilling fear factor ripples through to private colleges and even to secondary schools. By the same reasoning, presumably, the Lambda (lesbian) Society would have to welcome raging toxic cis-men and the

Black Student Union allow KKK members, but no one believes it would ever run in those directions. *Checkmate!*

Finally, if you thought the Left was already working hard enough to shut down religion and all its trappings as a source of power and influence in people's lives, the whole controlling climate change canard has provided them one more tool: carbon emissions. Why drive to church? *It's not necessary.* If sporting, arts, and concert events are to be restricted or banned because of their "needless" carbon footprints, how can other *unnecessary* gatherings escape the same fate? Even with church attendance declining, there are still all those trips to church, temples, and mosques. Some people waste even more time and energy going to confession, choir practices, council meetings, and potluck dinners. Others organize needless family gatherings, like Sunday dinners and Easter egg hunts. Some have the temerity to invite large numbers to Christmas parties. All unnecessary! *The church of the Left preaches to just forget "save your **soul"**—it's save the **planet**, you selfish a-hole!*

NO RIGHT OF SELF-DEFENSE

VIOLATION:
Achievement/Individualism/Self-Reliance, Guns

DO YOU THINK YOU HAVE A RIGHT OF SELF-DEFENSE? *Like against someone trying to knife you in the supermarket parking lot, or* *trying to bash your brains out in your own kitchen?* Yes? The United Nations disagrees. Their "Human Rights Council" says—*cynically, deceitfully, falsely*—that international law recognizes no such basic human right. On the contrary, they say, it is gun control—control *more severe and restrictive* than anything existing anywhere in the United States—that is the human right. Net, you are never to rely on yourself, but to put yourself at the mercy of criminals and the whim of the bureaucratic state to be there to protect you.

Remember what your mother told you if a bully punched you—"punch them right back"? Well, the UN says you had a *bad* mother. So did Democrat President Obama and his Secretary of State, John Kerry, who happily embraced the UN Arms Trade Treaty in 2013. Those two revered leaders of the Left who claim to be all knowing and wise are willfully myopic and ignorant when it comes to connecting the dots on self-preservation, self-defense, weapons broadly, and guns specifically. A read of "The Human Right of Self-Defense," a 120-page scholarly article with 593 citations, would have set the UN and Obama and Kerry straight, if they had wanted. It pointed out the UN Human Rights Council, in its 2006 conclusion that self-defense is not a human right, started off badly when it ignored the words of its own United Nations Universal Declaration of Human Rights, adopted the year the UN was formed in 1948. It got worse from there, ignoring more than *five centuries* of humanitarian international law.[464]

That same report that concluded self-defense is not a human right argued instead that a government's failure to *restrict* self-defense itself is a violation of human rights! A subcommittee of the Human Rights Council also proclaimed that all nations were required by law to implement the gun control measures of the report. Those included licensing for every gun, which could only be for a specific purpose, such as hunting. Even while enforcing that, governments were to commence **disarmament** programs to effect "destruction of small arms."

It really is just *too rich*: within a few months of concluding there is no human right to self-defense and pushing global disarmament, the UN launched into drafting its Arms Trade Treaty, which has as its purpose to limit or prohibit arms transfers **everywhere**. This is the one supported by Obama, Kerry, and the gun grabbers on the Left. It includes missiles, tanks, aircraft, and warships—*oh, and common weapons used for self-defense, like handguns, rifles, and shotguns.* Its defenders insist it has no effect whatsoever on American's Second Amendment rights, but the text says otherwise.

For those maintaining it applies only to international sales, it is not the *International* Arms Trade Treaty, but the Arms Trade Treaty. Further, the text has separate sections encompassing imports, exports, trans-shipments, and mere "transits"—all equally defined as a "transfer." It requires each government to regulate the transit "under its jurisdiction of conventional arms … through its territory in accordance with relevant international law." *In other words, **domestic**, not just international.* Minimally, that regulation includes recordkeeping or registration for each gun and, arguably, it may include restricting the sale entirely based upon the other aims of the treaty. To leave no doubt of its expansiveness, each government "is encouraged to apply the provisions of this Treaty to the broadest range of conventional arms," and is admonished that "national definitions shall not cover less than the descriptions used in relevant United Nations instruments." Finally, the treaty may be amended regularly to add as needed.[465]

A majority of the US Senate disagreed with Obama and Kerry and actually voted instead for an amendment forever preventing the adoption of the treaty and its tacit agreement with the UN's declaration of no right to self-defense. Obama waited three years until after Trump's election before nevertheless sending the treaty to the Senate to keep his base happy in the face of failure. Trump himself "unsigned" the treaty in 2019.[466] Even if what Kerry said about the treaty were 100% true—that it "will not diminish anyone's freedom"—and Trump slayed a toothless Hydra, even toothless Hydras are snakes and tend to grow new heads. The UN treaty was easily expandable. The UN also shockingly allows rogue nations like Iran and others touting sharia law to pontificate as virtuosos of "human rights." Submitting US citizens to a "superior" UN authority is laughable at best and dangerous at worst.

Enlightened Europeans, who the Left cite as superior in governance and morality, have already failed on the issue of self-defense. Most European countries make it difficult, if not impossible, to possess weapons. England, having seen the Russian Revolution against the monarchy, so distrusted its own people with guns that it disarmed after World War I and

found itself unable to defend against the Nazis without solic-
iting American hunters and farmers to send their extra guns
to the rescue. Throughout the twentieth century, Brits were
progressively disarmed by their own government. Since the
1950s, it has been forbidden to carry any item with the *intent*
of self-defense. As a result, London is increasingly dangerous, with knives the weapon of choice for criminals against
the empty, outstretched hands of their victims. During 2011
riots there, *baseball bats* saw a 5000% spike in Amazon sales
for citizens hoping for some option to defend themselves.[467]

In England, there are numerous cases of those prosecuted
for defending themselves during home invasions or burglar-
ies. *In their homes!* In 2018, the *Independent* newspaper was
forced to put up a webpage answering common questions
for an outraged citizenry, starting with "Am I entitled to kill
a burglar?"[468] This is all in spite of the English Bill of Rights
of 1689—still in force—that guaranteed the rights to possess
arms for personal defense. This is reinforced by both the
older common law and the newer European Convention on
Human Rights, yet the government and its courts clearly have
a modern bias against honoring it.

Governments in the US are guilty of the same: whether
you are prosecuted for wounding or killing in self-defense
depends in major part on the political beliefs of your prose-
cutor. It is just another reason to avoid San Francisco. Social
justice and criminal justice reform advocates add to this by
re-characterizing lawful self-defense—whether by police or
private citizens—as *legal execution*. When an armed home

invader is shot and killed by a homeowner, someone on the Left will invariably ask why they couldn't have just shot to *wound*, or even just *frighten*. Trayvon Martin, judged to have been justifiably killed when he attacked and knocked the smaller George Zimmerman to the ground and promised to kill him while he straddled and pummeled him, was hailed instead as the hero by the Left based upon his skin color. *He was a victim of gun violence!*

Of course, the biggest social justice and criminal justice reformer America has ever known is one Barack Hussein Obama. Struggling to get any success with his UN Arms Treaty, he turned to having his Department of Justice investigate police departments and a string of them-or-me police self-defense shootings made high profile by him and his social justice allies. Trayvon Martin was his favorite case to beat down self-defense laws such as "stand your ground." When local law enforcement could not find enough to charge Zimmerman, Obama's Department of Justice (DOJ) swooped in. Days later, Obama lionized Martin as a would-be son. The following year, just days after Zimmerman's acquittal, Obama lamented self-defense laws while comparing Martin to himself thirty-five years earlier.[469] [470] As a cherry on top, he honored the aggressor's parents with an invitation to the White House on the third anniversary of his death—to counter the news that his DOJ had just closed its own independent investigation of Zimmerman without any charges.[471]

What's the lesson? A basic human right like self-defense is increasingly threatened and subject to the Left's manipulation of all means possible: international law, domestic law, selective prosecution, race-baiting, identity politics, and electioneering. The barrel of that gun may be pointed at **you** at all times. *Be cautious of shooting back.*

NO GUNS

VIOLATION:
Guns, Achievement/Individualism/Self-Reliance

DEMOCRATS VOW TO TAKE YOUR GUNS![472] *If only it were just them.*

At a Democrat presidential debate in late 2019, candidate Beto O'Rourke answered for his support of confiscation of so-called assault weapons by famously exclaiming, "Hell, yes, we are going to take your AR-15, your AK-47!"[473] Across America, the Left's gun grabbers, mainstream media, think-tank wonks, and Democrat politicians all sucked in an exhilarated gasp thrilled that America was about to take a bold step forward. Then a sickening heat washed over them, and they slowly exhaled knowing that what they falsely claimed could never happen had just been admitted. But Beto continued to run his mouth, adding that for those not volunteering their guns, "that weapon will be taken from them and they will be fined, and if they should persist in continuing to use and to buy these weapons, then there will be other consequences in the criminal code."[474] *Don't worry, the government will take care of your gun ... and you too.*

The Democrat cleanup effort started apace. Senate Minority Leader Chuck Schumer stated, "I don't know of any other Democrat who agrees with Beto." "He gave his own opinion, OK? I think it was very harmful to make it look like all the Democrats," asserted Senator Joe Manchin, who has been a point person on gun control for Democrats. Senator Martin Heinrich was more forthright: "I think that was a bit of a gift to the NRA." Indeed, the National Rifle Association began using Beto's words in their fundraising immediately.[475] Academics also weighed in, believing that the Left's efforts to push even moderate gun control proposals would be hobbled for years by Beto's words used to raise suspicion of darker motives once concealed.[476] Beto's campaign was suspended in little more than a month.

End of story? Not at all. With former Vice President Biden looking like the 2020 Democrat nominee, he had Beto join him at a Texas rally and made a declaration: "You're going to take care of the gun problem with me. You're going to be the one that leads this effort." Then they left for a live-streamed dinner with Biden there confirming, "this guy can change the face of what we're dealing with, with regard to guns, assault weapons ... if I win, I'm coming for him." So the supposed "moderate" of the Democrats has embraced confiscation, though as classic Biden, he remains combative and confused. The very next day an auto worker confronted Biden over his gun confiscation plans and Biden lashed out on live television, telling the man he was "full of sh*t" and calling him "a horse's ass" while arguing he would certainly not take *all* guns, but "we'll take the AR-14s (sic) away." In 2019, Biden couldn't even field a softball from CNN's Anderson Cooper, who set him up with "to gun owners out there who say, well, a Biden administration means they're going to come for my guns . . ." only to have Biden interrupt with "BINGO. You're right, if you have an assault weapon."[477] Biden's campaign website stopped short of confiscation, calling for a new assault weapon ban and either buybacks or registration and taxation of existing weapons, but his own words betray his true position. *He is a much more accomplished politician than Beto.*

Biden comes out and says he would take guns, just not *all* of them—only those damned "assault weapons." But an ongoing favorite tactic of Democrats is to confound just what is an assault weapon and to play bait and switch to include any gun that uses the semi-automatic technology that is a century old. The Democrats' 2020 presidential wannabes routinely referred to common **semi-automatic** rifles like the AR-15 and AK-47 as "weapons of war." They are not. Armies issue selective-fire rifles—the **automatic** weapons that 99.999% of ordinary citizens do not possess. None of the world's armies issues semi-automatic rifles to their troops on the front lines of war. Hillary Clinton did the same throughout her campaigning, and it is an acknowledged tactic by gun control groups who will go to far greater lengths to deceive for their own purposes. A proposed assault weapon referendum in Florida was broadly written to ban the possession of virtually every semi-automatic long-gun.[478]

"Military-style" is similarly used—but the *majority* of guns in America have military origins. Pump shotguns are used by the military, so presumably, they are "military-style." Millions upon millions of pistols owned by ordinary citizens are 1911 semi-automatic types—the same gun issued to US military forces for 105 years. Even the six-guns used by Roy Rogers to shoot guns out of the bad guys' hands were the same Colt single-action revolvers as issued to the US Army. Shotguns, pistols, revolvers, rifles—all "military-style."

Increasingly, corporations are just as dogmatic as politicos. After the tragic massacre at the Parkland, Florida high school and resulting outcry to forever end evil simply by banning guns, Walmart and Dick's Sporting Goods weighed their interests for two weeks, assessing the liberal voices before acting to curtail legal gun sales. Following a Connecticut shooting in 2012, Dick's had "suspended" sales of "assault-style rifles" before quietly reinstating them a few months later in its outdoor and hunting retail chain. This time they said they meant it, and also ended sales of high-capacity magazines. They also decided to discriminate against Americans ages 18-20 by refusing to sell them guns regardless of the law permitting it.[479] After Walmart—who had stopped selling "assault rifles" in 2015—one-upped them by announcing not only would they also discriminate against ages 18-20, but they would even ban sales of "assault-style ... guns *and toys,*" Dick's said they would actually *destroy* the guns they had taken from their stores.[480][481] Walmart and Dick's can't take your weapons, but they can prevent you from ever getting them.

Leftists at America's top banks also want to prevent you

from owning a gun. Citigroup has insisted its customers no longer sell guns to those 18-20 or sell high-capacity magazines, among other restrictions. This applied to any customer that uses their banking services, borrows money, raises capital, or offers credit cards backed by Citigroup.[482] That would include every business from Walmart to internet sporting goods sites to your local gun store. Bank of America said they will no longer "underwrite or finance military-style firearms" and outright told gun manufacturers they would no longer do business together.[483] Ironically, the Trump administration had only months earlier ended a 2013 Obama DOJ program that evidenced the same intent: shut down the ability of *deplorable* organizations like gun manufacturers or distributors to finance their own activities. Under Obama's Operation Choke Point, not only banking regulators but the DOJ itself would pressure and investigate banks that financed "high risk" businesses like selling guns or ammunition.[484] This caused obvious disruption and harm to these businesses. *All to take your guns away.*

For those clinging to their guns and religion, be warned that one does not go with the other. The leadership of most mainstream Protestant denominations support gun control, regardless of the views of the parishioners filling the offering plates. The conservative Missouri Synod of the Lutheran Church advocates no infringement of Americans' Second Amendment rights, but the largest faction, the Evangelical Lutheran Church of America does.[485] The Methodist Church wants Congress to "regulate the importation, manufacturing, sale, and possession of guns and ammunition by the general public" to enable the "reduction of the availability of guns."[486] The Presbyterian leadership jumped on the gun control bandwagon fifty years ago and has made sure no one forgets, with resolutions repeated in 1976, 1988, 1990, 1991, 1996, 1998, 2000, and 2008. From 2014, their "Gun Violence Prevention Congregational Toolkit" included study sessions on "Gun Violence 101 and the Citizen's Test on Gun Violence in America" and "Guns in the US Today, Including 'Battleground America.'" Still not a believer? Read "Scripture Passages Addressing Gun Violence."[487]

The Catholic Church *officially* has no position on gun control. While the Catechism of the Catholic Church says self-defense even using lethal force is permissible and forgivable, not much else supports gun use or ownership. The universal magisterium (teaching exercised by either the pope or the worldwide bishops in concert with him) is silent. However, bishops may teach separate from the pope, and do. In 2000, the United States Conference of Catholic Bishops (USCCB) said they believed "handguns should be eliminated," which was a reiteration of a 1975 statement.[488] The pope himself in 2014 called "to all who sow violence and death by force of arms ... give up the way of arms," which sounded evenhanded, and he remained so even when subsequently alluding to mass shootings in America. But his bishops again were unequivocal. Following the 2018 Parkland shootings, that same USCCB called for "Catholics and all people of good will" to urge Congress to restrict "high-capacity weapons and ammunition magazines" and to "require universal background checks."[489] Just a few months later, Pope Francis finally came through, in a tweet even surpassing his US bishops with "let's ban all weapons."[490] *What do you pray for?*

The few in America who have studied and respect the Constitution may recall that the Second Amendment says something about Americans and guns. It doesn't *grant* a right, because our Founding Fathers insisted that certain rights were inalienable human rights *granted by a Creator* that no government could claim credit for, or overrule. The Founding Fathers thought you should be able to defend yourself, *specifically* against the government, and against any others not following natural or manmade laws. In 2008 and 2010, in landmark cases, our Supreme Court had to step in to rule that meant the *individual right* to bear arms, and to carry them outside the home for the same protection purpose.[491] But the Left detests the self-reliance that guns in the hands of law-abiding citizens displays. The Left detests the Constitution itself. The only right *people* should have is to *vote—for those handing them the free stuff and assuring them they will protect them.*

With the Democrats leading the way no longer needing to maintain the ruse of denying taking guns, a signal has been sent to every gun control group, every retailer, every bank, and every church group that the gloves are off. *America may now be disarmed, and government will protect you.*

NO AMERICAN FLAG

VIOLATION:
Nationalism/Patriotism

THE LEFT HAS ALREADY MADE ITS POINT that the national anthem cannot be tolerated because America is a historically racist and unjust society. Plus, didn't you know the song has lyrics that *glorify* slavery? Yes, it speaks of *freemen*, which are the opposite of slaves.[492] That's *discrimination* right there that is being celebrated!

Next, we have that little problem that the first American flag—the one with the circle of thirteen stars on a field of blue with thirteen red and white stripes—waved over states that had *slaves.* The same guy leading the protests against the national anthem saw to it that Nike quickly withdrew a special edition shoe that was to feature that flag. Nobody talks about it, but that reasoning eliminates another fourteen flags, up through the thirty-three-star flag that waved at the start of the Civil War, when states forming the Confederacy raised their own controversial flag.[493] For the longest time, the Left told us that *that* was the bad flag. So what is to be done with those fifteen American flags? Should they be *removed* from textbooks, history books, and encyclopedias? What about the internet? Should searches be *blocked*? Should it be *illegal* to put them on a website?

It's not a leap to say *any* flag that sprang from a nation that once tolerated slavery is unacceptable. But at what point is

228 Fifty-Six Things The Left Will Take Away From You

there forgiveness? It's been over 150 years. **America went to war to** *defeat* **slavery.** *No good?* Some today want reparations paid to descendants of slaves. What about the 400,000 Americans who died fighting to *free* slaves? Weren't they victims? What do *their* descendants get? What if those descendants and tens of millions more see something different in the American flag that creates solemnity and deep respect? Are their feelings to be *disregarded*?

Clearly, the answer is YES. The American flag—the one callously displayed right now in so many places—reportedly screams racism, injustice, imperialism, consumerism, and unbridled nationalism.[494] The Left comes up with all sorts of mumbo jumbo to justify trashing the flag. Before Trump's big "Salute to America" parade in Washington DC in 2019, the Revolutionary Communist Party of America released a vague statement that "there are people inside the borders of this country who stand with the people of the world." That became infinitely clearer at the event, when they burned an American flag while chanting, "America was never great."[495] In another example, a commissioner in Poughkeepsie explained his directive to remove flags from the backs of three fire engines: "they were a liability." Only after protests did the commissioners recognize "the importance and symbolism of the American flag."[496]

Students and spectators for Travelers Rest High School (TRHS) in South Carolina were blocked from bringing American flags to a football game, lest the opposing school take offense. That school has a minority Hispanic population (31%, compared to 35% white, and 30% African American), and the flag may have been previously used in taunting—of *other Americans!* How does that work? The other team even runs onto the football field carrying—*you guessed it*—an American flag. The principal went on record to say, "no object, sign, chants by students, etc. would be permitted if they compromise safety." The school itself assured the decision was made "in the spirit of patriotism."[497] Now with criticism coming from *both* school communities, the school reversed its enforcement against its imagined future infractions: "Instead of restricting possession of the flag, the TRHS administration will, if needed, address the misuse of the flag."[498]

Massachusetts's Hampshire College lowered the American flag to half-staff the day after Trump's election. Why? Its president said it had *nothing* to do with the election. It was instead "meant as an expression of grief over the violent deaths being suffered in this country and globally." *What?* A day later, the flag was burned, and it was then the college decided to no longer fly the flag at all. Now, a spokesman confessed, it was the "community" that told them "the flag is a powerful symbol of fear they've felt all their lives because they grew up as people of color, never feeling safe."[499] Again, protests ensued, and two weeks later, the flag went back up, but the college president did not back down, defending its removal because the flag itself can suppress "uninhibited expression of deeply held viewpoints."[500]

These instances are like scrums where the outcome of two sides pushing intensely against each other can turn on the slightest advantage. So far, patriots have only been winning by vigilance and sheer persistence. *The Left will not long put up with playing by the rules if they cannot win.*

NO COUNTRIES

VIOLATION:
Nationalism/Patriotism, Carbon Emissions

NO Border Wall! Build Bridges Not Walls! Families Have No Borders! No Hate No Racism No Borders! No Borders No Nations F*ck Deportation!

THE MOST VOCAL CRITICS OF AMERICA exercising its right to maintain its sovereignty and to control its borders—the activist sign carriers—do appear to be most concerned with allowing one and all to tap into the American dream, but in utter *disregard* of any laws. In some cases, they may selfishly have family members who would benefit by sidestepping the law. For most, in the name of a misplaced sense of justice or humanitarianism, they tout no borders or no border enforcement, with thoughts no deeper than the sloganeering of the protest signs. A few may just want a ride on the anarchy train wherever it takes them.

No matter their motivation, all these groups are dangerous to America. For them, laws that get in the way of their personal circumstances or convictions or musings are to be ignored. Their focus is only on the plight of those aliens wanting in, with no concern for the well-being of those citizens already here. They would overload and swamp the boat for all, especially any boat that they themselves are not on. Of course, the arguments for borders fall on deaf ears with them, whether to regulate the economy, ensure national security, or maintain health and welfare. But these people waving signs are at best *cheerleaders*, and not the players or managers.

The *players* are organizations with names like the New York Immigrant Coalition, the National Immigration Forum, and the Fair Immigration Reform Movement (FIRM).[501] *All* are well left of center and *all* advocate for illegal aliens to be made **legal**. The New York Immigrant Coalition has lobbied for driver licenses for illegals and wants broad expansion of entitlement programs to them.[502] The National Immigration Forum opposes border walls and border enforcement. For one of their fundraisers, they auctioned a life-sized, nude statue of Donald Trump entitled "The Emperor Has No Balls."[503] FIRM wants citizenship for **all** illegals and opposes **all** border security. FIRM is known to use children for demonstrations and human blockades. When they did not get the desired results, a spokesman said they would "switch tactics from persuasion to punishment."[504]

While Leftist immigration "reform" groups are also dangerous in their flaunting of laws and their urgings to open the gates and coffers to all, they still rank only as players— very *effective* players, but only players. The *managers* are those who have the ability to effect policy. In a 2019 presidential primary debate, ten Democrats were asked whether they supported extending universal health care to "undocumented immigrants," and all ten responded affirmatively.[505] They included one US Representative, four US Senators, and one former US Senator and Vice President. *These* are the managers. A number of them also oppose border walls and border enforcement and want illegal immigration decriminalized. These are the people the players seek to influence with their sit-ins, sign waving, and political contributions—their *money*.

Perhaps yet another group may be termed *owners*. The most powerful of the players with money and their largely silent mega-donor partners are these owners. Who funds the immigration groups? *Often*, teacher unions! They are disproportionately composed of Democrats, and their leadership is still more liberal than the membership itself. And *most often*: George Soros funded groups like his Open Society Network. Soros spends billions to bankroll his anti-free market and redistributionist "open society" ideals.[506] Many of the world's largest foundations also espouse and fund the liberal ideals of the Left, starting with immigration and going on from there.

But open borders and uncontrolled immigration are just the opening gambit for those who believe that the US should bow to other authority broadly. Where President Trump calls for "America First," they would put America *last*. As the darling of the Left, President Barack Obama raised this to an art form, and they long to return to the days of Obama bowing to foreign monarchs, apologizing for America, and setting policy to reduce America's position in global affairs so that others might take a greater hand. Where Trump embraced nationalism as the natural objective of the leader of a nation, Obama signed on to global gun control and climate change pacts, while joining other nations in providing a path for terrorist-fomenting Iran to become a nuclear power. The Democrat party and many of its most prominent politicians who support no borders for immigration also support no borders in US versus international law. Trump negotiates trade agreements one country at a time, while Democrats are quite happy with multilateral agreements that not only diminish American strength in negotiating terms, but also call for international tribunals to set rules and mediate disputes forevermore.

If you believe in big government as a source of power to be manipulated and profited from, how could you come up with a bigger government than *one for the whole world*?[507] This is what the real power brokers of the Left want. Destroying America's border security is just a preliminary step in destroying America's sovereignty. The tools to advance the strategy already exist. They go by the names United Nations, World Trade Organization, World Health Organization, World Bank, International Monetary Fund, Paris Climate Agreement, and many others. The EU has been a major initiative, and even as it overreached and the United Kingdom determined to leave, the EU doubled down. In the face of rising populism and nationalism that threatened it, the EU called for its own first-time military force and then saw twenty-one heads of member-states sign a resolution calling for even more integration.[508] [509]

In 2015, the UN vaulted past its founding vision of universal human rights to a new document that puts *rights* aside to record seventeen goals for **world governance by 2030**, with ninety-one numbered sections and 169 targets, at a cost of trillions of dollars.[510] Of course, the Left sells world government on the utopian ideals of no poverty and no wars.[511] They point out the current construct of nation-states is only an aberration of the past 400 years, and that defending borders and even cheering for national sports teams are just two of the ills of nationalism, with war and exploitation among the others.[512]

The push for one world government actually was popularized by the *Republican* presidential candidate—Wendell Willkie—at the height of World War II.[513] After the war, it quickly gained steam as a way to reimagine how the last war—*and the next*—could be erased. It persisted through the 1970s with both Democrats and Republicans (Nixon, yes; Reagan, never)—but now to include chiefly America and Europe, while excluding the Soviets as a way to defeat or at least stymie them.[514] With the end of the Soviet Union and its bloc as a threat, the one-worlders are again elites and utopians—and *Democrats*.

Why Democrats? *Easy!* **Climate change!** Climate change and big government go hand in hand—and no government can be bigger and better than a *world* government.[515] Climate change represents the biggest opportunity for Democrats and Leftists to control people and exert power. It is irresistible for them. It is the meaty bone to their slobbering jowls. *The world must finally unite!* With "science," it's so easy to dupe the populace, and the do-gooders want so much to help. And how better to grow government than to engage to fight Nature? *It can never be defeated, and it will never go away.* Few Democrats are transparent enough to mention climate change and one world government in the same breath; they leave that to Leftist organizations and writers to make the connection. But world government does not have to be one governing body for *all* issues when governments may convene to unite, issue by issue, and give over their decision-making and sovereignty to a larger body. The Paris Agreement was just such a one-government, one-issue accord.

Donald Trump backing America out of that slanted and largely ineffective agreement was taken as dashing out the brains of the proud newborn of the radical Left. *It is a blood feud they will never give up.*

TAKE WHAT YOU HAVE

NO EXTRAVAGANT POSSESSIONS OR PURCHASES

VIOLATION:
Inequality, Wealth

AS THE WORLD LEANS INTO SOCIALISTIC POLICIES or full embrace of socialism itself, there are pathbreaking calls to rid the fortunate of any signs of wealth. How can there *not* be? Socialism calls for the *sharing* of property, not the *possession* of it, especially not the possession of property deemed "exclusive" by the Left. *Get with the program.*

Starting in 2019, a school in northwestern England told parents it would start enforcing a ban on *expensive coats* worn by some children. "These coats cause a lot of inequality between our pupils. They stigmatize students and parents who are less well off and struggle financially."[516] In New Jersey, a school decreed that students would not be allowed to hire *limos* or *party buses*, or even use their parents' *own expensive cars* to get to the prom. Instead, each would pay fifteen dollars to ride on a chaperoned bus provided by the school. Why? Safety, of course. Oh, and *equity*. "We have students from various socioeconomic backgrounds," the superintendent stated, "and we wanted to provide an even playing field for all students."[517] The school also acknowledged that there had been no past safety issues to precipitate the change.[518] For good measure, to ensure all students would experience *equality of sadness*, the prom was also scheduled for a *Tuesday* night.

In Australia, one hundred schools take part in a "Poverty Proofing the School Day" effort to keep poorer children from being "stigmatized." They completely banned *pencil cases*, "so there's no comparison on the tables." Further, they require a "standard backpack" so they "don't have any designer goods." Teachers have been challenged to look at ways some children might be excluded. As a result, dress-up and fundraising days have been reduced. Even physical education classes are being scrutinized.[519] Another problem: did you understand that prompting students to *talk about* what they did over the weekend can *penalize those from low-income backgrounds? No? We thought so.* In America, ginned-up concerns have led schools to cancel Halloween in the name of equality.

So what's the strategy from the Left? *Get the equality and wealth-shaming message to the kids now, so they grow up believing it to be natural and good to hate the rich.* Bans are very effective, but they can catalyze resistance. Taxes are much sneakier, and *who doesn't like taxing those better off than they are?* The 2020 Democrat Presidential candidates talked incessantly of higher taxes on the wealthy (*repeal the Trump tax cuts for the rich*), including Senator Warren's extra 2% tax on *only* the wealthy. It's not an *income* tax, but a *net worth* tax, meaning once you have it, it will be taxed every year in perpetuity. *Take that rich pigs!* Except some foresee that it would have a disastrous trickle-down effect on those it is supposed to be sating—sinking stocks and retirement savings, and raising interest rates on mortgages and consumer debt.[520] But ... *take that rich pigs!*

In 1991, George H. W. "read my lips, no new taxes" Bush signed into law a 10% luxury goods tax on jewelry, watches, furs, private jets, many boats, and some cars. Democrat Clinton signed the bill to reverse it two years later after it sank the boat industry and torpedoed jobs.[521] It continued on autos until 2002, and a gas-guzzler tax that disproportionately affects the cars of the wealthy ($3,000 for a BMW) continues to this day. It can easily happen again. On the *Monopoly* board game, there is a space labeled "luxury tax." *Anyone* landing on it pays the luxury tax. *Take a lesson.*

In the old USSR—that's the Union of the Soviet **Socialist** Republic—luxury goods were virtually unknown. Only the highest party officials and their cronies were permitted luxuries. Anyone else caught with a luxury item would get attention from the apparatchik that might result in them disappearing. *But, hey, everyone else was equal.* That's something! Again, *take a lesson.*

In his first 2020 debate, Democrat Presidential candidate Michael Bloomberg, whose wealth is estimated at over sixty billion dollars, was asked a personal question: "Mayor Bloomberg, *should you exist?*"[522] It was in response to repeated assertions by rival Senator Bernie Sanders that billionaires just *should not exist.* Perhaps Senator Sanders' honeymoon in the USSR cemented that abiding notion of poverty and equality in his mind. Bernie draws an equivalency between Bloomberg's wealth and the bottom 125 million Americans. *Even it up!* The same equivalency could be applied to your "extravagant" home. It would house a lot of illegal aliens if operated instead as government housing. Until now, they've all felt *excluded.* *Even it up!* Your spending to vacation for a week at Disney World would do more good funding universal health care for the less fortunate. *Even it up!* Even your late model pickup truck—it could be sold to buy *three* Kia sedans. Two for them, one for you—*our compliments.*

Take a lesson.

NO INCOME TAXES–OR INCOME

VIOLATION:
Inequality, Private Ownership

THE MOST PROMINENT DEMOCRAT CANDIDATES in the 2020 presidential election horribly mismanaged how to pay for Medicare for All. It was objectively priced out to cost thirty-two trillion dollars over ten years. Annual expenditures on this one item would rival that of the *entire remaining federal budget.* All dancing around the issue as long as they could, Senator Elizabeth Warren finally had to concede a big number, and promptly plummeted in the polls. Senator Bernie Sanders had a deft touch: he simply argued that somehow every American would save enough to handily zero out the bill.[523] Of course, that is a ridiculous claim: comparing the 300,000,000+ people and the $3,000,000,000,000+ annual cost, that comes out to **$10,000 per person**—as if a family of five reliably spends *$50,000* on health care *every year*. With that average, for every family that only spends just $25,000, another would have to spend *$75,000*.

It is no surprise that Bernie can count on no one doing the math, or calling him on it if they did. But most understand that his claim sounds fishy on its face. Don't forget, his claimed savings even comes after giving *thirty million more* access to government-paid health care. And add in all the *efficiency* reaped by the government running health care—just like with the Veterans' Administration! Bernie's real mistake is in its stopping *too short*. Translations of *Mein Kampf* reveal Hitler to have written the masses more easily fall victim to the *big lie* than to any small lie. It was picked up by the OSS (the predecessor of the CIA) in their wartime psychological profile of him.[524] Bernie has gone to school on the USSR and Cuba, but somehow missed the Nazis.

No, Bernie should have extended his plan not just to have the government pay for health care, but for *everything*. What is the slogan, the big lie? **NO MORE TAXES!**

How? When Americans rely on the government for *everything*, it is folly to pay out for everyone's support only after taking in a similar amount in taxes. Why not eliminate all those debits and credits back and forth? Why not have the government **keep your income** to pay your—*and everyone else's*—support? There really is no need for individual accounts. *The server in the prison mess hall does not have to account for each meal served to each inmate—he need only serve up **the same bowl of slop to all.***

The organizing principle quickly approaches that of the Soviet Union: the government owns all the means of production and wealth creation, everyone works for the government because there is no private enterprise, all live in government housing because there may be no landlords, and nothing is available if not from the government because the government owns anything that may be acquired. Think of it as a big, happy family where mommy and daddy divvy up whatever everyone already shares—the "kids" need no income to get along. Perhaps you *can* uniquely have a framed family portrait or a prosthetic leg that can't be easily modified for another. Maybe a higher-level government job gets you a nicer apartment, or at least access to more stylish *shoes*. But you don't *own* anything, and you don't need to.

This is the dream of the Left—to have the power to control everything and to make the decisions for everyone. How else to stamp out *inequality*? Does it look a little too much like the *communist* Soviet Union? (And how did *that* turn out?) Does it smack just a bit of *totalitarianism*? Well, *maybe* on paper, holds the Left, but the difference is, *"we are **good** people"*! Be assured that Hitler, Stalin, Mao, Castro, and Pol Pot felt the same. *And Idi Amin was supposed to be a great guy when you got to know him.*

There are not just analogs for comparison in the

government's bad record in managing health care with the Veterans' Administration and the Obamacare false promises, there are analogs for their managing *entire populations*. Look to how the Native Americans have fared with their "management" by the government. *Can't happen today?* Look to African Americans and their fate in being supported and "lifted" by so many government programs starting in the twentieth century. Federal, state, and local governments continue to work together to give them just enough to be compliant and predictable with only occasional flare-ups while keeping them in the dependent and Democrat fold. *That is the great experiment that is to now instead become the norm.*

NO INHERITANCE

VIOLATION:
Inequality, Wealth, Private Ownership, Self-Reliance

HOW LONG WOULD IT TAKE TO OVERCOME the income inequality the Left is fixated on without massive, imminent changes? Let's see—if we tax Michael Bloomberg's sixty billion dollars with a 10% *annual* confiscatory surcharge—taking six billion—but his portfolio investments appreciate 10%, we would get nowhere fast. Confiscate 20% every year, and with his remaining wealth still appreciating 10%, after ten years, he would still be worth about eighteen billion of pure inequality.

Why screw around? TAKE IT ALL. *Starting now!* Of course, we use Michael Bloomberg as just an example representing all those with wealth. We get even more from Bill Gates and Jeff Bezos and a few others, and less from the rest of us. But "lesser" people with a million or even a couple hundred grand have the same income inequality versus upside-down debt college students, negative net worth minorities, and skid row crack addicts. *Lesser people are worth a good confiscation too!* And think how much *better* the students, minorities, and addicts will *feel* about themselves! *It's a good bet they'll be voting Democrat from here on.*

Senator Bernie Sanders would have a government take-over of so much of the economy—health care, pharmaceuticals, fossil fuels, and so on—and would hand trillions back every year starting most prominently with Medicare for All, that there's a case not to even collect taxes and then hand it back. We could just have the government *keep **all** income* and simplify the logistics and accounting. Sanders already touts this type of savings with having a monolithic government program. So move to *no* income and *no* taxes—just an entitlement! Kind of like an account at the company store. But abolishing income doesn't solve income inequality the way the Left has come to define it. Now there even can be no disparity of *wealth*.

How do you get to a leveling of wealth? "Give" everything to the government, stupid! *They will take care of you.* Close out the bank accounts, and by "bank accounts," we don't mean just checking accounts and Christmas clubs, but brokerage accounts, retirement plans, and college savings plans (remember, college will be *free*). Ultimately, there would be no private ownership of businesses either—no private enterprise—but we are getting too far ahead. *Just concentrate on **no savings** and **no wealth.***

How do you get that done? Some people talk about only prying their guns from their *cold, dead* hands, but many more feel even stronger about their *money*. And therein is the solution: *cold, dead* hands. Don't try 20% annual confiscations, don't start by taking retirement savings—think BIG. And wait until they're DEAD.

Just ban *inheritances*.[525] [526]

Estate taxes and required distributions of inherited IRAs have already paved the way for *reducing* inheritances. Since the majority of wealth in America is held by the oldest people, completely *banning* inheritances and sending the proceeds to the government can erase a majority of wealth inequality in just a generation or two—thirty to forty years. Meanwhile, young Wesley, Jr. and Courtney can plan accordingly, including voting for the free stuff the Democrats and the Left are slinging.

Uncertainty about estate taxes? *No problem, count on 100%.* Worried about the terms and continuation of the family trust? *Don't worry—it's gone.* Planning to pass on the family farm or small business to the kids and grandkids? *It **will** go to the kids—**all the kids of America**.*

Of course, no inheritances and no personal wealth provide a huge dependency dividend to the Left. They don't like family or religion or private enterprise getting in the way of the government they control and that is the source of their power. People who think and act like they are self-reliant are the worst—they are just too much work to control and to bend to the wishes of the Left. *Come on, go along easy.* Separating the self-reliant from their wallets may make more of them more receptive to "I'm here to help—I'm with the government."

At the very least, banning inheritance is a great white privilege remover.

NO PERSONAL PROPERTY

VIOLATION:
Inequality, Wealth, Private Ownership, Self-Reliance

AS REFERENCED IN THE DISCUSSION OF NO INCOME TAXES and no income, it would be so much easier to legislate away inequality if everyone owned just the same. And who better than *government* to push that legislation, take over running everything, and decide how to redistribute it "equally"? In explicating the case for a totalitarian state where there is no income tax ... because there is no *income* ... because there is no *private ownership* ... little time was spent on what giving up private ownership actually looks like. It can be done in any number of ways, and it's already gotten started. Short of no personal property is the position of no personal property *of a certain type*. That is addressed here.

Property is at the heart of the Left's war on "inequality." It has historical significance, too. Much is made of the Founding Fathers agreeing for the purpose of the census that slaves should only count for 3/5 of a person, but another notable exclusion was that all those males who did not own property (real estate, not fancy clothes) did not get a vote.[527] Why should someone who had no skin in the game get a call on where the game pieces are placed? So once, property impacted voting *rights*, but today it continues to impact voting *preferences*. People with property tend to be on the Right; those without property, on the Left. So here's the Left's position: *take away property!*

Income redistribution is all about the Left enforcing their vision of equality. *Tax the rich, give to the poor!* Give tens of millions of the poor uninsured health care coverage under Obamacare, and legislate the prices higher for the middle class to pay for it.[528] Push up the income taxes in Lefty havens like California, New Jersey, and New York to pay for the massive social programs of the nanny state.[529] Democrat identity politics pushes the haves vs. have-nots divisiveness at every turn. They say rich banks are out to get students. Rich credit card companies are out to get consumers. Rich oil companies are out to crush every millennial's dream of a Green New Deal. Rich drug companies are out to sacrifice everyone's health to the almighty dollar. The rich top 2% of the country are out to keep everyone else in the universe in their place. Rich is *bad*. Wealth is *bad*. Rich wealth creates *inequality*.

Take it away! It's been done before. The US has had times more than once when the marginal income tax rate was around 90%.[530] *Nine for me, one for you, says Uncle Sam!* Estate taxes have devastated family fortunes at death. It would not be hard to make 401k retirement savings plans unable to be inherited at all. There's no *right* to have a savings account of any kind. The means are already available to confiscate wealth.

In Europe, there's a movement to ban private ownership of cars—whether for "green" or socialistic motives is to be debated.[531] Government already runs housing for millions. Who needs to *own* a house? Those are the two biggies for most people. But the Left wants a clean sweep to include everything. One high school in England said they banned certain types of expensive coats because the coats "cause a lot of inequality between our pupils."[532] Other schools have used the same rationale to ban Halloween costumes. There's not much need to buy things the government won't let you use. *Plain brown jumpsuits for all will do.* Regulating clothing? How about jewelry? Makeup? What about branded versus generic tampons? And why just at *school*? Isn't there inequality *everywhere*?

Self-reliance is also anathema to the Left, just a block or two down the road past inequality. The self-reliant take issue with being made dependent, but the Left insists. Wealth and personal property just facilitate self-reliance, so one is as bad as the other. Self-reliance doesn't go away with the expensive coats. It will require the totalitarian transformation where all personal property is banned and confiscated. Is that twenty years off? Fifty? *Ever?* Much depends on what happens in the near-term. If America embraces socialist concepts like Medicare for All, and the Green New Deal, both of which turn major portions of the economy over to government ownership or overregulation, it will hurtle down that path.

NO PRIVATE HOMES

VIOLATION:

Carbon Emissions, Inequality, Wealth, Private Ownership, Self-Reliance

THIS CONFISCATION WINS THE PRIZE for running afoul of nearly half the dire concerns of the Left—*five different sicknesses for which they demand a cure.*

Climate change is relatively no more than a once every 10,000-year weather report: *"Our local earth region will see elevated temperatures today and continuing for the next nine thousand years, with a cold front then moving through."* The people calling the shots on the Left recognize serendipity when they see it. "You never want a serious crisis to go to waste. And what I mean by that is an opportunity to do things that you think you could not do before," famously schemed Rahm Emanuel, Obama's Chief of Staff.[533] The smart money on the Left pushes battling climate change as their favorite new ploy to increase government dominance over its subjects. They either get to run the government and control who gets favored, or they hang out in the private sector and get the government contracts to have a chance at helping and a sure shot to get rich—*or both*.

So the *smart people* at the top are smart enough to see the opportunity, figure out how to uniquely benefit from it, *and* get the *dummies* below to do their work for them. They use things like fear tactics ("we have just ~~twelve~~ nine years to save the earth"), faked authority ("all scientists agree . . ."), and appeals to people's plain good intentions ("if we all join in we can all contribute in some way") to manipulate the fearful, overwhelmed, and well intentioned as dummies. Millions are called to rise up. Blueprints like the Congressional Green New Deal bill text and its policy statement spinoffs prove inscrutable and incomplete.[534] They shrewdly decline to outline its vast effects and tentacles, and certainly make no effort to place any true cost on its dictates. What if you were told you would give up your home and be relocated to an apartment—*possibly government housing*—to do your part in fighting climate change? *Ready to go?*

When the controlling concern of government is minimizing carbon emissions, there just is no case to be made for private homes. Plot out your square footage per person—*the government will*. Every extra, "unnecessary" square foot is an assault on the planet, destroying green space, consuming resources to construct, and then consuming more resources to operate and maintain. *Even sick people can share a tiny hospital room with a stranger and get well, so why can't you live in your own small but neat apartment in a building of 156 small but neat apartments?* Do it for the *planet*! Do it for the *children*! *Do it for the Democrats and Leftists who will reap power and money for telling you what is good for you!*

If the climate change rationale doesn't sway you, perhaps the inequality one will: under our current system, the Left declares you are either one who has more than you deserve, or one who deserves more than you have. America is **not** the land of *opportunity*; America is nothing but the land of *inequality*. How can that be fixed, *quickly*? Well, the principal source of wealth for a majority of Americans is their home. So go for the gusto—get rid of their homes! It conveniently comes out to the same answer as to how millions of Americans can combat climate change. The Left also vilifies wealth, so this particular battle against inequality serves two noble purposes simultaneously. Again, every single-family home can be changed to multiunit housing. With a socialist President and Congress you can drive people out at once, or to manage the risk of social disorder, choose to draw it out. Perhaps forbid single-family homes from being inherited or sold upon the death of the current owner. Every home would have to be converted to apartments or knocked down and rebuilt. Second or vacation homes, the prize of the wealthy, could be confiscated outright.

Confiscation—the taking by the government—gets to whether private ownership is to be encouraged, or even permitted. The Left is increasingly successful in convincing younger Americans that capitalism is bad and socialism is good. Incremental steps to government control and ownership that previous generations would have seen through and resisted are now seen favorably: health care termed a human right that others must pay for and "free" college education among them. Many young people see no reason why the oil, pharmaceutical, and insurance companies should not be owned by the government. Next comes, "why should *any* private companies be allowed to profit?" And if private companies cannot profit, they cannot exist. This includes not just Wall Street behemoths, but the family florist business with six locations and the guy who owns the local convenience store. Once the government is running and owning everything, there is a lot less opportunity for wealth creation, and there won't be lots of people who can afford big homes, or any single-family home at all. That may take awhile, and allow inequality to persist, so better just to cut it off. *Take the homes now.* People in the Soviet Union did okay in their government apartments. Our government is good at running things, and your apartment house won't be any different. *Don't worry.*

The real prize of banning home ownership is the injury to self-reliance. Self-reliance is at the heart of America, with frontier courage, capitalism, and self-determination all hallmarks of the American experience. We are told by the Left, in many different ways, that self-reliance is not needed — we have a safety net for you. In fact, self-reliance is no longer even desired. *Get in order, fall into line. Do what you're told.* For all their other schemes to work smoothly, the Left cannot have independent-minded people standing up to them.

It's tough to be self-reliant from apartment 26B. That's the plan!

NO PRIVATE ENTERPRISE

VIOLATION:

Inequality, Wealth, Private Ownership, Self-Reliance

BUILDING A BRIDGE HALFWAY across to the other side just makes no sense. Either build none, or *get it done*. The Left, the Democrats, the Democratic Socialists, the garden-variety socialists, the social justice warriors, the reparations demanders, the media, and the academics are ready to get it done. You can't convert major portions of American industry to government control, multiply the welfare state, tax at such high rates that you might as well just keep all the money, and confiscate wealth to overcome inequality, but still *keep* private property and private enterprise. *Get it done*. It's time.[535][536]

Once American industry is run *by* the government, then all income and support comes *from* the government. Businesses no longer in business have no workers and no paychecks. If there *are* paychecks, or just chits, they will come from the government. If government runs housing, then there are no landlords, and there is no home ownership—just occupancy. If government employs you and houses you, it is a small step to ban private property—after all, it is *government* money that would have to buy you your designer clothing, your artwork, and your Mercedes. That won't happen. There will be no room for businesses big or small. *You mean you work for yourself, and we don't control you?* The family insurance agency, bed and breakfast, and pizza shop will all be gone. *Government can do it better!* And even if it can't, you're not going to have the chance to demonstrate otherwise.

This would be a huge victory for the Left, and the start of it was unflinchingly a topic of everyday conversation with the 2020 Democrat Presidential hopefuls. They want the government to take over health care—another 20% of the economy—at a cost equal to all current federal spending added together. They want the fossil fuel industry out of business. They want an astronomically priced Green New Deal that is much more FDR-style socialist New Deal than green. They want *more* social welfare programs, and they want them to apply to *more* people, including illegal aliens who aren't even Americans. They want college paid for by "other people's money." They want to outright confiscate wealth from the "wealthy." They want a Wall Street "speculation" tax that actually covers *every trade* in *everyone's accounts*, whether you are wealthy or not. They want income redistribution broadly. They want reparations.[537] The Left wants the middle class to believe that they can massively expand government and handouts without taxing them, and many are gullible or dumb or oblivious enough to shuffle along and believe they will get more than they pay out. *Free, free, it's FREE!*

The Left hates all institutions that compete with government as a source of power in people's lives: family, religion, private enterprise, and plain old-fashioned *reliance in self.* They must all be destabilized on the way to being destroyed or overpowered. But it is private enterprise that is particularly feared by the Left because, unlike any of the others, and certainly unlike government, it can actually *create* value. Deposits at banks create value when the funds are lent out at rates higher than those to acquire the deposits. Stocks go up in value as companies compete successfully, grow, and get a return on the capital used in the business that is greater than the rate required to acquire the funds to start.

If your goal is to grow government as a source of your power—running it and getting to be the one in charge of not only policy, but the government purse strings to reward your supporters (and buy votes!) and hobble your enemies—then you *must* be *against* private enterprise. You can either destroy it or take it for your own. You would be faced with a similar choice to Hitler. *Hmm, do I bomb the sands of Northern Africa, or do I take it for myself for its oil reserves—something I do not possess? Do I continue to ally with the Soviet Union, or do I invade and destroy a few parts of it to get to the vast natural resources (including labor) left over? Deutschland über alles!* Of course, taking it away from a direct opponent is like a double win—suddenly you have more, and they have less. Flip the poles, and the power instantly flows in the other direction.

This is the Left's calculation. Until 2020, no one was willing to talk about actually going fast versus going slow. They are today openly talking about taking it over, starting **now**. Once the plan is revealed, there is no value in going slow and allowing the other side time to defend. Things will happen fast. **Things *are* happening fast**.

CONTROL THE FUTURE BEFORE IT ARRIVES

NO NONCONSENSUAL SEX–WITH *ROBOTS*

VIOLATION:
Politically Incorrect Thought

THE LEFT IS ALWAYS THINKING — always way out in front of you. So just in case you've been thinking about raping an object that does not exist, they have already thought long and hard to prevent it. Sex robots have received titillating press, but none exist. Yes, sex *dolls* exist—and they aren't just $19.99 blow-up dolls anymore. And yes, a series of companies have designed and tried to refine sex robots combining artificial intelligence and attractive features. But those *robots* have been no more than talking heads with moving eyes and mouths. No, there have been no *full body* sex robots. No, once again, there have been no robots with smart, wired up moving parts *down there*.

Perhaps more disturbing than the subject of rape of robots is that there is already a sizeable portion of academia making a living off of *writing about the rape of robots*. How about studying reducing rape of *humans*? Or work on hunger, or world peace? No, instead, we get "intellectuals" prescribing how we should have sex with humanoid machines that don't exist. The other little flaw with this endeavor is that while you *could* have sex with a robot—just as you could have sex with a knothole in a tree—you *cannot* have nonconsensual sex with a robot because it is not a human for the granting or withholding of consent. And for the final rub, unless and until we get a whole new area of law for interactions with robots, it's also not legally possible to *rape* a robot.

But never mind all that. What do the experts, published in the prestigious *International Journal of Social Robotics*, tell us now about how to behave in bed with these futurebots? Surprise, surprise, they *disagree*. Go figure. One two-professor team urges the use of their "virtue ethics" and says it could be facilitated by providing the robots with a module that can initiate a sexual consent scenario.[538] You see Pollyanna, *even robots and human partners will have to agree on the sex to take place.* It would be *good* for the human to be rejected now and again to practice how to take that well when they are actually with humans. The robot would be like your parents, teaching you the right way to treat others, but *better* because your parents aren't there for you when you are having sex (*hopefully*). Then we have a third professor with the opposite view, that a robot that could refuse consent to sex is *bad*. Every pervert will want the fembot that can say "no" just to play out the scenario of *raping* it! Robot rape with an everlasting "get out of jail free" card will only encourage the robot abuser to practice the same on real humans.[539] *At the same time we are creating robots, we are creating monsters!*

Stay tuned for our dissenting professor's subsequent

treatise, "Robotics Has a Race Problem," (yes, *really*) in which he notes that the "existing social robots have white surfaces." But, he adds, to instead make them "Black, Brown, or Asian risks representing people of these races as slaves."[540] *Now what's the right answer?* Oh, and the sex robots are all *female*, so that's *sexist!* To be *inclusive*, could any be designed to deliberately be misshapen or malfunctioning to appear *disabled*? Or is that *appropriating* disabled culture? What about religion? Maybe it is there that there can be a solution rather than the same old human problems transplanted to a whole new field of play. *Can we make some attractive to jihadists so they can have sex with virgins without having to so often first kill the innocents they label infidels?*

NOTES

URLs all last visited 5/20. nd = not dated.

POLITICALLY INCORRECT THOUGHT

1   http://www.ala.org/advocacy/intfreedom/hate 2020 hate speech and hate crime

2   https://www.heritage.org/civil-society/commentary/the-origins-hate-speech 10/18

3   http://www.chicano.ucla.edu/research/hate-speech-media 2009

4   https://www.splcenter.org/fighting-hate/extremist-files/groups nd

5   https://www.dailymail.co.uk/news/article-7769709/
Fox-host-Pete-Hegseth-BANNED-Twitter-sharing-manifesto-Pensacola-shooter.
html 12/19

ACHIEVEMENT/INDIVIDUALISM/SELF-RELIANCE

6   https://www.nytimes.com/2019/08/27/us/sat-adversity-score-college-board.html

7   https://www.pewsocialtrends.org/2016/06/27/1-demographic-trends-and-economic-well-being/

8   https://www.newyorker.com/news/our-columnists/the-many-sins-of-college-admissions 10/19

9   https://www.politico.com/magazine/story/2019/08/02/joe-biden-investigation-
     hunter-brother-hedge-fund-money-2020-campaign-227407

10   https://money.com/joe-biden-net-worth-2020-democratic-presidential-candidate/
     4/19

GUNS

11   https://www.hawaii.edu/powerkills/20TH.HTM nd Death By Government

FAMILY SANCTITY

12   https://responsiblehomeschooling.org/policy-issues/current-policy/parent-qualifi-
     cations/ 2020

13   https://www.ncregister.com/daily-news/does-california-law-deny-parents-right-
     to-opt-out-of-gender-education 5/18

14   https://www.acf.hhs.gov/sites/default/files/cb/cm2018.pdf Child Maltreatment
     pdf download pp. 7, 9

15   https://pjmedia.com/zombie/2015/10/8/interrupting-whiteness-education-confer-
     ence-blame-white-teachers-and-students/

16   https://www.washingtontimes.com/news/2018/apr/26/democratic-professors-out-
     number-republicans-10-to-

17   https://www.cdc.gov/nchs/data/nvsr/nvsr68/nvsr68_13-508.pdf 11/19 unmarried
     births by race p. 25

18   http://www.nbcnews.com/id/39993685/ns/health-womens_health/t/blacks-strug-
     gle-percent-unwed-mothers-rate/#.Xpu99y-ZN2Z 11/10

19   http://www.pewsocialtrends.org/2015/12/09/the-american-middle-class-is-losing-
     ground/

20   https://www.brookings.edu/blog/social-mobility-memos/2018/06/05/seven-rea-
     sons-to-worry-about-the-american-middle-class/

21   https://www.valuepenguin.com/average-student-loan-debt nd

22   https://www.aei.org/research-products/report/for-richer-for-poorer-how-fami-
     ly-structures-economic-success-in-america/ 10/14

RELIGION

23   https://en.wikipedia.org/wiki/Religion_in_China nd

24   https://en.wikipedia.org/wiki/USSR_anti-religious_campaign_(1928–1941) nd

25   https://encyclopedia.ushmm.org/content/en/article/nazi-racism-an-overview nd
     Holocaust Encyclopedia

26   https://en.wikipedia.org/wiki/Religious_views_of_Adolf_Hitler nd

27   https://www.washingtonpost.com/five-myths-about-church-and-state-in-america/2011/04/21/AF2SlBQE_story.html

28   https://www.becketlaw.org/case/littlesisters/ 2020

29   http://www.gopusa.com/nordstrom-banned-salvation-army-kettles-because-they-made-lgbtq-employees-uncomfortable/?omhide=true 12/19

PRIVATE ENTERPRISE/CAPITALISM/PRIVATE OWNERSHIP

30   https://www.investopedia.com/articles/active-trading/080715/if-you-would-have-invested-right-after-apples-ipo.asp

WEALTH

31   https://www.politifact.com/truth-o-meter/statements/2016/jul/26/bernie-s/dnc-bernie-sanders-repeats-claim-top-one-tenth-1-o/

INEQUALITY

32   https://www.foxnews.com/media/elizabeth-warren-trump-environmental-racism 7/19

33   https://www.brookings.edu/blog/the-avenue/2019/10/03/black-household-income-is-rising-across-the-united-states/

34   https://www.forbes.com/sites/evangerstmann/2019/06/06/dispelling-myths-about-the-gender-pay-gap/#3def183046fa

35   https://www.asanet.org/sites/default/files/savvy/images/press/docs/pdf/ASARace-Crime.pdf 9/97 criminal justice "racism" pp. 3, 21

36   https://www.city-journal.org/html/myth-criminal-justice-racism-10231.html 10/15

37   https://religionnews.com/2019/11/12/fbi-report-jews-the-target-of-overwhelming-number-of-religious-based-hate-crimes-2/

NATIONALISM/PATRIOTISM

38   https://www.newsweek.com/betsy-ross-flag-meaning-history-racist-1447174 7/19

39   https://www.nytimes.com/2012/04/03/science/civil-war-toll-up-by-20-percent-in-new-estimate.html

GENDER DIFFERENTIATION

40   https://archive.attn.com/stories/8109/starbucks-other-chains-gender-neutral-bathrooms 5/16

41   https://quillette.com/2019/05/03/a-victory-for-female-athletes-everywhere/

ANIMAL USE

42   https://www.animallaw.info/statute/fl-initiatives-amendment-13-ban-wagering-dog-races

CARBON EMISSIONS

43   https://democrats.org/wp-content/uploads/2018/10/2016_DNC_Platform.pdf

NO PLASTIC BAGS
VIOLATION: CARBON EMISSIONS

44   http://www.allaboutbags.ca/papervplastic.html 2012

45   https://reason.com/2019/04/11/california-plastic-bag-bans-spur-120-per/

46   https://www.ncsl.org/research/environment-and-natural-resources/plastic-bag-legislation.aspx 1/20

NO VALEDICTORIANS
VIOLATION: ACHIEVEMENT/INDIVIDUALISM/SELF-RELIANCE, INEQUALITY

47   https://us.blastingnews.com/lifestyle/2017/06/more-american-high-schools-say-goodbye-to-valedictorians-001779323.amp.html Left rationale

48   https://www.businessinsider.com/schools-not-crowning-valedictorians-2017-6 48 valedictorians

49   https://www.wsj.com/articles/farewell-valedictorian-high-schools-drop-tradition-of-naming-top-student-1507301285 10/17

50   https://www.npr.org/templates/story/story.php?storyId=10693512 6/07 for AP classes

51   https://www.simplemost.com/schools-phase-out-valedictorians/10/17 reinstate

52   https://professionals.collegeboard.org/guidance/applications/rank 2020 squeezed out of the top 10%

53   https://www.wcpo.com/news/local-news/warren-county/mason/mason-high-school-eliminating-valedictorian-salutatorian-recognition 5/19 against AP classes

54   https://www.wlwt.com/article/mason-does-away-with-valedictorian-salutatorian-to-reduce-competitive-culture/27422423 5/19

55   https://www.baltimoresun.com/maryland/anne-arundel/bs-md-class-rank-trend-20190626-story.html academic stress, challenging homes, UC professor

56   https://theconversation.com/long-considered-a-high-honor-the-valedictorian-tradition-faces-an-uncertain-future-115789 5/19 history, UK professor

57   https://www.newsobserver.com/news/local/article230433284.html 5/19 sports

NO GUNS ON MILITARY BASES
VIOLATION: GUNS, ACHIEVEMENT/INDIVIDUALISM/SELF-RELIANCE

58   https://humanevents.com/2019/12/19/soldiers-without-guns/ overview

59   https://www.change.org/p/let-dod-personnel-defend-themselves-on-base 2020 death tally

60   https://www.theguardian.com/us-news/2015/jul/28/congress-loosen-gun-restrictions-military-outposts-chattanooga Coalition, Odierno

61   https://www.military.com/daily-news/2016/04/14/army-chief-opposes-soldiers-carry-concealed-firearms-base.html Milley Senate hearing

62   https://apps.dtic.mil/dtic/tr/fulltext/u2/a272176.pdf 2/92 DoD Directive

63   https://www.npr.org/2014/04/03/298754420/should-soldiers-be-armed-at-military-posts "posted conspicuously," Murphy

64   https://www.marinecorpstimes.com/news/your-marine-corps/2015/07/18/marine-recruiters-told-not-to-wear-uniforms-after-attack/

65   https://www.thetrace.org/2015/10/defense-bill-congress-guns-military-bases-background-checks/ no action

66   https://www.businessinsider.com/pentagon-private-firearms-military-base-open-carry-2016-11 Milley

67   https://fas.org/irp/doddir/dod/d5210_56.pdf 11/16 DoD change

68   https://www.ammoland.com/2019/12/defiance-through-compliance-the-deep-state-hoodwink-on-gun-free-military-bases/#axzz6ANdvZGQF Pensacola, Trump

69   https://www.conservativereview.com/news/sitting-ducks-soldiers-disarmed-bases/ 12/19 Pensacola, Trump

NO MEN'S ROOM—OR WOMEN'S ROOM
VIOLATION: GENDER DIFFERENTIATION, INEQUALITY

70   https://williamsinstitute.law.ucla.edu/publications/trans-adults-united-states/ 6/16 0.6% identify as transgender in US

71   https://www.nbcnews.com/feature/nbc-out/record-4-5-percent-u-s-adults-identify-lgbt-gallup-n877486 5/18

72   https://news.gallup.com/poll/259571/americans-greatly-overestimate-gay-population.aspx 6/19

73 https://www.glaad.org/files/aa/2017_GLAAD_Accelerating_Acceptance.pdf

74 https://transequality.org/sites/default/files/docs/usts/USTS-Executive-Summary-Dec17.pdf 12/16 Transgender Survey

75 https://tall.life/height-percentile-calculator-age-country/

76 https://www.pcc.edu/queer/district-efforts/all-user-restrooms/ 2020 all-user

77 https://www.kgw.com/article/news/local/urinals-banned-portland-building/283-74b0d059-0d32-465f-804a-c3f8dacebd28 9/19 flexibility

78 https://peopleqm.blogspot.com/2017/07/no-more-queueing-at-ladies-room.html 7/17 Ghent Univ. study

79 https://www.nydailynews.com/life-style/unisex-bathrooms-eliminate-long-restroom-lines-women-article-1.3332829 7/17

80 https://www.interiorsandsources.com/article-details/articleid/22601/title/gender-neutral-restrooms 5/19 design code

81 https://www.machronicle.com/some-still-pissed-about-the-gender-neutral-restrooms/ 10/19 plywood

82 https://www.nationalreview.com/2019/11/gender-neutral-bathrooms-pointless-wasteful-sexist/

83 https://psmag.com/magazine/how-social-bias-is-segregating-americas-bathrooms

84 https://bppblog.com/2018/04/17/gender-neutral-restrooms-require-new-choice-architecture/ London School, UNC

85 https://archive.org/stream/RulesForRadicals/RulesForRadicals_djvu.txt 1971 p. 139

NO RELIGIOUS REFUSALS
VIOLATION: RELIGION

86 https://www.pbs.org/newshour/science/there-is-no-gay-gene-there-is-no-straight-gene-sexuality-is-just-complex-study-confirms 8/19

87 https://en.wikipedia.org/wiki/Defense_of_Marriage_Act nd

88 https://www.scotusblog.com/2015/06/opinion-analysis-marriage-now-open-to-same-sex-couples/

89 https://en.wikipedia.org/wiki/Same-sex_marriage_in_the_United_States nd

90 https://www.americanprogress.org/issues/religion/reports/2019/04/11/468041/religious-liberty-no-harm/ Left overview, adoptions

91 https://billofrightsinstitute.org/cases/ 2020 SCOTUS religion cases through 2010

92 https://www.freedomforuminstitute.org/first-amendment-center/supreme-court-cases/ SCOTUS 1A cases 2000 through 2019

93 https://www.nbcnews.com/news/us-news/supreme-court-declines-hear-pharmacy-s-religious-objections-case-n600261 6/16

94 https://www.pri.org/stories/2018-01-08/supreme-court-wont-hear-challenge-mississippi-anti-lgbt-religious-freedom-law 1/18 MS

95   https://altoday.com/archives/2814-marshall-yates-will-obama-use-the-irs-to-si-lence-religious-organizations-over-same-sex-marriage 5/15

96   https://www.deseret.com/indepth/2019/9/22/20869076/8-religion-related-cases-to-watch-when-the-supreme-court-is-back-in-session adoptions

97   https://thehill.com/opinion/judiciary/363285-the-supreme-courts-gay-cake-case-matters-to-all-americans 12/17 state examples

98   https://www.washingtontimes.com/news/2017/jul/19/gay-megadonor-going-after-christians-punish-wicked/

99   https://www.supremecourt.gov/opinions/17pdf/16-111_j4el.pdf 6/18

100 https://www.americanbar.org/groups/crsj/publications/human_rights_magazine_home/the-ongoing-challenge-to-define-free-speech/not-a-masterpiece/ 6/18 law school dean

101 https://encyclopedia.ushmm.org/content/en/article/nazi-racism-an-overview nd Holocaust Encyclopedia

102 https://www.annefrank.org/en/anne-frank/go-in-depth/why-did-hitler-hate-jews/ nd

103 https://www.npr.org/sections/health-shots/2019/05/09/721532255/whats-behind-a-rise-in-conscience-complaints-for-health-care-workers

104 https://www.npr.org/sections/health-shots/2019/11/06/776765601/judge-scraps-con-science-rule-protecting-doctors-who-deny-care-for-religious-reas

105 https://www.nationalreview.com/2015/02/persecution-gordon-college-da-vid-french/

106 https://www.nationalreview.com/2015/05/gordon-college-keeps-its-faith-and-its-accreditation-david-french/

107 http://www.abajournal.com/news/article/8th-circuit-reinstates-legal-challenge-by-videographers-who-wont-make-same-sex-wedding-videos 8/19 MN

NO BAD WORDS
VIOLATION: POLITICALLY INCORRECT THOUGHT

108 https://newsroom.haas.berkeley.edu/study-shows-the-social-benefits-of-politi-cal-incorrectness/ 9/19

109 https://tsl.news/opinion-its-time-to-stop-saying-politically-correct/ 11/18

110 https://www.zerohedge.com/news/2017-03-04/british-university-bans-all-political-ly-incorrect-words-heres-list man, Christian name, polio victim

111 https://www.phillymag.com/news/2012/03/13/pop-language-quiz-racist-racist/ an-gel food, blackball, Chinaman, Native Americans, Oriental, voodoo economics

112 https://libertynewsnow.com/the-new-liberal-list-of-politically-incorrect-words/ article1948 8/15 person of . . .

113 https://imgur.com/gallery/P06AB7a 1/18 100 terms including black, man . . .

114 https://www.npr.org/sections/codeswitch/2013/09/19/224183763/is-it-racist-to-call-a-spade-a-spade

115 https://www.rd.com/culture/words-with-offensive-origins/ nd eenie meenie, ghetto

116 https://nypost.com/2018/05/26/pc-police-wont-let-us-use-these-words-anymore/ ableist

117 https://www.dailymail.co.uk/news/article-5094791/A-Z-politically-correct-madness.html 11/17 Jamaican Stew, twerking, violate,

118 https://slate.com/human-interest/2013/08/miley-cyrus-vma-performance-white-appropriation-of-black-bodies.html

119 https://listverse.com/2015/08/25/10-most-absurd-things-to-ban-on-politically-correct-college-campuses/ grammar, ableist, Mt. Holyoke, UC

120 https://www.glaad.org/reference/transgender nd

121 https://www.newyorker.com/news/news-desk/trouble-teaching-rape-law 12/14

122 https://www.thedailybeast.com/the-university-of-californias-insane-speech-police 4/17

123 https://www.thecollegefix.com/california-professors-instructed-not-to-say-america-is-the-land-of-opportunity/ 6/15

124 https://reason.com/2014/11/18/at-uc-davis-students-cant-register-until/

125 https://www.insidehighered.com/news/2013/11/25/ucla-grad-students-stage-sit-during-class-protest-what-they-see-racially-hostile

126 https://dailybruin.com/2013/11/14/ucla-grad-students-stage-sit-in-following-recent-discrimination-report

NO LETTERS "T" OR "X" IN THE ALPHABET
VIOLATION: RELIGION

127 https://www.loyolapress.com/our-catholic-faith/scripture-and-tradition/jesus-and-the-new-testament/jesus-in-history/symbols-for-jesus nd

128 https://www.ancient-symbols.com/christian_symbols.html 2020

129 https://fox8.com/2019/02/22/controversial-statue-of-president-mckinley-sold-in-california-city-of-canton-to-become-new-owner/

130 https://www.nytimes.com/2017/08/23/sports/ncaafootball/espn-robert-lee-virginia.html

NO ROCK AND ROLL—OR COUNTRY, OR RAP
VIOLATION: INEQUALITY, POLITICALLY INCORRECT THOUGHT

131 https://www.indiewire.com/2020/01/stephen-king-criticized-ava-duvernay-diversity-art-1202203184/

132 https://www.newyorker.com/culture/culture-desk/do-this-years-best-picture-oscar-nominees-pass-the-bechdel-test 3/18

NO UNDERWEAR
VIOLATION: CARBON EMISSIONS

133 https://www.treehugger.com/sustainable-fashion/microfibers-may-be-small-they-re-enormous-problem.html 3/17

NO ETHNIC RESTAURANTS
VIOLATION: POLITICALLY INCORRECT THOUGHT, INEQUALITY

134 https://la.eater.com/2017/11/21/16459554/yamashiro-history-hollywood-pho-tos-los-angeles

135 https://www.dailywire.com/news/la-times-probes-prominent-japanese-restaurant-paul-bois 4/18

136 https://www.laweekly.com/white-guy-pad-thai-channels-bangkok-street-food-in-side-an-rv-trailer/ 2/16

137 https://www.pastemagazine.com/articles/2017/06/cultural-appropriation-food-jus-tice.html

138 https://www.laweekly.com/when-white-guys-cook-pad-thai-and-tacos-results-will-vary/ 1/17

139 https://www.laweekly.com/downtowns-white-boy-tacos-cart-serves-pulled-pork-and-whiskey-steak-tacos/ 1/17

140 https://www.researchgate.net/publication/323158780_Racial_Plagiarism_and_Fashion 10/17

141 https://qz.com/909817/instagram-photos-of-ethnic-food-are-perpetuating-rac-ist-stereotypes/ 2/17

142 https://fivethirtyeight.com/features/how-msg-got-a-bad-rap-flawed-science-and-xenophobia/ 1/16

143 https://www.bbc.com/news/world-us-canada-47892747 4/19 appropriation, Lucky Lee's

144 https://www.nbcnews.com/news/asian-america/chinese-restaurant-opened-white-woman-shuts-down-8-months-after-n1098486 12/19

145 https://www.mic.com/articles/177642/these-white-cooks-bragged-about-stealing-tortilla-recipes-from-mexico-to-start-a-portland 5/17 "stealing" still in the url

146 https://www.portlandmercury.com/blogtown/2017/05/22/19028161/ this-week-in-appropriation-kooks-burritos-and-willamette-week post pulled

147 https://www.wweek.com/news/2017/12/19/may-17-ww-reviews-kooks-burritos-and-a-war-over-cultural-appropriation-breaks-out/ death threats

148 https://www.tastingtable.com/dine/national/portland-kooks-burritos-cultural-ap-propriation-restaurant-list 5/17 POC list

149 https://archive.attn.com/stories/17361/heres-why-someone-made-list-restau-rants-fight-cultural-appropriation 5/17 POC list excerpts

150   https://www.latimes.com/food/story/2019-11-27/tiki-bar-problems

151   https://scholararchive.ohsu.edu/concern/etds/qb98mf98m?locale=en 6/19 pdf
       download "Commodity Racism, Cultural Appropriation, and the Perpetuation
       of Oppressive Food Discourse," pp. vi, 9, 17

NO GENDER-BASED MEDICAL EXAMS
VIOLATION: GENDER DIFFERENTIATION, INEQUALITY

152   https://www.theblaze.com/news/gay-man-impregnates-transgender-partner-who-
       identifies-as-male-but-alas-was-born-a-female 1/19

153   https://www.dailymail.co.uk/news/article-7833589/Transgender-man-39-gives-
       birth-non-binary-partners-baby.html 12/19

154   https://www.politico.com/story/2019/06/27/julian-castro-debate-abortion-1385950

155   https://thinkprogress.org/not-only-women-have-abortions-is-pro-choice-rhetoric-
       catching-up-with-that-reality-b2a2c70efd05/ 6/19

156   https://melmagazine.com/en-us/story/the-trans-men-who-get-abortions 7/19

157   https://psmag.com/social-justice/reducing-discrimination-against-trans-peo-
       ple-in-healthcare 10/18

158   https://www.nyu.edu/students/health-and-wellness/services/tnbgnc-health-well-
       ness.html nd

159   https://transcare.ucsf.edu/guidelines/physical-examination 6/16

160   https://www.optionsforsexualhealth.org/wp-content/uploads/2019/07/FQPN18-
       Manual-EN-BC-web.pdf BC

161   https://www.telegraph.co.uk/news/uknews/1419023/Doctors-in-trouble-for-not-
       giving-man-cervical-smear.html 1/03

162   https://www.redstate.com/alexparker/2019/12/03/man-identifying-lesbian-previ-
       ously-sued-get-woman-waxing-files-human-rights-complaint-refused-gynecologi-
       cal-exam/

NO WOMEN'S SPORTS
VIOLATION: GENDER DIFFERENTIATION, INEQUALITY

163   https://arcdigital.media/sport-is-a-human-right-so-let-trans-women-compete-2db-
       252184fe

164   https://thefederalist.com/2019/12/04/male-transjacking-will-ultimately-end-wom-
       ens-sports/

165   https://www.theguardian.com/sport/2019/sep/24/ioc-delays-new-transgender-
       guidelines-2020-olympics

166   https://www.outsports.com/2019/12/3/20993190/inclusion-sports-transgender-ath-
       letes-propaganda-mosier-patricio-telfer

167 https://www.aclu.org/blog/lgbt-rights/transgender-rights/banning-trans-girls-school-sports-neither-feminist-nor-legal 3/19

168 https://www.outsideonline.com/2401736/juniper-eastwood-transgender-runners#-close 6/19

169 https://www.transathlete.com/k-12 2020 18 states

170 http://www.ncaa.org/static/champion/a-time-of-transition/ Fall 2019 Champion magazine

171 https://www.courant.com/sports/high-schools/hc-sp-transgender-high-school-track-lawsuit-20190618-20190618-4mjx7gllrjarlpidhnjeecfosq-story.html 6/19

172 https://www.nbcnews.com/feature/nbc-out/connecticut-gop-honor-girls-suing-over-transgender-sports-policy-n1143466 2/20

173 http://www.adfmedia.org/files/SouleComplaint.pdf 2/20

174 https://ctmirror.org/2019/12/31/best-of-2019-transgender-sports-debate-polarizes-womens-advocates/

175 https://dailycaller.com/2019/02/24/male-runners-connecticut-track/ GMA video "run faster"

176 https://www.wsj.com/articles/states-weigh-measures-to-stop-transgender-athletes-from-competing-in-womens-sports-11578393001 1/20

177 https://www.metroweekly.com/2019/11/majority-of-americans-oppose-transgender-athletes-in-womens-sports-poll-finds/

178 https://www.redstate.com/alexparker/2019/10/08/new-study-reveals-americans-really-think-transgender-athletes-womens-sports/

179 https://www.outsports.com/2019/12/3/20993190/inclusion-sports-transgender-athletes-propaganda-mosier-patricio-telfer

180 https://ctmirror.org/2019/12/31/best-of-2019-transgender-sports-debate-polarizes-womens-advocates/

181 https://www.sciencedaily.com/releases/2019/07/190723092111.htm abandon gender binary

NO GREETING CARDS
VIOLATION: CARBON EMISSIONS

182 https://www.dontsendmeacard.com/infographic.html nd

183 https://newrepublic.com/article/116595/valentines-day-environmental-travesty 2/14

184 https://corporate.hallmark.com/citizenship/hallmark-community/sustainability? nd

185 https://www.americangreetings.com/corporate/about-us/sustainability nd

NO MATHEMATICS
VIOLATION: INEQUALITY, SELF-RELIANCE

186 https://www.k12.wa.us/sites/default/files/public/socialstudies/pubdocs/Math%20 SDS%20ES%20Framework.pdf 8/19 Seattle framework

187 https://www.edweek.org/ew/articles/2019/10/11/seattle-schools-lead-controver-sial-push-to-rehumanize.html

188 https://www.chicagotribune.com/lifestyles/sns-tns-bc-edu-math-racist-20191010-story.html NAACP lobbying

189 https://www.wsws.org/en/articles/2019/12/06/ethn-d06.html BLMAS

190 https://files.eric.ed.gov/fulltext/EJ1166672.pdf 12/17 Gutiérrez JUME

191 https://www.campusreform.org/?ID=10342 1/18 Brooklyn College

192 https://www.educationnext.org/the-long-reach-of-teachers-unions/ 2010

193 http://www.nea.org/home/ProfessionalPay.html 2019 for higher pay

194 http://www.nea.org/home/59488.htm 2019 against testing

195 https://blog.prepscholar.com/average-sat-scores-over-time 10/19

196 https://www.statista.com/statistics/185025/average-salary-of-teachers-in-public-schools-since-1980/ 3/20

197 https://www.insider.com/how-much-countries-around-the-world-spend-on-edu-cation-2019-8

198 http://www.oecd.org/pisa/publications/pisa-2018-results.htm Snapshot of Student Performance link: country rankings

199 https://www.seattletimes.com/seattle-news/data/seattle-schools-have-biggest-white-black-achievement-gap-in-state/ 5/16

200 https://www.seattletimes.com/education-lab/seattle-public-schools-has-a-new-performance-report-the-achievement-gap-isnt-part-of-it/ 11/19

201 https://files.eric.ed.gov/fulltext/EJ1166672.pdf 12/17 Gutiérrez JUME

202 https://www.hoover.org/research/seattle-schools-propose-teach-math-educa-tion-racist-will-california-be-far-behindseattle 10/19

NO PETS
VIOLATION: ANIMAL USE, INEQUALITY

203 https://www.beefmagazine.com/blog/animal-rights-activists-ramping-ef-forts-abolish-animal-ag 8/16

204 https://www.vice.com/en_us/article/3d4yxy/why-these-vegans-are-protesting-ber-nie-sanders-rallies 3/16 Species Equality Act

205 https://www.nbcnews.com/news/us-news/seaworld-orlando-debut-new-killer-whale-show-start-2020-n1106941 12/19

206 https://www.beefmagazine.com/blog/losing-animal-rights-war 5/16 circus

207 https://harvardpolitics.com/culture/the-face-on-your-plate/ 4/12

NO CASKETS AND BURIALS
VIOLATION: CARBON EMISSIONS, RELIGION, INEQUALITY

208 https://www.consumer.ftc.gov/articles/0301-funeral-costs-and-pricing-checklist
nd

NO DISPOSABLE ITEMS
VIOLATION: CARBON EMISSIONS

209 http://www.opc.ca.gov/2014/10/plastic-bag-ban-signed/

210 https://www.usatoday.com/story/news/nation-now/2018/09/20/plastic-straws-barred-full-service-restaurants-california/1373655002/

211 https://www.businessinsider.com/plastic-water-bottle-airport-ban-san-francisco-sfo-2019-8

212 https://www.bloomberg.com/news/articles/2019-04-28/starbucks-sbux-dunkin-dnkn-brace-for-coffee-cup-bans-fees 4/19

213 https://www.sfchronicle.com/restaurants/article/To-go-coffee-cups-could-become-a-thing-of-the-14821391.php 11/19

214 https://thespoon.tech/new-california-law-sets-protocol-for-reusable-food-and-drink-containers/ 7/19

215 https://associatedcoffee.com/blog/its-time-to-re-think-the-disposable-coffee-cup/ 8/16 chart

216 https://www.sightline.org/2019/01/04/why-youre-still-not-bringing-a-reusable-mug-for-your-daily-coffee-2/ 1/19

217 https://www.foodandwine.com/news/berkeley-california-reusable-metal-coffee-cups-program 9/19

NO SYNTHETIC FIBER CLOTHING
VIOLATION: CARBON EMISSIONS

218 https://www.vox.com/the-goods/2018/9/19/17800654/clothes-plastic-pollution-polyester-washing-machine also buy less clothing

219 https://www.frontiersin.org/articles/10.3389/fmars.2018.00039/full fish

220 https://www.plymouth.ac.uk/news/washing-clothes-releases-thousands-of-microplastic-particles-into-environment-study-shows 9/16

NO FLORISTS
VIOLATION: CARBON EMISSIONS

221   https://www.bloomsbyheinau.com/eco-flowers nd

222   https://www.scientificamerican.com/article/environmental-price-of-flowers/ 2/09

223   https://www.policyforum.net/love-hurts-environmental-risks-in-the-cut-flower-industry/ 2/16 history

224   https://ethicalunicorn.com/2019/02/19/what-is-ethical-sustainable-floristry/

225   https://www.vox.com/the-goods/2019/2/12/18220984/valentines-day-flowers-roses-environmental-effects

NO CHRISTMAS TREE AND LIGHTS
VIOLATION: VIOLATION: CARBON EMISSIONS, RELIGION

226   https://www.zillow.com/blog/legal-rights-against-holiday-noise-166614/ 12/14

227   https://scholar.google.com/scholar_case?case=11524565241868904841&hl=en&as_sdt=6&as_vis=1&oi=scholarr 12/94 Christmas lights AR

NO CELEBRATIONS
VIOLATION: CARBON EMISSIONS, FAMILY SANCTITY, RELIGION

228   https://www.which.co.uk/news/2017/08/eu-vacuum-cleaner-ban-2017-everything-you-need-to-know/

229   https://www.usnews.com/news/elections/articles/2019-11-20/democrats-unite-behind-severity-of-climate-change

230   https://www.latimes.com/politics/story/2019-12-19/democrats-debate-climate-change

231   https://cnsnews.com/news/article/penny-starr/md-schools-ban-religious-holidays-impoverishes-education-group-says 11/14

232   https://www.usatoday.com/story/news/nation/2018/12/07/nebraska-principal-leave-after-banning-christmas-decorations/2235496002/

NO VACATIONS
VIOLATION: CARBON EMISSIONS

233   https://yourmileagemayvary.net/2019/03/14/how-much-is-walt-disney-worlds-electric-bill/

NO SPORTING, ARTS, OR CONCERT EVENTS
VIOLATION: CARBON EMISSIONS

234   https://www.dailykos.com/stories/2019/1/14/1826238/-What-s-the-carbon-footprint-of-the-Superbowl-Or-the-Avengers-films-Or-the-blogosphere many links

235   https://www.theguardian.com/sport/2006/oct/29/features.environment opinion: How sport is killing the planet

236   https://www.forbes.com/2007/01/19/super-bowl-green-sports-biz-cz_ad_0119green.html#11499d845579

237   https://www.esquire.com/food-drink/drinks/a28842420/ball-aluminum-cups-sustainability-beer-pong/ 8/19 .25

238   https://www.ecowatch.com/ball-sustainable-aluminum-cup-2640121437.html 8/19 .25 (v .17 for red solo cup, but as low as .08-.12)

239   https://www.espn.com/racing/news/story?id=2002571 3/05 EPA asked NASCAR to switch six years ago

240   https://www.athleticbusiness.com/stadium-arena/sports-venues-racing-to-achieve-carbon-neutrality.html 8/08 neutral games via offsets

241   https://www.rubiconglobal.com/blog/sustainability-super-bowl/ 2/18 examples

242   https://www.forbes.com/sites/uhenergy/2017/12/11/big-sports-events-have-big-environmental-footprints-could-social-licenses-to-operate-help/#7c033d8c50cf 7X footprint to attend events

NO RETAIL SHOPPING
VIOLATION: CARBON EMISSIONS

243   https://www.cnn.com/2019/12/19/business/2019-store-closings-payless-gymboree/index.html

244   https://www.fool.com/investing/2019/08/21/fedex-drops-ground-delivery-for-amazon-is-internat.aspx

245   https://www.citylab.com/equity/2019/07/andrew-yang-plan-malls-greyfields-2020-election-democrats/593440/

246   https://www.forbes.com/sites/pamdanziger/2017/12/04/why-malls-should-add-residential-to-their-repurposing-plans/#2e888aab5dd2

NO LAND DEVELOPMENT
VIOLATION: CARBON EMISSIONS, INEQUALITY

247   https://psmag.com/environment/utah-anti-public-lands-agenda 10/18

248   https://calmatters.org/explainers/californias-worsening-wildfires-explained/ 10/19

NO HOME MEALS OR KITCHENS
VIOLATION: CARBON EMISSIONS, SELF-RELIANCE

249 https://www.npr.org/sections/thesalt/2019/04/22/716010599/meal-kits-have-smaller-carbon-footprint-than-grocery-shopping-study-says

NO MEAT
VIOLATION: ANIMAL USE, CARBON EMISSIONS

250 https://en.wikipedia.org/wiki/The_Sexual_Politics_of_Meat nd

251 https://civileats.com/2019/10/22/meat-matters-10-years-of-changes-in-animal-agriculture/

252 https://www.vox.com/future-perfect/2019/1/29/18197907/clean-meat-cell-plant-impossible-beyond-animal-cruelty

253 https://www.vice.com/en_us/article/3d4yxy/why-these-vegans-are-protesting-bernie-sanders-rallies 3/16

254 https://reducetarian.org/why/ nd

255 http://www.thenewjournalatyale.com/2015/03/everyday-evil/ DxE

256 https://www.sfgate.com/bayarea/article/Armed-with-fake-blood-animal-rights-activists-10154372.php 10/16 DxE

257 https://www.vice.com/en_us/article/3d4yxy/why-these-vegans-are-protesting-bernie-sanders-rallies 3/16

258 https://www.beefmagazine.com/blog/animal-rights-activists-ramping-efforts-abolish-animal-ag 8/16 destroy industry

259 https://harvardpolitics.com/culture/the-face-on-your-plate/ 4/12

260 https://theintercept.com/2018/03/02/consumers-are-revolting-against-animal-cruelty-so-the-poultry-industry-is-lobbying-for-laws-to-force-stores-to-sell-their-eggs/

261 https://www.beefmagazine.com/blog/animal-rights-activists-ramping-efforts-abolish-animal-ag 8/16 veganism

NO POLITICAL PARTIES
VIOLATION: POLITICALLY INCORRECT THOUGHT

262 https://www.pbs.org/newshour/show/in-memoriam-david-brinkley 6/03

263 https://www.conservapedia.com/Walter_Cronkite nd

264 http://archive.mrc.org/projects/rather20th/welcome.asp nd

265 https://www.hollywoodreporter.com/features/dan-rather-reflects-his-dramatic-829780 10/15

266 http://transcripts.cnn.com/TRANSCRIPTS/1910/21/cnnt.02.html 10/19

267   https://www.washingtonpost.com/politics/2020/01/20/president-trump-made-16241-false-or-misleading-claims-his-first-three-years/

268   https://perezhilton.com/donald-trump-hitler-comparisons-twitter-celebrity-reactions-immigration-comments/ 6/18 Streisand

269   https://www.businessinsider.com/celebrities-who-are-against-donald-trump-2016-6#america-ferrera-7 Louis C.K., Midler, Cher

270   https://www.foxnews.com/entertainment/celebs-trump-threat-iran-airstrike-soleimani 1/20 Arquette(s), Messing, Reiner, Leguizamo, Howard, Cheadle, McGowan

271   https://www.forbes.com/sites/michaeltnietzel/2019/12/09/more-than-five-hundred-law-professors-write-a-letter-favoring-impeachment-what-effects-will-it-have/#52e2998137d9

272   https://abcnews.go.com/Politics/1100-doj-officials-call-william-barr-resign/story?id=69030388 2/20

273   https://en.wikipedia.org/wiki/January_2019_Lincoln_Memorial_confrontation nd

274   https://www.washingtontimes.com/news/2020/jan/13/reza-aslan-likely-be-sued-over-now-deleted-punchab/

275   https://www.aol.com/article/entertainment/2019/01/22/jim-carrey-labels-covington-catholic-students-as-baby-snakes-in-new-artwork/23650004/

276   https://www.washingtontimes.com/news/2019/jan/22/kathy-griffin-deletes-nazi-sign-smear-from-stream-/

277   https://en.wikipedia.org/wiki/January_2019_Lincoln_Memorial_confrontation nd

278   https://thehill.com/opinion/campaign/457044-why-democrats-demonizing-trump-supporters-destroys-accurate-polls

279   https://www.foxnews.com/entertainment/celebs-trump-threat-iran-airstrike-soleimani 1/20 Arquette(s), Messing, Reiner, Leguizamo, Howard,, Cheadle

280   https://www.washingtonpost.com/news/the-fix/wp/2016/03/07/the-hitler-ification-of-donald-trump/ Louis C.K., SNL

281   https://www.cheatsheet.com/entertainment/celebrities-who-have-spoken-out-against-donald-trump.html/ 4/18 Oswalt, Louis C.K.

282   https://www.businessinsider.com/celebrities-who-are-against-donald-trump-2016-6#america-ferrera-7 Louis C.K., Midler, Cher

283   https://www.businessinsider.com/de-niro-trump-racist-white-supremacist-2019-1 De Niro

284   https://en.wikipedia.org/wiki/Nazi_Party nd

NO ACTUAL HISTORY
VIOLATION: POLITICALLY INCORRECT THOUGHT

285   https://welcome.topuertorico.org/reference/taino.shtml 2020

286   https://www.britannica.com/topic/Carib 2020

287 https://www.sciencedaily.com/releases/2020/01/200110073731.htm cannibalism

288 https://en.wikipedia.org/wiki/Slavery_among_Native_Americans_in_the_United_States nd

NO JOURNALISM
VIOLATION: POLITICALLY INCORRECT THOUGHT

289 https://www.americanpressinstitute.org/journalism-essentials/what-is-journalism/elements-journalism/ nd

290 https://americanpressassociation.com/principles-of-journalism/ nd

291 https://thefederalist.com/2019/10/15/anderson-cooper-casually-vindicates-hunter-biden/

292 https://www.youtube.com/watch?v=wdlvUU_dsSc 11/16 Martha Raddatz

293 https://www.foxnews.com/us/nick-sandmann-covington-catholic-case-reopened 10/19

294 https://www.politico.com/blogs/media/2014/05/survey-7-percent-of-reporters-identify-as-republican-188053

295 https://www.investors.com/politics/editorials/media-bias-left-study/ 11/18

296 https://www.thecrimson.com/article/2019/10/22/act-on-a-dream-petitions-crimson/

297 https://www.nationalreview.com/2019/10/harvards-student-newspaper-chooses-ethical-journalism-over-pc-mobs-demands/

298 https://www.bostonherald.com/2019/11/11/harvard-student-government-sides-with-anti-ice-protesters-against-newspaper/

299 https://www.thecrimson.com/article/2019/11/18/anti-crimson-protest-champagne-showers/

NO TOY GUNS
VIOLATION: GUNS

300 https://time.com/barbie-new-body-cover-story/ 1/16

301 https://lammily.com/gave-kids-barbie-doll-doll-realistic-proportions-say-next-really-says/ 8/16

302 https://www.rochesterfirst.com/news/state-consumer-group-asking-hasbros-to-stop-making-assault-style-toy-weapons/?utm_medium=social&utm_source=facebook_News_8_WROC_Rochester 12/19

NO HALLOWEEN
VIOLATION: POLITICALLY INCORRECT THOUGHT

303   https://thehill.com/opinion/civil-rights/413813-cultural-appropriation-turns-halloween-into-a-nightmare 10/18

304   https://www.themorningwatchmsu.com/post/at-it-again-msu-instructing-students-what-to-wear-for-halloween 10/19

305   http://www.lspirg.org/costumes nd

306   https://northcooknews.com/stories/514086405-evanston-elementary-school-spooked-out-of-celebrating-halloween-this-year 10/19

307   http://www.hngnews.com/monona_cottage_grove/article_1ba52c5f-ecef-53b9-b4d2-1978f5e522a9.html 10/19

308   https://www.history.com/topics/halloween/history-of-halloween 11/09

NO COMEDY SHOWS
VIOLATION: POLITICALLY INCORRECT THOUGHT

309   https://dailyiowan.com/2019/09/26/no-laughing-matter-ui-professor-weighs-in-on-the-politically-correct-comedy-debate/

310   https://www.vanityfair.com/hollywood/2019/09/snl-shane-gillis-fired-nbc

311   https://www.vulture.com/2019/09/snl-shane-gillis-racist-homophobic-remarks.html

312   https://ew.com/awards/2018/12/06/kevin-hart-responds-oscars-controversy/

313   https://www.billboard.com/articles/events/oscars/8492982/kevin-hart-oscar-hosting-controversy-timeline 1/20

314   https://thebodyisnotanapology.com/magazine/what-can-we-laugh-at-now-political-correctness-and-humor/ 7/19

315   https://www.bostonmagazine.com/news/2019/11/18/rozzie-square-theater-sexist-jokes/ shut down mid-show

316   https://nypost.com/2018/12/05/former-snl-writer-booted-off-stage-at-columbia-university/

317   https://www.nbc-2.com/story/40504869/comedian-shares-his-side-of-the-story-after-joke-led-to-911-call-after-naples-show 5/19

318   https://www.chicagotribune.com/entertainment/theater/ct-ent-petedavidson-vic-theatre-non-disclosure-agreement-20191202-okagits4tjeyhf4haauo2v-75su-story.html

319   https://www.salon.com/2015/06/10/10_famous_comedians_on_how_political_correctness_is_killing_comedy_we_are_addicted_to_the_rush_of_being_offended/

320   https://ew.com/article/2015/06/08/jerry-seinfeld-politically-correct-college-campuses/

321 https://www.theatlantic.com/magazine/archive/2015/09/thats-not-funny/399335/
college circuit

322 https://www.sandiegouniontribune.com/opinion/the-conversation/
sd-mel-brooks-comedians-say-political-correctness-killing-comedy-20170922-ht-
mlstory.html

323 https://torontosun.com/opinion/columnists/furey-theres-still-risque-comedy-out-
there-but-the-politically-correct-dont-want-you-to-find-it 7/19 Rogen, Borat

NO FEMININE PRODUCTS
VIOLATION: GENDER DIFFERENTIATION

324 https://www.cnn.com/2019/10/22/health/always-period-gender-symbol-re-
moved-transgender-nonbinary-trnd/index.html

325 https://www.cnn.com/2019/05/26/us/gillette-ad-transgender-man-trnd/index.html

NO MEN'S-OR WOMEN'S-CLOTHING OR STORES
VIOLATION: GENDER DIFFERENTIATION, INEQUALITY

326 https://www.today.com/style/victoria-s-secret-hires-first-transgender-model-fol-
lowing-criticism-t160127 8/19

327 https://corporate.target.com/article/2015/08/gender-based-signs-corporate

328 https://www.pri.org/stories/2015-01-30/forget-mens-and-womens-clothing-one-de-
partment-store-going-unisex

329 https://www.nytimes.com/2019/02/19/style/gender-neutral-clothing.html

330 https://www.beautyindependent.com/gender-neutral-pioneer-the-phluid-proj-
ect-beauty/ 1/20

331 https://www.cbc.ca/radio/noworneverver/gender-identity-challenge-change-and-cel-
ebration-1.4684642/at-this-clothing-store-there-are-no-men-s-and-women-s-sec-
tions-1.4692042 8/18

NO DEGREES, DIPLOMAS, OR EXIT EXAMS
VIOLATION: INEQUALITY, POLITICALLY INCORRECT THOUGHT

332 https://www.stradaeducation.org/measuring-the-value-of-education/are-col-
lege-degrees-becoming-obsolete/ 8/19

333 https://www.opensecrets.org/industries/totals.php?cycle=2018&ind=I1300 2019

334 https://www.inacol.org/news/making-learning-personal-eliminate-gaps-and-en-
sure-mastery-through-proficiency-based-diplomas/ 5/16

335 https://www.fairtest.org/graduation-test-update-states-recently-eliminated 5/19

336 https://edsource.org/2015/governor-signs-bill-allowing-diplomas-for-students-who-failed-exit-exam/88698 CA

337 https://www.manhattan-institute.org/html/positive-effects-exit-exams-1731.html 5/04

338 https://www.fairtest.org/graduation-test-update-states-recently-eliminated 5/19

339 https://www.nydailynews.com/opinion/ny-oped-new-yorks-regents-diplomas-in-the-balance-20200116-fmkg74nh5bhgpjggoxox753ywa-story.html

340 https://www.scpr.org/news/2015/11/17/55689/elimination-of-high-school-exit-exams-leads-to-ris/ Los Angeles

341 https://ed.sc.gov/newsroom/public-information-resources/high-school-exit-exam-elimination/ 4/14

342 https://www.fairtest.org/graduation-test-update-states-recently-eliminated 5/19

343 https://www.npr.org/sections/ed/2015/06/07/411786246/in-chicago-at-risk-students-are-being-misclassified

344 https://apps.npr.org/grad-rates/ TX and others

345 https://www.americaspromise.org/2019-building-grad-nation-report 6/19 90% goal

346 https://nces.ed.gov/programs/digest/d18/tables/dt18_221.10.asp 2017 statistics

347 https://blog.prepscholar.com/average-sat-scores-over-time 10/19

348 https://www.scpr.org/news/2015/12/15/56257/us-high-school-graduation-rate-hits-record-high/

NO MALE ARTISTS
VIOLATION: INEQUALITY

349 https://www.newyorker.com/culture/culture-desk/do-this-years-best-picture-oscar-nominees-pass-the-bechdel-test 3/18

350 http://eleven-thirtyeight.com/2016/09/stages-within-stages-the-minority-report-year-two/ Diversity Scoring

351 https://www.snapmunk.com/female-founder-developing-rotten-tomatoes-diversity-scoring/ 2/16

352 https://news.artnet.com/art-world/baltimore-museum-women-art-1730058 12/19

353 https://www.rollingstone.com/culture/culture-news/comedian-iliza-shlesinger-sued-over-women-only-comedy-show-253680/ 12/17

354 https://www.statesman.com/news/20171123/austin-closes-book-on-one-alamo-drafthouse-wonder-woman-complaint

355 https://www.theguardian.com/music/2018/dec/19/statement-swedish-women-only-music-festival-guilty-gender-discrimination

356 https://www.statementfestival.se/faq 2020 translated from Swedish

NO BEAUTY PAGEANTS
VIOLATION: INEQUALITY, GENDER DIFFERENTIATION

357 https://www.theatlantic.com/entertainment/archive/2018/06/miss-america-the-inner-beauty-pageant/562070/

358 https://www.usatoday.com/story/entertainment/celebrities/2019/12/19/miss-america-2020-changes-ditching-atlantic-city/2696772001/

359 https://www.missamerica.org/sign-up/ nd

360 https://www.vice.com/en_us/article/qvjdxm/miss-america-used-to-ban-abortion-and-still-bans-moms-wives-and-divorcees 3/17

361 https://www.advocate.com/commentary/2018/9/11/miss-america-wants-change-it-still-bans-trans-women

362 https://www.pressofatlanticcity.com/missamerica/miss-america-leaving-atlantic-city-again/article_00bd823d-213e-560b-914c-f4aa4bb1008a.html 7/19

363 https://variety.com/2019/tv/news/tv-ratings-miss-america-2020-nbc-1203449866/ 12/19

364 https://interestingengineering.com/miss-america-2020-wows-judges-and-audience-with-her-science-experiment 12/19

365 https://en.wikipedia.org/wiki/Miss_Earth nd

366 https://www.washingtonpost.com/world/2018/12/17/miss-spain-becomes-first-transgender-woman-compete-miss-universe-pageant/

367 https://www.npr.org/2019/12/22/790553874/transgender-woman-sues-miss-usa-pageant

NO DATING FREEDOM
VIOLATION: INEQUALITY, POLITICALLY INCORRECT THOUGHT

368 https://www.vice.com/en_uk/article/9kejae/i-asked-reddit-trans-dating-advice?utm_source=dlvr.it&utm_medium=twitter 11/19

NO MARRIAGES LIMITED TO ONLY TWO PEOPLE
VIOLATION: INEQUALITY, FAMILY SANCTITY, RELIGION

369 https://www.gao.gov/new.items/d04353r.pdf 1/04

370 https://www.law.cornell.edu/supremecourt/text/14-556 nd

371 https://www.nolo.com/legal-encyclopedia/marriage-rights-benefits-30190.html nd

372 https://splinternews.com/ban-marriage-1820022167 11/17

373 https://splinternews.com/ban-marriage-1820022167 11/17

NO POLICE
VIOLATION: INEQUALITY

374   https://en.wikipedia.org/wiki/Flower_Power_(photograph) nd

375   https://www.redstate.com/alexparker/2019/12/04/irate-transgender-activists-con-demn-local-government-involving-murderous-police-trying-honor-dare/ 6/19

376   https://www.mndaily.com/article/2018/04/acdisarm

377   https://www.thecollegefix.com/uc-davis-police-chief-decries-resolution-to-disarm-campus-cops-as-officer-killed-in-line-of-duty/ 6/19

378   https://www.thecollegefix.com/university-of-chicago-students-demand-cam-pus-police-be-disarmed/ 6/18

379   https://www.chicagomaroon.com/article/2018/4/4/ucpd-officers-involved-shooting-53rd-kimbark-ave/

380   http://cardozolawreview.com/are-police-obsolete-police-abolition/ post 2018

381   https://www.rollingstone.com/politics/politics-news/policing-is-a-dirty-job-but-nobodys-gotta-do-it-6-ideas-for-a-cop-free-world-199465/ 12/14

382   https://www.thenation.com/article/archive/abolish-police-in-stead-lets-have-full-social-economic-and-political-equality/ 4/15

383   https://www.inquirer.com/opinion/commentary/police-abolish-criminal-jus-tice-reform-20200102.html also disempower, disarm, and disband.

384   https://www.bl.uk/learning/timeline/item107460.html nd Black Panther

NO PRISONS
VIOLATION: INEQUALITY

385   https://www.teenvogue.com/story/what-is-prison-abolition-movement 12/19 links to headline search and author

386   https://www.teenvogue.com/story/history-black-radical-group-move-infa-mous-bombing-by-police 5/20

387   https://www.teenvogue.com/story/what-is-prison-abolition-movement 12/19 also moratorium, decarceration, and excarceration

388   https://www.theguardian.com/cities/2019/dec/09/rikers-20-inside-the-battle-to-build-four-new-prisons-in-new-york-city

389   https://www.sentencingproject.org/publications/decarceration-strate-gies-5-states-achieved-substantial-prison-population-reductions/ 9/18

390   https://www.afro.com/census-bureau-higher-percentage-black-children-live-sin-gle-mothers/ 12/16

391   https://www.vox.com/policy-and-politics/2017/6/19/15764176/prisons-abolition-al-ternatives 6/17

392   https://berniesanders.com/issues/criminal-justice-reform/ 2020

393 https://cnsnews.com/article/national/susan-jones/sanders-wouldnt-just-legal-ize-marijuana-hed-help-minorities-start 2/20

394 https://therealnews.com/stories/why-does-teen-vogue-need-a-labor-column 9/19

395 https://berniesanders.com/issues/reinvest-in-public-education/ 2020

NO PARENTAL RIGHTS
VIOLATION: FAMILY SANCTITY

396 https://www.gopusa.com/?p=29207?omhide=true 8/17 WA teaching, CA gender reveal

397 https://www.tolerance.org/about 2020

398 http://2009bookclubblog.blogspot.com/search?updated-max=2010-03-12T09:45:00-08:00&max-results=7 *All Colors*, teach six elements, biracial couples

399 http://2009bookclubblog.blogspot.com 3/10 O'Saurus

400 http://www.usingtheirwords.org/6elements/ 2012 social justice for elem. students

401 https://courageousconversation.com/about/ 2017 PEG

402 https://pjmedia.com/zombie/2015/10/8/interrupting-whiteness-education-confer-ence-blame-white-teachers-and-students/ 10/15 PEG

403 https://courageousconversation.com/seminars/leading-while-white-coura-geous-conversation-for-activism-from-application-to-interruption/ 2017 PEG

404 https://www.seattlepi.com/local/article/School-district-pulls-Web-site-after-exam-ples-of-1205162.php 6/06

405 http://www.fourmilab.ch/fourmilog/archives/seattle_schools_racism_2006-05-29/searace.htm

406 https://nationalseedproject.org/white-privilege-unpacking-the-invisible-knapsack 2020 hetero privilege

407 https://nationalseedproject.org/SEED-Directors-and-Year-Round-Staff/peg-gy-mcintosh 2020 fraudulence

408 https://nationalseedproject.org/impact/social-justice 2020 multicultural world citizens

409 https://nationalseedproject.org/about-us/history 2020 3 million

410 https://www.washingtontimes.com/news/2019/jun/10/coloradans-face-seri-ous-threats-to-parental-rights/

411 https://mynorthwest.com/1665798/parental-rights-washington-immoral/ 1/20

412 https://www.aclu.org/other/laws-restricting-teenagers-access-abortion 2020

413 https://www.plannedparenthood.org/learn/teens/preventing-pregnancy-stds/pa-rental-consent-and-notification-laws 6/18

414 https://democrats.org/where-we-stand/party-platform/ 9/16 pdf download p. 41

415 https://en.wikipedia.org/wiki/Sports_school nd Soviet Union

416 https://www.ushmm.org/wlc/en/article.php?ModuleId=10007820 nd Holocaust Museum Nazi Youth

417 https://www.history.com/news/how-the-hitler-youth-turned-a-generation-of-kids-into-nazis 8/18

418 https://www.dailymail.co.uk/news/article-7216087/China-separates-Muslim-children-parents-brainwashing-them.html 7/19

419 https://www.acf.hhs.gov/sites/default/files/cb/cm2018.pdf Child Maltreatment pdf download pp. xiii, 3, 9, also education personnel source

420 https://www.acf.hhs.gov/sites/default/files/cb/cm2012.pdf Child Maltreatment pdf download p. 29

421 http://www.wnd.com/2011/11/372409/ Does your child belong to the state? *My Two Dads*

422 https://www.youtube.com/watch?v=EUyP3N1tz6g 6/14 NJ spinning pencil

423 https://www.theatlantic.com/national/archive/2014/07/arrested-for-letting-a-9-year-old-play-at-the-park-alone/374436/

424 https://www.theatlantic.com/national/archive/2014/07/this-widows-4-kids-were-taken-because-she-left-them-home-alone/374514/

425 https://newsmaven.io/pinacnews/eye-on-government/cops-and-cps-strip-search-six-kids-including-4-year-old-over-mom-s-muffin-run-srZXVzC4VkKTYLh6UMmkfg 6/19

426 https://reason.com/2020/01/30/child-services-medical-abuse-wisconsin/

427 https://www.nbcnews.com/news/us-news/hundreds-parents-say-kids-wrongly-taken-them-after-doctors-misdiagnosed-n1096091 12/19

428 https://parentalrights.org/understand_the_issue/supreme-court/ nd

429 https://govtrackinsider.com/proposed-constitutional-amendment-would-enshrine-parental-rights-in-the-constitution-9e5304f2d8f7 2/19

430 https://coloradotimesrecorder.com/2020/02/conservatives-are-pushing-for-parental-rights-in-colorado-heres-what-that-means/20973/

431 https://thehill.com/homenews/state-watch/380485-utah-becomes-first-state-to-pass-free-range-parenting-law 3/18

NO FAMILIES
VIOLATION: FAMILY SANCTITY, WEALTH

432 https://www.cdc.gov/nchs/data/nvsr/nvsr68/nvsr68_13-508.pdf 11/19 unmarried births by race p. 25

433 http://www.nbcnews.com/id/39993685/ns/health-womens_health/t/blacks-struggle-percent-unwed-mothers-rate/#.Xpu99y-ZN2Z 11/10

434 https://www.heritage.org/poverty-and-inequality/report/the-war-poverty-after-50-years#_ftn2 9/14 welfare marriage penalty

435 http://www.pewsocialtrends.org/2016/06/27/1-demographic-trends-and-economic-well-being/ black disparities

436   https://www.washingtonpost.com/news/the-fix/wp/2015/07/07/when-did-black-americans-start-voting-so-heavily-democratic/?utm_term=.850270a7539d

437   http://www.pewsocialtrends.org/2015/12/09/the-american-middle-class-is-losing-ground/

438   https://www.brookings.edu/blog/social-mobility-memos/2018/06/05/seven-reasons-to-worry-about-the-american-middle-class/

439   https://www.valuepenguin.com/average-student-loan-debt nd

440   https://www.cnsnews.com/news/article/terence-p-jeffrey/obama-was-first-president-spend-more-welfare-defense 1/17

441   https://blogs.lse.ac.uk/usappblog/2017/10/31/how-obamas-welfare-legacy-helps-explain-the-roots-of-trump-supporters-rage/

442   https://www.heritage.org/welfare/commentary/obama-gutted-work-requirements-welfare-why-trump-right-restore-them 8/17

443   https://onenewsnow.com/business/2019/12/16/almost-6m-off-food-stamps-after-all-time-high-under-obama

444   https://www.cnbc.com/2019/12/29/how-the-affordable-care-act-transformed-the-us-health-care-system.html 30 million

445   https://www.forbes.com/sites/theapothecary/2017/03/22/yes-it-was-the-affordable-care-act-that-increased-premiums/#268b8cc211d2

446   https://www.pewresearch.org/fact-tank/2017/09/14/as-u-s-marriage-rate-hovers-at-50-education-gap-in-marital-status-widens/

447   https://www.usatoday.com/story/opinion/2019/04/07/males-risk-boy-crisis-identity-america-future-addiction-suicide-column/3331366002/

448   https://www.cbsnews.com/news/life-expectancy-for-american-men-drops-for-a-third-year/ 10/19

449   https://www.manhattan-institute.org/html/leaving-boys-behind-public-high-school-graduation-rates-5829.html 4/06

450   https://www.cnbc.com/2019/04/30/stephen-moore-says-the-decline-in-male-earnings-is-big-issue-for-the-economy.html

451   https://www.usatoday.com/story/news/nation/2012/12/07/edie-windsor-gay-marriage-supreme-court/1737387/

NO RELIGION
VIOLATION: RELIGION, POLITICALLY INCORRECT THOUGHT, CARBON EMISSIONS

452   https://www.thepublicdiscourse.com/2010/10/1920/ separation of church and state

453   https://www.pewforum.org/2009/05/14/shifting-boundaries4/ *Everson* and the Wall of Separation

454   https://law.jrank.org/pages/22878/Everson-v-Board-Education-Significance.html 2020

455   https://billofrightsinstitute.org/cases/ nd landmark Supreme Court religion cases

456   https://www.nytimes.com/2018/09/26/us/politics/julie-swetnick-avenatti-kav-enaugh.html

457   https://www.chicagotribune.com/columns/john-kass/ct-federal-judge-catholic-kass-met-0913-20170912-column.html Durbin, Feinstein

458   https://www.afa.net/activism/action-alerts/2018/democratic-senator-attacking-reli-gious-views-of-secretary-of-state-nominee-mike-pompeo/ 4/18 Booker

459   https://www.pewforum.org/2019/10/03/religion-in-the-public-schools-2019-up-date/

460   https://cruxnow.com/church-in-the-usa/2016/10/clinton-campaign-fire-criti-cal-emails-catholic-church/ Podesta, Palmieri

461   https://www.cnsnews.com/blog/craig-bannister/texas-dem-defends-pro-life-col-leagues-litmus-test-any-one-issue-just-wont-work 4/17 Perez

462   https://www.nationalreview.com/2017/01/democrats-christian-voters-endur-ing-problem/ KKK

463   https://www.regent.edu/acad/schlaw/student_life/studentorgs/lawreview/docs/issues/v24n2/02Paulsenvol.24.2.pdf 2011 *Christian Legal Society v. Martinez*

NO RIGHT OF SELF-DEFENSE
VIOLATION: ACHIEVEMENT/INDIVIDUALISM/SELF-RELIANCE, GUNS

464   https://www.researchgate.net/publication/228177997_The_Human_Right_of_Self-Defense 10/07

465   https://treaties.un.org/doc/Treaties/2013/04/20130410%2012-01%20PM/Ch_XXVI_08.pdf Arms Trade Treaty

466   https://www.factcheck.org/2019/05/trumps-deceptive-arms-trade-treaty-argument/

467   https://www.theguardian.com/uk/2011/aug/11/uk-riots-amazon-withdraws-trun-cheons

468   https://www.independent.co.uk/news/uk/crime/kill-burglar-self-defence-what-law-allow-richard-osborn-brooks-reasonable-force-murder-household-er-a8290441.html#explainer-question-4

469   https://famous-trials.com/zimmerman1/2293-zimmermanchrono nd

470   https://www.theguardian.com/world/2013/jul/19/trayvon-martin-obama-white-house

471   https://time.com/3725290/obama-trayvon-martin-parents/ 2/15

NO GUNS
VIOLATION: GUNS, ACHIEVEMENT/INDIVIDUALISM/SELF-RELIANCE

472   https://abcnews.go.com/Politics/heres-2020-democrats-differ-gun-control/sto-ry?id=62970498 2/20

473   https://www.realclearpolitics.com/video/2019/09/12/beto_orourke_hell_yes_we_
      are_going_to_take_your_ar-15.html

474   https://www.washingtonexaminer.com/news/beto-orourke-we-will-use-criminal-
      code-against-people-who-refuse-to-turn-in-ar-15s 10/25/19

475   https://thehill.com/homenews/campaign/462377-orourke-gun-confisca-
      tion-talk-alarms-democrats 9/21/19

476   https://www.economist.com/democracy-in-america/2019/10/22/how-beto-orourke-
      has-helped-americas-gun-lobby

477   https://www.dallasnews.com/news/politics/2020/03/10/beto-hell-yes-orourkes-en-
      dorsement-has-joe-biden-fending-off-allegation-that-hes-a-gun-grabber/

478   https://www.tallahassee.com/story/news/2019/07/29/florida-ag-ashley-moody-
      seeks-block-assault-weapons-ban/1861073001/

479   https://www.usatoday.com/story/money/2018/02/28/dicks-sporting-goods-bans-
      sales-assault-weapons-after-parkland-florida-school-shooting/380382002/

480   https://www.washingtontimes.com/news/2018/mar/1/walmart-bans-sales-toy-
      guns/

481   https://www.businessinsider.com/dicks-destroys-assault-guns-after-parkland-
      shooting-2018-4

482   https://www.nytimes.com/2018/03/22/business/citigroup-gun-control-policy.html

483   http://thehill.com/policy/finance/384906-gop-chairman-pushes-bank-of-america-
      citigroup-on-gun-policies 4/18

484   https://thehill.com/blogs/pundits-blog/civil-rights/348379-doj-stops-operation-
      choke-point-for-now-but-congress-must-end 8/17

485   http://download.elca.org/ELCA%20Resource%20Repository/Community_Vio-
      lence_GunsSPR93.pdf 1993

486   https://www.newsmax.com/fastfeatures/christian-gun-control-liber-
      al-church/2015/05/07/id/643119/

487   https://www.presbyterianmission.org/ministries/peacemaking/gun-violence-re-
      sources/ 2020

488   https://www.catholic.com/magazine/online-edition/what-does-the-church-say-
      about-gun-control 2/16

489   https://www.miamiarch.org//CatholicDiocese.php?op=Article_what-does-the-
      church-say-about-gun-controlt 2/18

490   https://townhall.com/tipsheet/timothymeads/2018/04/29/pope-francis-bans-all-
      weapons-n2475765

491   https://www.everycrsreport.com/reports/R41750.html 4/11 Heller and McDonald

NO AMERICAN FLAG
VIOLATION: NATIONALISM/PATRIOTISM

492   https://www.cnn.com/interactive/2018/07/us/national-anthem-annotated/

493   https://247wallst.com/special-report/2019/06/28/here-are-the-27-different-us-flags-and-how-they-got-that-way/4/

494   https://www.shrm.org/resourcesandtools/hr-topics/employee-relations/pages/displaying-u.s.-flag-offensive.aspx 9/19

495   https://www.cnn.com/2019/07/04/politics/flag-burned-outside-white-house-july-4th/index.html

496   https://www.poughkeepsiejournal.com/story/news/local/2016/08/18/arlington-firefly-flag-again-but-not-all-satisfied/88957642/

497   https://www.greenvilleonline.com/story/news/local/2016/08/27/tr-principal-says-american-flag-has-been-used-taunt-berea-students/89485158/

498   https://www.greenvilleonline.com/story/news/education/2016/08/29/tr-police-chief-disagrees-tr-principals-flag-decision/89538622/

499   https://www.cnn.com/2016/11/23/us/hampshire-college-no-american-flag/index.html

500   https://www.thecollegefix.com/college-that-removed-american-flag-after-trumps-election-is-on-the-brink-of-collapse/ 2/19

NO COUNTRIES
VIOLATION: NATIONALISM/PATRIOTISM, CARBON EMISSIONS

501   https://www.influencewatch.org/?s=immigration+reform+advocacy+organization 2020

502   https://www.influencewatch.org/non-profit/new-york-immigrant-coalition/ 2020

503   https://www.influencewatch.org/non-profit/national-immigration-forum/ 2020

504   https://www.influencewatch.org/non-profit/fair-immigration-reform-movement-firm/ 2020

505   https://www.realclearpolitics.com/video/2019/06/27/all_dem_candidates_raise_hand_when_asked_if_illegal_immigrants_should_get_health_care_coverage_at_debate.html

506   https://www.influencewatch.org/organization/soros-network-open-society-network/ 2020

507   https://www.conservapedia.com/One-world_government 2020

508   https://www.businessinsider.com/eu-countries-agree-mega-army-2017-11

509   https://en.news-front.info/2019/05/11/21-european-heads-of-state-sign-stronger-europe-manifesto-demanding-more-eu-integration/

510   https://www.americanthinker.com/articles/2018/10/the_un_wants_to_be_our_world_government_by_2030.html

511   https://www.theguardian.com/global-development/2015/jan/19/sustainable-development-goals-united-nations

512   https://metro.co.uk/2016/07/20/what-would-the-world-look-like-if-we-didnt-have-any-nations-6016745/

513 https://www.laprogressive.com/whos-afraid-of-world-government/ 11/09

514 https://www.salon.com/2013/09/20/elites_strange_plot_to_take_over_the_world/

515 https://worldbeyondwar.org/imagine-therere-countries/ nd

NO EXTRAVAGANT POSSESSIONS OR PURCHASES
VIOLATION: INEQUALITY, WEALTH

516 https://www.usnews.com/news/education-news/articles/2018-11-16/high-school-bans-expensive-winter-coats-to-stop-poverty-shaming

517 https://dailycaller.com/2019/03/01/high-school-seniors-banned-prom-limos/

518 https://abc7ny.com/new-jersey-high-school-bans-limos-party-buses-for-prom/5159925/ 2/19

519 https://www.bbc.com/news/uk-england-44075878 5/18 Australia

520 https://www.wsj.com/articles/warrens-2-cents-come-at-your-expense-11573515899 11/19

521 https://www.wsj.com/articles/SB10418077299767946664 6/03

522 https://nypost.com/2020/02/19/even-moderator-skewers-mike-bloomberg-at-democratic-debate-should-you-exist/

NO INCOME TAXES—OR INCOME
VIOLATION: INEQUALITY, PRIVATE OWNERSHIP

523 https://www.newsweek.com/bernie-sanders-claims-every-study-out-there-says-medicare-all-will-save-money-1489149 2/20

524 https://www.theday.com/article/20190826/OP02/190829763

NO INHERITANCE
VIOLATION: INEQUALITY, WEALTH, PRIVATE OWNERSHIP, SELF-RELIANCE

525 https://www.theatlantic.com/business/archive/2011/06/why-do-we-allow-inheritance-at-all/240004/

526 https://www.theguardian.com/commentisfree/2017/jul/24/utopian-thinking-fund-welfare-state-inheritance-tax

PERSONAL PROPERTY
VIOLATION: INEQUALITY, WEALTH, PRIVATE OWNERSHIP, SELF-RELIANCE

527 https://www.businessinsider.com/when-women-got-the-right-to-vote-american-voting-rights-timeline-2018-10

528 https://www.forbes.com/sites/theapothecary/2017/03/22/yes-it-was-the-affordable-care-act-that-increased-premiums/#268b8cc211d2

529 https://taxfoundation.org/state-individual-income-tax-rates-and-brackets-for-2020/

530 https://www.taxpolicycenter.org/statistics/historical-highest-marginal-income-tax-rates 2020

531 https://www.theguardian.com/commentisfree/2017/oct/23/owning-car-thing-of-the-past-cities-utopian-vision

532 https://www.cnn.com/2018/11/16/uk/poverty-proof-school-gbr-scli-intl/index.html

NO PRIVATE HOMES
VIOLATION: CARBON EMISSIONS, INEQUALITY, WEALTH, PRIVATE OWNERSHIP, SELF-RELIANCE

533 https://www.wsj.com/articles/SB122721278056345271 11/08 Emanuel audio link

534 https://www.congress.gov/116/bills/hres109/BILLS-116hres109ih.pdf 2/19 Green New Deal

NO PRIVATE ENTERPRISE
VIOLATION: INEQUALITY, WEALTH, PRIVATE OWNERSHIP, SELF-RELIANCE

535 https://time.com/5422714/what-is-democratic-socialism/10/18

536 https://journalstar.com/opinion/columnists/george-will-socialism-now-about-confiscation/article_49de7c56-3653-534a-9fff-cf52322034fb.html 2/19

537 https://www.cnn.com/2019/07/31/politics/2020-democratic-debate-socialism/index.html

NO NONCONSENSUAL SEX–WITH *ROBOTS*
VIOLATION: POLITICALLY INCORRECT THOUGHT

538 https://www.researchgate.net/publication/335986790_Designing_Virtuous_Sex_Robots 11/19

539 https://link.springer.com/article/10.1007%2Fs12369-017-0413-z 6/17

540 https://research.monash.edu/en/publications/robotics-has-a-race-problem 7/19

ACKNOWLEDGMENTS

PATTY, MY WIFE OF FORTY YEARS, gets marquee space on anything of worth I do. I also want to thank my parents, Sam and Betty, for the drive and freedom to achieve. My sons, Marshall, Sheridan, and Ashton, have provided me the grounding that good kids teach their parents.

I have had many excellent teachers over the years, but a few especially stand out: Robert Santarelli (fifth and sixth grade), Helga Rist (four years of high school German), Dr. Henry Hoerner (school district superintendent), Dr. James Hansz (undergraduate marketing class and activities), and Rev. Ronald VanBlargan (my Lutheran pastor). I am indebted.

Two of my business superiors also taught me a lot and let me run to the end of a long leash: John Greeniaus and Doug Conant, both at Nabisco. Thanks, guys.

Somewhere along the way, a person's words or a book's passage—I can't remember which—impressed upon me that you can learn something from everyone. From some, you learn what to do, and from others, you learn what not to do. For this reason, I also want to acknowledge the biggest jackasses and a-holes I have encountered. You sure taught me something!

About the Author   291

ABOUT THE AUTHOR

CEO, LAWYER, COLLEGE PROFESSOR, AND SCHOLAR, Wynn Willard is uniquely experienced to see the big picture and explain it. Teaching at a large state university and going to law school as an older, seasoned executive revealed to him the folly and fealty of the Left. Amazed at the destructiveness of the Left's radical agenda, he has documented hundreds of examples and fit them into a revealing framework.

wynnwillard.com

Made in the USA
Las Vegas, NV
09 June 2021

24464030R00173